COLLEGE
UnMazed

Your Guide to Navigate the High School to College Maze

by

Dr. Amanda Sterk
Dr. Timothy Poynton
Dr. Richard Lapan

Copyright © 2022 College UnMazed®, all rights reserved.
Dr. Amanda Sterk, Dr. Timothy Poynton, and Dr. Richard Lapan, 2022
Published by College UnMazed, LLC.

College UnMazed and their associated logos are trademarks of College UnMazed, LLC. No part of this publication may be reproduced, stored in a retrieval system, transmitted in any form or by any means, electronic, mechanical, photocopying, recording, or otherwise, without prior written permission of College UnMazed, LLC. For information regarding permission visit our website at www.collegeunmazed.com, contact us at info@collegeunmazed.com, or write to:
College UnMazed, LLC.
2229 SW 43rd Ter.
Cape Coral, Florida
33914
ISBN: 978-1-957556-00-0 (Paperback)
ISBN: 978-1-957556-01-7 (Digital Online)
Library of Congress Control Number: 2022901248
Printed February 2022

MEET THE AUTHORS

Dr. Amanda Sterk is the Director of Accelerated Programs at Florida Southwestern State College, where she works with students, parents, school counselors, and school districts to understand and participate in accelerated learning programs in SW Florida. Dr. Sterk is active in multiple college and career readiness programs, such as the Florida Alliance of Dual Enrollment Partnerships, Florida College Access Network, and FutureMakers (Talent Hub). After 19 years in education, she brings her passion for helping students realize their full potential through academic planning and college decision-making. Her responsibilities include content creation, presentation, and collaborator relations.
Contact: asterk@collegeunmazed.com

Dr. Amanda Sterk
Educator, Curriculum Writer and Speaker

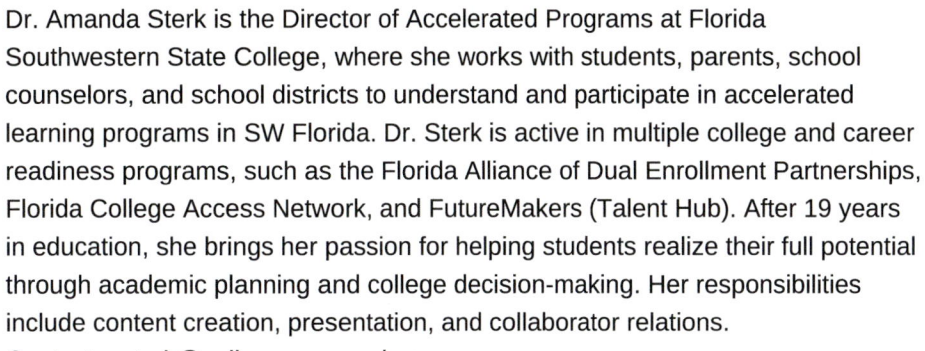

Dr. Timothy Poynton is a professor and counselor educator committed to improving the transition from high school into young adulthood through his research and teaching. A former school counselor, Dr. Poynton is currently an associate professor in the Department of Counseling and School Psychology at the University of Massachusetts Boston. Dr. Poynton has published several research articles and book chapters related to school counseling, career development, and college readiness, and was recognized in 2011 as the Counselor Educator of the Year by the American School Counselor Association. His responsibilities include technology, school-based analysis, and assessment.
Contact: tpoynton@collegeunmazed.com

Dr. Timothy Poynton
Professor and Counselor Educator

Dr. Richard Lapan is a professor, counselor educator, and psychologist committed to transforming the profession of school counseling from an ancillary support service to a comprehensive program central to the academic, personal development, and social justice/diversity mission of every school. The effectiveness of these efforts was recognized in 2006 when Dr. Lapan won the prestigious Counselor Educator of the Year award from the American School Counselor Association (ASCA). His responsibilities include research, innovation, and curriculum development.
Contact: rlapan@collegeunmazed.com

Dr. Richard Lapan
Professor and Counselor Educator

TABLE OF CONTENTS

INTRODUCTION: SECTION 1 — p.5-9
Your Guide through the High School to College Process
Why College? — p.5
College UnMazed — p.6
Self & College Knowledge Map — p.8

CHAPTER 1: YOU FACTOR — p.10-17
Develop a Plan for the Future Based on Your Goals and Strengths
Step 1: The 8 Strengths of the You Factor — p.11
Step 2: Case Study – Emily — p.12
Step 3: Strengthening Your You Factor — p.14

CHAPTER 2: ACADEMIC FACTOR — p.18-27
Understand How to Build the Academic Skills and Plan Needed for College and Career Success
Step 1: The Academic Factor & College Admissions — p.18
Step 2: Case Study – José — p.24
Step 3: Developing Your Academic Factor — p.26

CHAPTER 3: CAREER FACTOR — p.28-42
Enhance Your Career Knowledge and College and Career Decision-Making
Step 1: The Career Factor — p.29
Step 2: Exploring Career Pathways — p.30
Step 3: Case Study – Alex — p.35
Step 4: Developing Your Career Factor — p.37

CHAPTER 4: MONEY FACTOR — p.43-53
Become Financially Literate and Savvy to Pay for College
Step 1: Managing the Costs of College — p.45
Step 2: Know Key College Finance Terms — p.46
Step 3: Case Study – Sholondo — p.50
Step 4: Understand Net Price — p.52

INTRODUCTION: SECTION 2 — p.54-58
Learn about LEADS and the 6 Keys of College Fit
LEADS Strategy Map — p.54
LEADS — p.56
6 Keys of College Fit — p.57

TABLE OF CONTENTS

CHAPTER 5: LIST   p.59-65
Identifying Colleges and Gathering Information

Step 1. Use Online Resources   p.59
Step 2. Learn about College Attributes   p.61
Step 3: Review Case Study – Alex   p.63
Step 4. Develop Your Own List   p.64

CHAPTER 6: EXPLORE   p.66-81
Gathering and Analyzing Information

Step 1: Dig Deeper using the 6 Keys of College Fit   p.67
Step 2: Explore Admission Factors   p.71
Step 3: Explore Your You Factor to Make the Most of College Visits   p.74
Step 4: Review Case Study – Sholondo   p.78

CHAPTER 7: APPLY   p.82-105
Critiquing and Prioritizing Colleges

Step 1: Understand Overall Fit and Chance of Admission   p.83
Step 2: Review Case Study – Emily   p.84
Step 3: Choose the Best Combination of Colleges Where You Will Apply   p.89
Step 4: Develop and Submit Competitive College Applications   p.92

CHAPTER 8: DECIDE   p.106-122
Comparing Offers and Making a Commitment

Step 1: Learn about Types of College Admission Decisions   p.107
Step 2: Review Case Study   p.108
Step 3: Make Your Final Decision   p.116

CHAPTER 9: SUCCEED   p.123-131
Creating Financial, Academic, and Social College Success Plans

Step 1: Establish Financial, Academic, and Social Strategies to Succeed in College   p.124
Step 2: Learn about College Success Plans   p.126
Step 3: Develop Your Own College Success Plans   p.129
Step 3: Reflect on Accomplishments and Next Steps   p.131

RESOURCES   p.132-139

High School Planning Checklist for Success   p.132
Referenced Links & Resources   p.138

YOUR COLLEGE UNMAZING

Using research informed practices, this workbook provides engaging content to promote self-discovery and college knowledge. We believe that all students have a path to success, and *College UnMazed* helps you make informed decisions about your future. Students will follow a sequential path to build the necessary skills for college and career success.

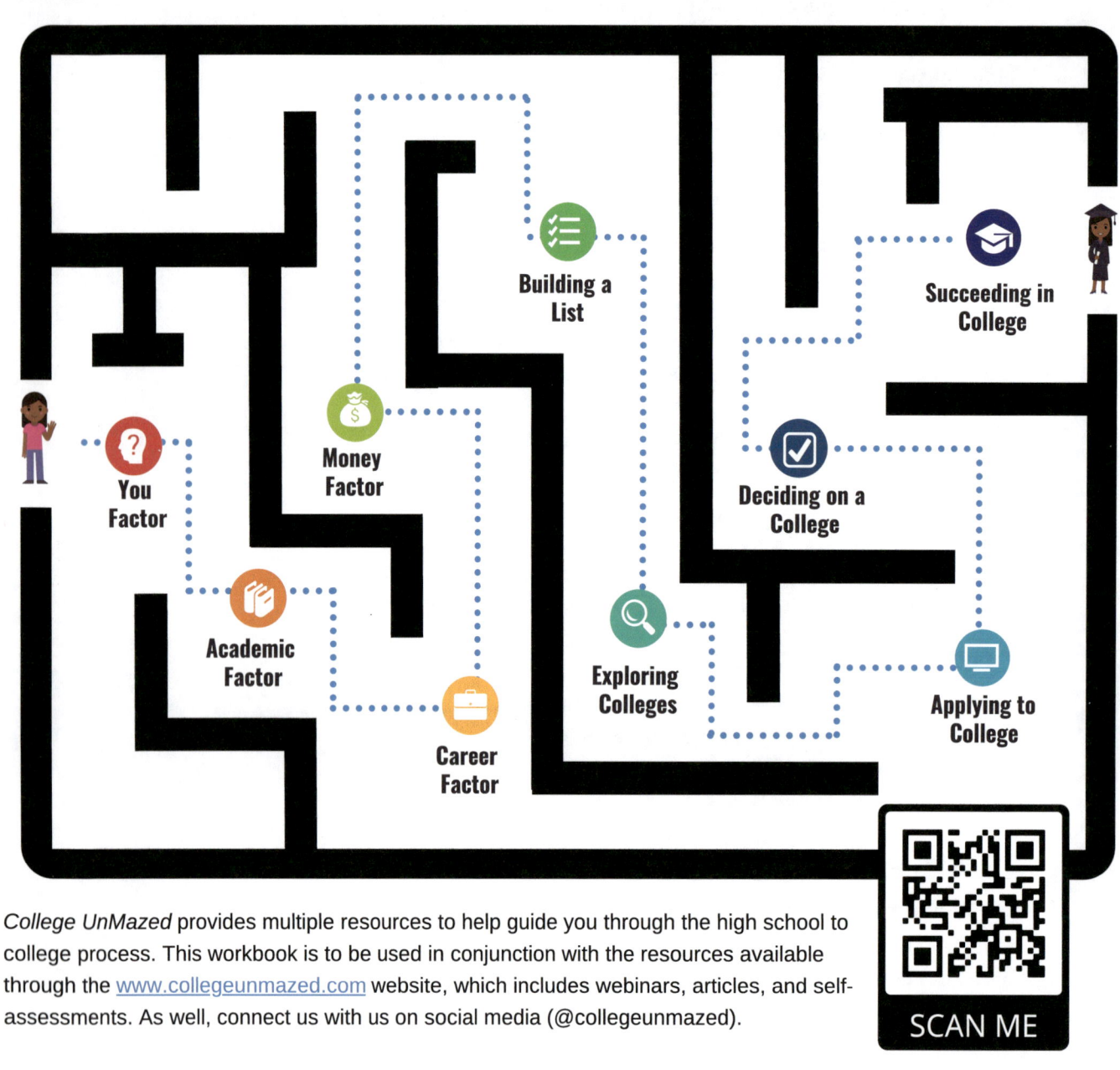

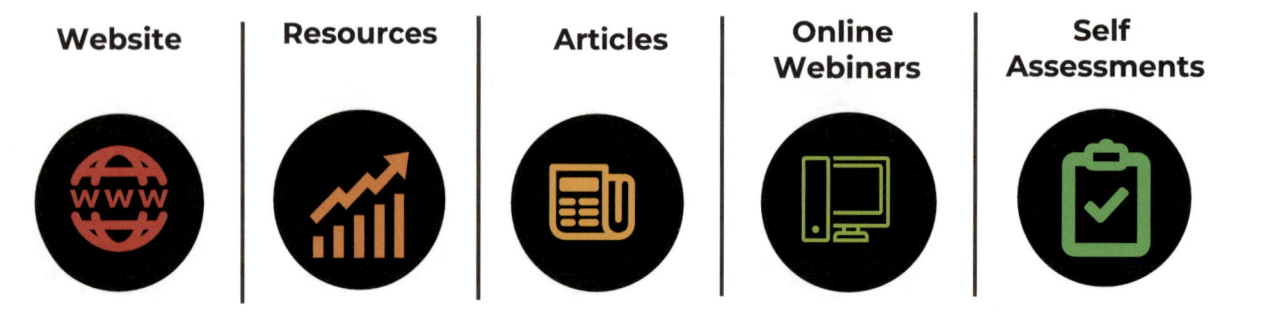

The maze path proceeds through the following steps:
- You Factor
- Academic Factor
- Money Factor
- Career Factor
- Building a List
- Exploring Colleges
- Deciding on a College
- Applying to College
- Succeeding in College

College UnMazed provides multiple resources to help guide you through the high school to college process. This workbook is to be used in conjunction with the resources available through the www.collegeunmazed.com website, which includes webinars, articles, and self-assessments. As well, connect us with us on social media (@collegeunmazed).

SCAN ME

| Website | Resources | Articles | Online Webinars | Self Assessments |

SECTION 1: INTRODUCTION

This book helps students and their families successfully find their way through the maze that is the college decision-making process. Choosing the right college is one of the most emotional, expensive, and important decisions students and families will make. This book will helps students and their families successfully find their way through the maze that is the college-choice process. By providing you with critical information, examples, and activities, you learn how to better prepare yourself for college while in high school and then make an informed decision about which college is right for you and your family. This book teaches you a strategy you can use to reduce the bewildering anxiety and stress often associated with college decision-making. You will become a more informed consumer of college information, and then be able to use this information to make decisions that meet you and your family's needs, hopes, and dreams.

The good news is you are in control of your own success. Career achievement and satisfaction in life is not up to the college you attend; it is up to you. CEOs of major corporations and genius award winners come from lots of different colleges – they come from state universities most people have not heard of, as well as the Ivy League colleges everyone has heard of. College is what you make of it – your success is not about what college can make of you. And please take this next point to heart: there are plenty of good colleges that will help you to become the kind of person you, and your family, want. There are lots of colleges out there that want you to become one of their alumni. Our job in this book is to help you make the most of your time in high school so you are ready to make a truly informed decision about which college is right for you and prepare you for success at that college.

Why College?

With the increasing costs of going to college, students and their families are now, more than ever before, asking, "Why college?" The simple answer is that there are many good reasons to attend college, even with how expensive it can be. There is easily over 50 years of research pointing out the advantages of going to and graduating from college. The good outcomes include wide-ranging benefits, such as enhanced personal growth, significant intellectual development, lifelong friendships and partnerships made, and access to alumni networks accessed that can provide vocational and social benefits over your life course.

And, yes, money–you are likely to make more money by graduating from college. People with a Bachelor's degree earn on average $1,000,000 more across their lifetimes than people with only a high school diploma. A college education has become one of the biggest investments a family makes, second only to a home mortgage. Despite this, college is still a great financial investment. To see returns on the investment of your time and money in a college education, however, you must graduate and get your degree.

To succeed in the 21st-century workplace, you are increasingly likely to need a postsecondary degree or certificate to secure a well-paying job. Current projections indicate that 60% of jobs will require some type of specialized postsecondary degree or certification by 2025. Recent data from the Lumina Foundation (2020) found that while the number of people earning postsecondary degrees and certificates are on the rise, there will be many high-paying jobs that go unfilled because not enough workers will be qualified. What does that mean for you? It means that now is a great time to pursue a postsecondary education, as there are many high-paying and personally rewarding opportunities awaiting you!

SECTION 1: INTRODUCTION

Figure Intro 1.1

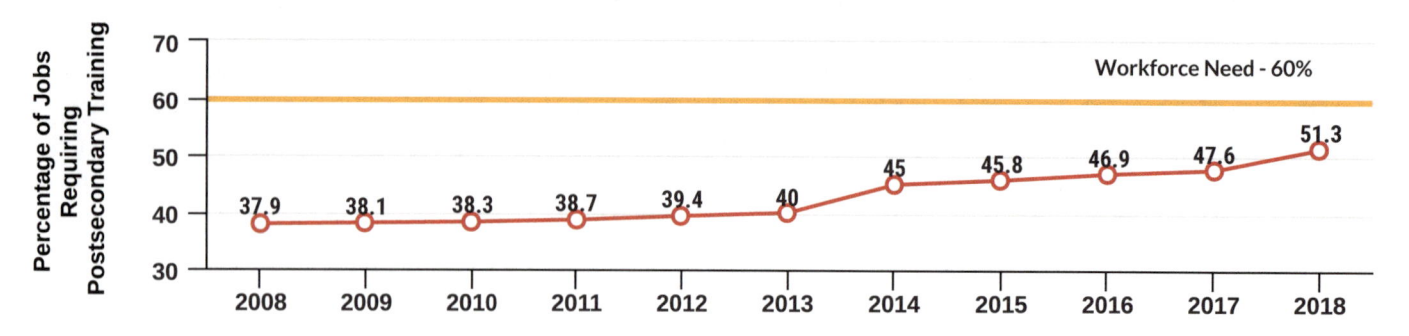

[Line chart: Percentage of Jobs Requiring Postsecondary Training — Workforce Need - 60%
2008: 37.9; 2009: 38.1; 2010: 38.3; 2011: 38.7; 2012: 39.4; 2013: 40; 2014: 45; 2015: 45.8; 2016: 46.9; 2017: 47.6; 2018: 51.3]

The reason why more jobs need a degree or credential is that the global economy is shifting away from an industry-based economy to a knowledge-based economy (Lumina Foundation, 2020). Even though most jobs created today require an education beyond high school, only half of Americans ages 25-64 hold a degree or credential.

The chart below shows the median annual wages in the U.S. by education level, showing that pay increases significantly as the amount of education completed increases. On average, if you have a Bachelor's degree, you will earn $461 more every week than if you only had a high school diploma. That is nearly $24,000 a year or $1 million dollars in extra income across a 40-year career. To reap these rewards, you must graduate from college and earn some type of degree or certificate.

Figure Intro 1.2

Median Annual Wages in the U.S. by Education/ Training Level

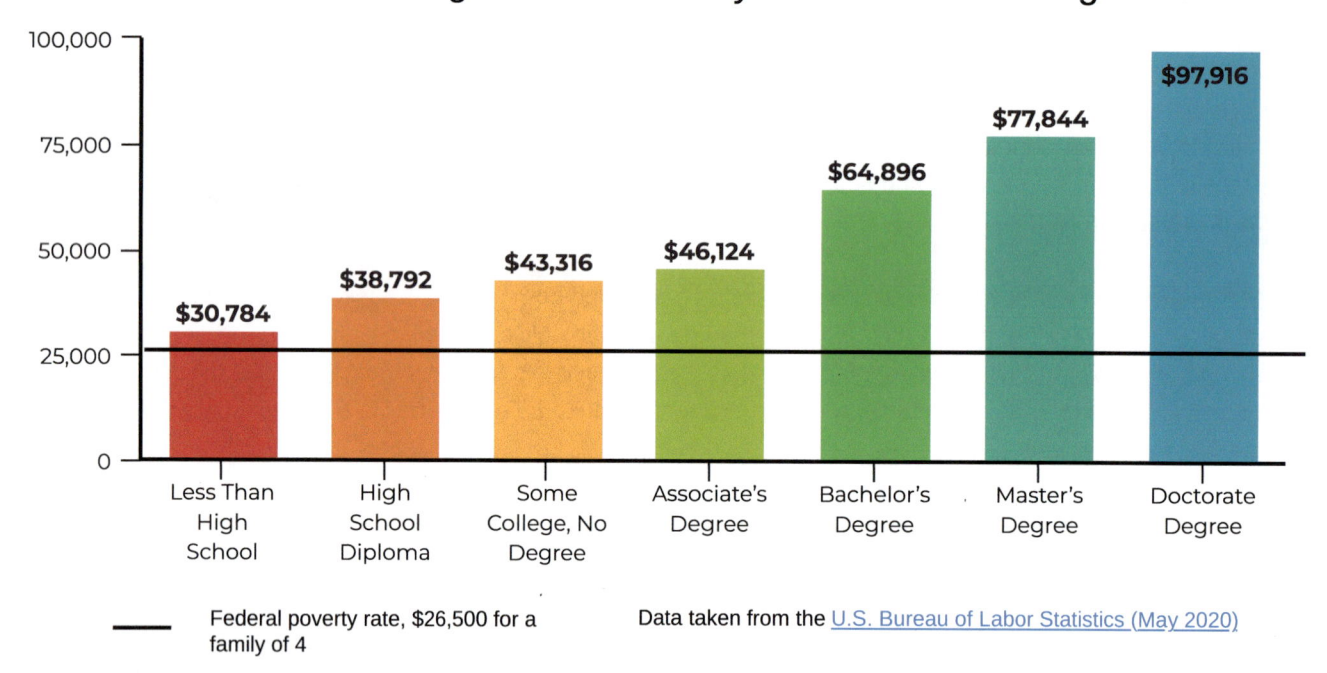

[Bar chart:
- Less Than High School: $30,784
- High School Diploma: $38,792
- Some College, No Degree: $43,316
- Associate's Degree: $46,124
- Bachelor's Degree: $64,896
- Master's Degree: $77,844
- Doctorate Degree: $97,916

Federal poverty rate, $26,500 for a family of 4
Data taken from the U.S. Bureau of Labor Statistics (May 2020)]

College UnMazed

This book is presented in two sections. Section 1 shows you how to build a foundation not only for college success but also for lifelong career success and satisfaction. You will be taken step by step through 4 critical factors to help you make the most of your high school experience and prepare you for your college experience: the You Factor, the Academic Factor, the Career Factor, and the Money Factor. Good preparation leads to good decisions, and getting to know your personal, academic, career, and financial strengths and needs will help you be well prepared to make informed college decisions.

Section 2 of *College UnMazed* will then teach you a strategy for making informed college decisions. Our strategy will help you apply to the right colleges for you, and ultimately, help you make a truly informed decision on which college to attend. The LEADS strategy (List, Explore, Apply, Decide, and Succeed) is a step-by-step decision-making process where you will reduce the thousands of college choices in the United States to a more manageable group of colleges where you will apply. The LEADS strategy is built to be used with freely available online college information systems. It relies heavily on gathering and using information on each college you are considering. You will assess how well each college fits by using the 6 Keys of College Fit: Academic Match, Career Match, Financial Match, Personal Match, Student Outcomes, and Student Support. Each of these keys adds unique and invaluable information that must be considered if you are to make an informed college decision.

How to Use This Book

College UnMazed is set up as a workbook, with the intent that you learn and then apply the information to best meet your goals and special attributes. We wrote *College UnMazed* based on research (ours and other academics), our own experiences as practitioners helping parents and students through the process, and current trends and information from college and career experts.

College UnMazed incorporates a higher-order thinking strategy that is specifically designed to provide critical college and career knowledge in a scaffolded way so you are ready for each step you must take to make it through the maze that is college decision making. We suggest you not only read the book but also engage in all the activities and resources. By doing so, you will be well-prepared and able to clearly articulate and use critical college knowledge to your advantage. If you are currently a high school senior, the goal of our book is for you to make a truly informed decision about which college to attend. If you are a high school junior, sophomore, freshman, middle school student, or non-traditional college student, our goal for you is to show you how to get ready for college and make an informed decision when it is your time to do so.

We, the three authors of this book, have come together to share our expertise and life experiences to provide you, the reader, an approach based on rigorous research to help you and your family with the wonderful and, at times, daunting life opportunity, which college is. Combined, the three of us, your authors, have spent more than 85 years being involved in college (as college students, graduate students, counselors advising students and families about college, and as college professors and researchers of college success and satisfaction). We have lived and worked inside of many different types of colleges. We see it from the inside out. We are parents of past and future college going children. We are award-winning researchers in student development and are school-based practitioners. We want you to be successful and satisfied. Your good outcomes will match a calling that brought us into the helping profession so we could promote growth and development for others.

Please Talk to Your Family About College

For most of you, your family has watched you grow for many years now – and to get to this point in your life, has likely helped you make most of the decisions thus far. Where you live, what school system you attend, what activities you participated in, even (when you were younger) who you spent time with outside of school were all largely determined by your family. The college decision process you are undertaking requires you to take responsibility for making decisions, while at the same time being open to the input and feedback of important people in your life. Being open means you are listening, communicating, discussing, and hearing their opinions and concerns for you. *College UnMazed* is designed to provide you the tools to have these conversations. If both you and your family are reading this book together and taking it seriously, you will have meaningful conversations that accomplish what you both want – a college education that will lead to a satisfying and fulfilling future.

Let's begin!

INTRODUCTION - SECTION 1

Figure Intro 1.3

YOU FACTOR

8 STRENGTHS
- Agency
- Positive Beliefs
- Effective Goals
- Knowing Yourself
- Becoming a Successful Student
- Character for Workplace Success
- College Knowledge
- College Support Network

ACTIVITIES
- Work Experience
- Community Involvement
- Creative Pursuits
- Major-Specific Activities
- School Clubs & Activities
- Leadership

MONEY FACTOR

MONEY SOURCES
- Gift Aid
  - Institutional
  - National
  - State
  - External
- Loans
  - Subsidized
  - Unsubsidized
  - Parent Plus
- Work Study
- External
- Out-of-pocket
- Savings/529

MONEY TERMS
- Award Letter
- EFC/SAI
- FAFSA/CSS Profile
- Cost of Attendance
- Net Price

SE... COL... KNOW...

Learning and... college kno... building a se... make infor...

8

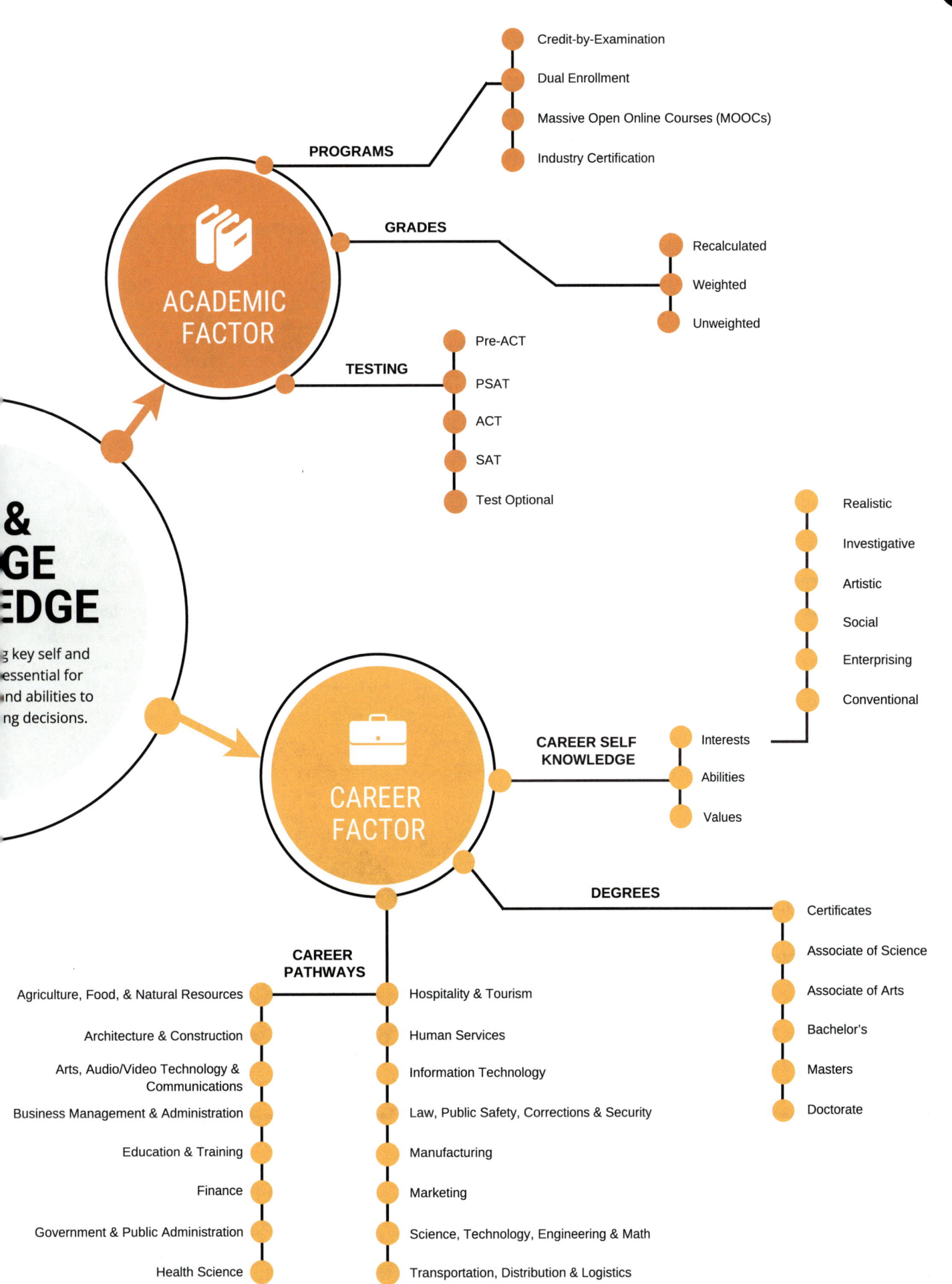

COLLEGE UNMAZED

ACADEMIC FACTOR

- **PROGRAMS**
  - Credit-by-Examination
  - Dual Enrollment
  - Massive Open Online Courses (MOOCs)
  - Industry Certification
- **GRADES**
  - Recalculated
  - Weighted
  - Unweighted
- **TESTING**
  - Pre-ACT
  - PSAT
  - ACT
  - SAT
  - Test Optional

& KNOWLEDGE

key self and essential for and abilities to ng decisions.

CAREER FACTOR

- **CAREER SELF KNOWLEDGE**
  - Interests
    - Realistic
    - Investigative
    - Artistic
    - Social
    - Enterprising
    - Conventional
  - Abilities
  - Values
- **DEGREES**
  - Certificates
  - Associate of Science
  - Associate of Arts
  - Bachelor's
  - Masters
  - Doctorate
- **CAREER PATHWAYS**
  - Agriculture, Food, & Natural Resources
  - Architecture & Construction
  - Arts, Audio/Video Technology & Communications
  - Business Management & Administration
  - Education & Training
  - Finance
  - Government & Public Administration
  - Health Science
  - Hospitality & Tourism
  - Human Services
  - Information Technology
  - Law, Public Safety, Corrections & Security
  - Manufacturing
  - Marketing
  - Science, Technology, Engineering & Math
  - Transportation, Distribution & Logistics

CHAPTER 1
You Factor

Develop a Plan for the Future Based on Your Goals and Strengths

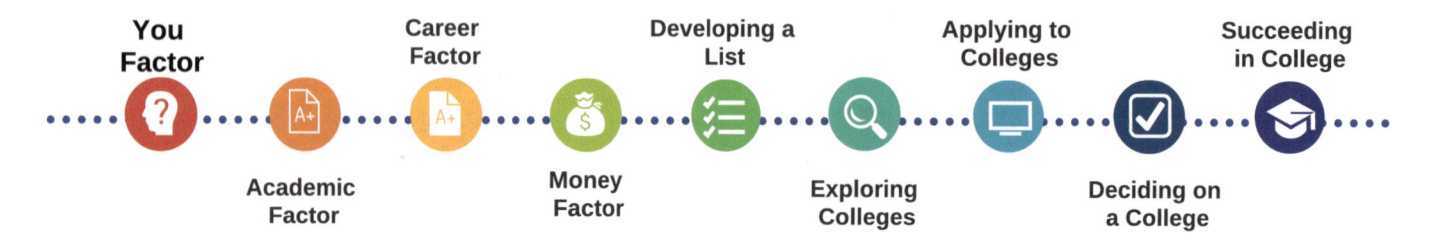

You Factor — Academic Factor — Career Factor — Money Factor — Developing a List — Exploring Colleges — Applying to Colleges — Deciding on a College — Succeeding in College

The You Factor is what helps you create your unique identity and focuses on learned strengths that will help you succeed in college and your career. The focus of this chapter is on the You Factor and how you can maximize 8 Strengths essential to your success and satisfaction. In subsequent chapters, we will show you how these 8 Strengths of the You Factor connect to the Academic Factor, Career Factor, and Money Factor. Many colleges use the You, Academic, Career, and Money Factors when making admission decisions. These four factors can be strengthened to work together on your behalf. The Academic Factor consists of things like your Grade Point Average (GPA), the rigor and level of the classes you take in high school, and ACT/SAT test scores. The Career Factor entails an exploration of your interests, passions, and goals to find focus and direction in your educational and occupational pathway. The Money Factor focuses on the multiple ways to make higher education affordable to meet your financial needs. The You Factor describes the 8 Strengths underpinning all 4 factors.

Your You Factor Steps

1. The 8 Strengths of the You Factor. You will be introduced to the 8 Strengths of the You Factor that create your unique identity and help you to become college and career-ready.

2. Case Study – Emily. Through a case study, you will be shown how these 8 Strengths assist high school students enhance their college and career readiness.

3. Strengthening Your You Factor. Through activities, you will be assisted in supporting the development of your 8 Strengths and become a college-ready student who is both well-rounded and focused.

Figure 1.1

COLLEGE UNMAZED

Step 1: The 8 Strengths of the You Factor

Our 8 Strengths model is built around what colleges look for as indicators that a student will be successful at their university. College admissions officers ask the question, "How do I know this student will be successful at our university?" Students that integrate the 8 Strengths will demonstrate to admissions officers that they can and will be successful at their college and persist through to graduation. When you incorporate the 8 Strengths early into your high school career, they can help you build a set of skills that will last a lifetime – and help you stand out in the sea of college applicants. In this chapter, we want to help you do 2 things – grow your You Factor and then learn how to use it when you apply to college.

Research shows that your chances of being satisfied and successful in college and a career increase greatly if you get stronger in 8 ways. Each of these 8 Strengths works together to make you college and career-ready. You are better prepared to succeed if you intentionally and assertively use each of these behaviors every single day.

Below you will find a brief description of each of the 8 Strengths: please read these carefully. To help you see how these strengths impact a college application, a case study is provided and then analyzed. Finally, to help you see where you are in your own development of the 8 Strengths, you will complete a self-assessment activity.

8 Strengths of College and Career Readiness

Figure 1.2

1. Agency
You have direction in life and are actively preparing yourself to pursue something meaningful and important to you and are ready to take advantage of expected and unexpected opportunities.

2. Positive Beliefs
You have the self-confidence to seize on new opportunities, persevere through adversity, and believe that your talents and capabilities grow through your own efforts.

3. Effective Goals
You have developed educational and career goals that guide your choices and actions for your success today and in the future. Your goals are SMART – specific, measurable, attainable, realistic, and timely.

4. Knowing Yourself
You understand how your interests, personality, skills, and work values fit best with different postsecondary educational and Career Pathways.

5. Becoming a Successful Student
You demonstrate the ability to take control over both the academic skills and learning strategies needed for lifelong learning success.

6. Character for Workplace Success
You get along with others, work as part of a team, are flexible, and dependable, can follow rules, be a leader, and not be overcome by emotions such as anxiety, anger, and depression.

7. College Knowledge
You have learned critical information about colleges, e.g., cost, financing, scholarships; how to apply; college cultures; choosing a college major; and terminology like *demonstrated interest* and *early action decision*s.

8. College Support Network
You have a well-established network of people (parents, family, relatives, siblings, peers, mentors, teachers, and school counselors) who will actively support you in your college-going journey.

CHAPTER 1: YOU FACTOR

Step 2: Case Study–Emily

> Emily is a high school sophomore beginning to take a strong interest in her academic work and hopes to attend college. While neither of Emily's parents went to college, they believe it is important for her to go to college and expand her career choices. Emily sees the hard work her parents have put in every day for the last 10 years to start and run their own small business. With three siblings, and Emily being the oldest, Emily has a lot of responsibility around the house and works part-time at a local restaurant where she cleans tables, washes dishes, and serves ice cream. Emily enjoys working in this restaurant and was promoted after three months. Emily likes to be given responsibility and enjoys the pressure when the restaurant gets busy.
>
> When Emily spoke to her high school counselor to plan for courses that would help her get ready for college over the next two years, the counselor recommended AP Psychology and additional science courses at the honors or AP level. Emily is a good student, with a 3.5 GPA out of 4.0. Emily was a volunteer peer mediator last year and joined the school's Psychology Club this year, as she very much enjoyed helping people solve their problems. The advisor for the Psychology Club also teaches the AP Psychology class, and Emily has developed a good relationship with the teacher. Emily is considering that Psychology might be a good college major and something to explore further. Emily has always done well in science classes and very much enjoyed her Biology class this year. She is not currently thinking about a science-related major for college.
>
> Emily has a wide range of interests. She was a starting defender on the high school's winning soccer team and promoted to co-captain of the team. When not playing soccer, Emily likes to hang out with friends.
>
> The high school counselor, Emily's teachers, and the soccer coach all report that she has a solid work ethic and is liked by peers and adults in school. Emily's attendance is excellent.

How Well Developed are Emily's 8 Strengths?

Agency: Emily is starting to take on and do well in academically rigorous coursework. She is also taking advantage of opportunities to develop and explore her interest in Psychology, which arose from her volunteering as a peer mediator and joining the Psychology Club. Having a part-time job and talking to her parents and school counselor about her future after high school are positive steps in beginning to become college and career ready.

Positive Beliefs: Emily enjoys her classes and expects to do well in more advanced coursework next year. She also likes attending school and looks forward to the days she works at the restaurant. This demonstrates self-confidence and a willingness to take on challenges.

Effective Goals: Emily's emerging goal that Psychology could be the right college major is rooted in her experiences as a peer mediator and member of the Psychology Club. This has given her the opportunity to interact with other people who have similar interests. This is an effective, age-appropriate goal for a high school sophomore. Emily can use the next two years of high school to further explore her interests and develop more specific, measurable, attainable, and timely goals.

Knowing Yourself: Emily is progressing in self-understanding, and her interest in Psychology is developing. However, science is another area she should explore further so that she does not prematurely close the door on a wide range of interesting and rewarding college majors and careers. Emily is starting to know what she likes and does not like and is eager to further her self-exploration.

Becoming a Successful Student: Emily is doing well in academic classes, has a strong GPA, and has excellent attendance. Emily is demonstrating that she is becoming the kind of student who will do well in rigorous high school courses and later in college courses.

Character for Workplace Success: Emily has good habits such as dependability (e.g., good attendance), showing initiative (e.g., getting a job, joining school activities), and demonstrates several positive aspects of character. Emily's friendships, participation on a sports team, and successful relationships in school and at work are additional strengths of character that will help her realize her future college and career aspirations.

College Knowledge: Emily is a first-generation student as neither parent attended college. First-generation college students have, on average, less college knowledge than students from families with at least one college-educated parent/guardian. It will be important for Emily to learn about college admissions procedures, financial aid, and what life is like at college to help her make an informed, effective decision about which college to attend.

College Support Network: Relationships with others in several areas of Emily's life – her counselor, teachers, parents, supervisors, coworkers, and peers – are important sources of active support in Emily's college-going journey. Emily does not need to go through the college-choice process alone. It will be very helpful to her if she regularly engages in discussions about going to college with the people in her support network.

ACTIVITY 1.1: My 8 Strengths

Now it is your turn to see how developed your 8 Strengths are. Read through the 8 Strengths on the chart below and put an "X" above each strength that corresponds to the level where you believe you are (beginning, developing, or proficient). After completing *College UnMazed*, you may want to return to this activity and see where your areas of growth have been.

For students using a digital version of this workbook and needing downloadable worksheets, visit www.collegeunmazed.com/downloads.

Beginning: I am just starting to develop this strength and know that I need to improve.
Developing: I can list a few specific ways in which I demonstrate this strength but need to continue developing this strength.
Proficient: I have integrated this strength into my life and can show my knowledge through my daily actions.

Proficient								
Developing								
Beginning								
	Agency	Positive Beliefs	Effective Goals	Knowing Yourself	Becoming a Successful Student	Character for Workplace Success	College Knowledge	College Support Network

Talk to people in your College Support Network about your assessment of the 8 Strengths. Here are some questions to guide your discussions:

- Right now, what strengths help you to be college and career ready?

- What strengths do you need to improve on?

- What can you do right now to improve your chances for success and satisfaction in high school? Your future education and career?

CHAPTER 1: YOU FACTOR

Step 3: Strengthening Your You Factor

Your high school years can be used to explore your interests and abilities and to begin using the unique talents that you have. Your talents and interests can lie in many different areas – whether you are interested in science, theater, athletics, music, art, volunteering, etc., high school is a time to begin exploring different areas because it will help guide you to what college to attend, and ultimately, what career you might pursue.

Importantly, high school is a place to develop your 8 Strengths. This becomes a crucial part of your college application through your high school transcript, résumé, essay, and letters of recommendation. How you grow and engage your 8 Strengths will show college admissions representatives your You Factor and what you have done to cultivate and grow it. This will provide evidence of both how and why you will be successful at their college.

Ways to Develop Your 8 Strengths

There are many ways you can develop your 8 Strengths. Several of the most common and important ways are discussed below. Colleges look favorably on students who have developed themselves in these areas.

Figure 1.3

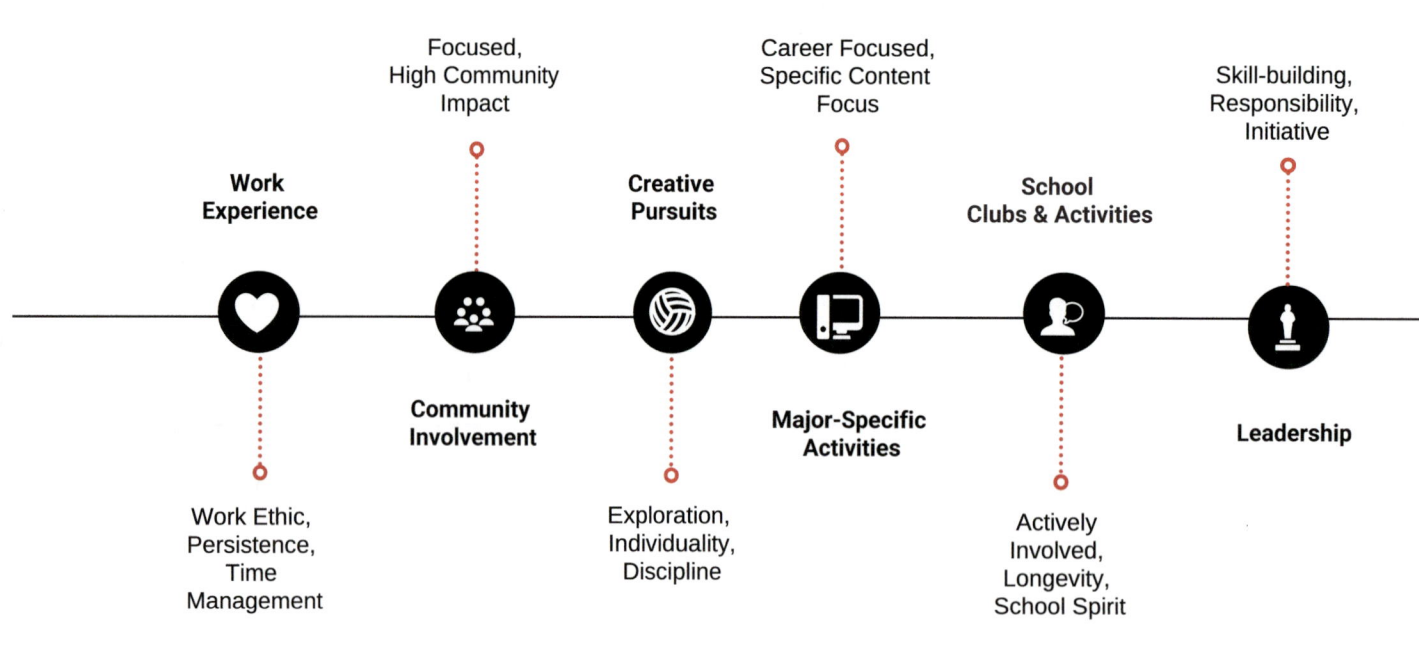

Category	Key Attributes
Work Experience	Work Ethic, Persistence, Time Management
Community Involvement	Focused, High Community Impact
Creative Pursuits	Exploration, Individuality, Discipline
Major-Specific Activities	Career Focused, Specific Content Focus
School Clubs & Activities	Actively Involved, Longevity, School Spirit
Leadership	Skill-building, Responsibility, Initiative

- **Work experience:** While finding part-time work for a teenager often will not be in a field of interest, working in a collaborative, fast-paced environment can show colleges you have the broad set of skills they are looking for, which includes skills such as being responsible, time management, and a strong work ethic. You can also reflect on what you enjoy and perhaps do not enjoy about your work environment to help you consider future career opportunities.

    Case Study Example: Emily has a part-time job, so she is already developing this valuable skill set.

- **Community involvement:** Colleges often look favorably on students who have participated in community service and volunteer activities. Achieving targeted goals through high impact community service can be powerful in building your You Factor more deeply with your community.

    Case Study Example: Emily's volunteer experience as a peer mediator in her school is a good example of community involvement. Emily might also consider volunteering with organizations outside of the school community. For example, volunteering at a non-profit organization, like the National Alliance on Mental Illness (NAMI) that provides resources, small groups, and mental health education, would be great exposure to the field of Psychology.

- **Creative pursuits:** High school is a time to explore your identity and creativity. It is a time to think outside of the box and explore unique opportunities for self-expression and personal growth. Possible activities could include being an entrepreneur, learning a new technological skill, participating in social activism, traveling abroad, and exploring other cultures and identities.

  Case Study Example: With the help of the Psychology Club, Emily could look at opportunities to take on some creative endeavors. Running a Suicide Prevention Week at the school by making posters, creating flyers, and organizing with other students could be a great activity.

- **Major exploration activities:** While we do not believe that all high school students should be deciding on a college major before they leave high school, exploring possible majors you may find interesting is a very good idea. For example, if you are interested in healthcare, you could volunteer at a hospital. This would help you learn about a wide variety of healthcare careers that you might find fitting for you. Did you know that about one-third of all college students change their major? That is because as people take more classes and have more experiences, they can make more informed decisions about college majors that are right for them. So, get started early – explore where you might fit best in the world of work as soon as possible. Work-based learning opportunities like job shadowing, apprenticeships, and internships can be extremely helpful.

  Case Study Example: The last two activities mentioned, NAMI and Suicide Prevention Week, are also college major exploration activities. So, while Emily is building those skills, she is also exploring Psychology as a major. Taking the AP Psychology class next year will help Emily see what college-level classes in Psychology will be like.

- **School clubs & activities:** Your school and community are likely to have activities you can be involved in, such as sports, martial arts, music, art, theater, debate, technology, and so forth. It is best for you to find something you can dedicate time to and actively be involved in for an extended period of time, as opposed to a large number of activities to which you are not very committed. Focus and find extra-curricular activities that are both meaningful and help to develop your 8 Strengths. It is better to be deeply involved in a couple of areas than it is to be spread too thin across many areas.

  Case Study Example: Emily shows commitment and active active engagement by being a part of the school's Psychology Club, peer mediation program, and soccer team.

- **Leadership:** Colleges tend to like applicants who have demonstrated leadership. There are many activities you can be involved in that will give you the opportunity to take on responsibility, work with others, and assume a leadership role. For example, you can be on the student council at your high school, be in charge of a school campaign, have a more senior position at your job, or help lead a community or volunteer project.

  Case Study Example: Emily is co-captain of the soccer team, was promoted at work and could become an officer in the Psychology Club. She is beginning to demonstrate leadership skills in multiple areas. Being open and willing is key.

Activity 1.2: Your 8 Strengths Activities

Review the 8 Strengths and Emily's activities above and how she is building her 8 Strengths. Write below some activities you are doing right now to build your 8 Strengths.

CHAPTER 1: YOU FACTOR

Be a "T" Shaped Student

Figure 1.4

Often parents and students hear the myth that students need to be involved in as many extra-curricular activities as they can. This can lead to students and their parents being overextended. The myth that "you should do it all" is just that, a myth. In terms of college admissions, it is better to be a "T"-shaped – you need to be both well-rounded and strength-focused.

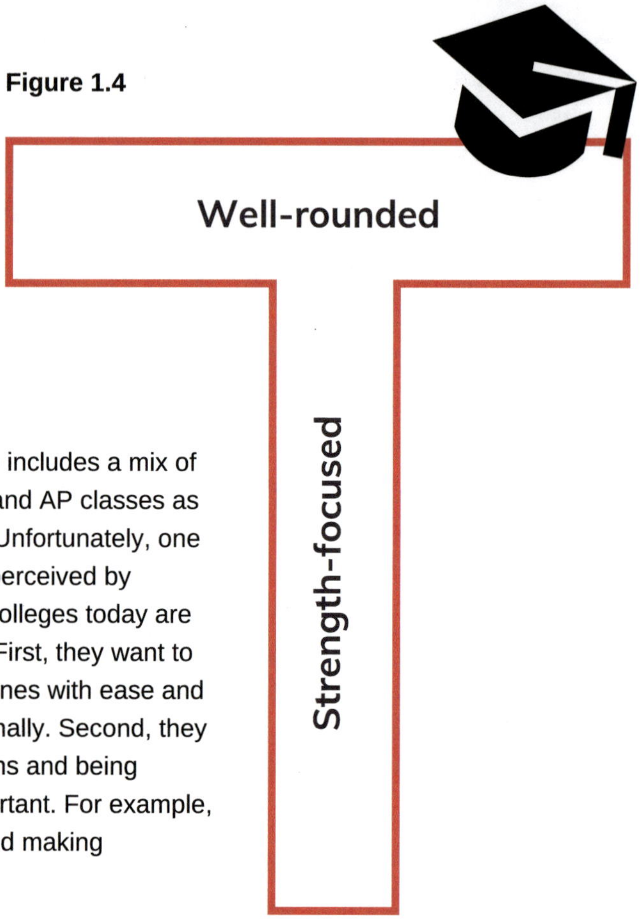

Many people believe that the secret recipe for getting into college includes a mix of community service, school clubs, athletics, and as many honors and AP classes as your school has. This can lead students to be stretched too thin. Unfortunately, one of the problems with students who try to do it all is that it can be perceived by colleges as lacking focus and not having a specialized skill set. Colleges today are often looking for applicants who showcase two strong attributes. First, they want to see a broad set of skills to be able to work across multiple disciplines with ease and confidence – being well-rounded personally, socially, and emotionally. Second, they want to see where students are the most focused on their passions and being unique. Admission factors like this are becoming even more important. For example, more colleges are going test-optional (discussed in Chapter 2) and making admission decisions based on the 8 Strengths.

Well-rounded, strength-focused students know how to work in small teams, solve problems, and demonstrate initiative and persistence to keep going when issues arise. Focused students have a strong passion for specific coursework, school activities, community engagement, and/or extra-curricular work. Together, students who are both well-rounded and strength-focused are "T"-shaped.

Activity 1.3: Building Your You Factor

You have been introduced in this chapter to the 8 Strengths and the You Factor. As mentioned, students will build these through activities they do while in high school and the support network they build. In this activity, you will be examining your support networks and some activities you can do to enhance your You Factor.

Step 1: Think of at least three people in your life that can help guide you through your high school years. This could be a teacher, spiritual leader, coach, advisor, school counselor, community member, etc. who you think is influential in your life. A recommendation is to think of people from various occupations (like one teacher, one coach, and one community member), but that is not necessary. Fill in the chart.

Step 2: Explore some activities in your community and school that you would like to be involved in or already are. Think of why that activity is meaningful to you and why you think that is building your You factor. Fill in the chart on the next page.

COLLEGE UNMAZED

List   Describe   Steps

List 3 people, groups, or communities that provide you with social support.	Describe how each of your supports helps you, or could help you, with emotional, tangible, informational, and/or social needs.	What specific steps could you take to better utilize your supports?
List 3 activities that can help build your You Factor.	Describe how each of your activities helps build your 8 Strengths.	What specific steps could you do to utilize the resources around you (school, community, family, friends, etc.)?

Chapter Summary

In Chapter 1 you explored your 8 Strengths (Agency, Positive Beliefs, Effective Goals, Knowing Yourself, Becoming a Successful Student, Character for Workplace Success, College Knowledge, and College Support Network) and how those skills are developed through your You Factor, which focuses on your unique strengths, passions, interests, and future goals. You were asked to explore activities and support systems that can help you grow your You factor. You should note that your high school years are a time learn more about yourself, others, and the world around you. Your personal ideas and skills will continue to evolve and change over time as you learn more. You should embrace these opportunities and continually reflect on what you liked and did not like at every step of the way.

At-Home Discussion

After describing each of the 8 Strengths to your family, ask them how much Agency they see in you. Write their answer below. *Yes, see a lot of agency. Thrive to see what I can do in life.*

Which You Factors does your family see as being most important to your success in college? Write their answer below.

They think agency and Effective goals are the most important. Also Knowing Yourself.

Review High School Planning Checklist in Resources on page 132. What are some next action steps that you need to take in the next month, six months, and year?

Mind Factor, Developing a list, Exploring colleges, Applying to colleges, Deciding on a college, Succeeding in college.

CHAPTER 2
Academic Factor

Understand How to Build the Academic Skills and Plan Needed for College and Career Success

You Factor · **Academic Factor** · Career Factor · Money Factor · Developing a List · Exploring Colleges · Applying to Colleges · Deciding on a College · Succeeding in College

In this chapter, you will learn how to develop your Academic Factor, one of the foundational components needed to succeed in college. What you do academically while in high school will set the stage for your academic success in college later. You will now explore what the Academic Factor is and how to look for opportunities to build and grow it. We will show you how your 8 Strengths are critical to the development of your Academic Factor.

Your Academic Factor Steps

1. The Academic Factor and College Admissions. You will be introduced to the Academic Factor and how it relates to college admissions. High school coursework, grades, and standardized test scores are discussed in relation to what college admissions personnel value and find important when making admission decisions.

2. Case Study – José. Through a case study example, you will be shown how the 8 Strengths can support the development of your Academic Factor.

3. Developing Your Academic Factor. Through activities, you will be shown how to take charge of the development of your own Academic Factor in high school.

Step 1: The Academic Factor & College Admissions

The Academic Factor as it relates to college admissions consists primarily of three areas: 1) your academic coursework, 2) your grades in that coursework, and 3) your standardized test scores on college entrance exams (ACT/SAT). College admission counselors rely heavily on these three factors when making admissions decisions. Every year, the National Association for College Admission Counseling (NACAC) surveys college admissions directors across the United States to identify what is important to them when reviewing applicants. The results of their latest 2019 survey are summarized in Figure 2.1 on the next page.

The factors ranked as most important by admissions directors – grades in all courses, grades in college prep courses, strength of curriculum, and admission test scores – comprise the Academic Factor as covered in this chapter. It is important to note here that the courses you choose to take and your grades in those courses are more important than admission test scores to colleges. More than 9 out of 10 admissions directors say that grades in all courses and grades in college prep courses are important. More than 8 out of 10 admissions directors say that the strength of the curriculum (e.g., taking honors and AP courses) is moderately or considerably important.

Please note, we are not trying to say that things like your essay, extracurricular activities, or recommendation letters are not important. However, it is true that these things are not as important as the rigor of the classes you choose to take in high school, your grades in those classes, and your admission test scores – all of which we review next in this chapter.

Figure 2.1

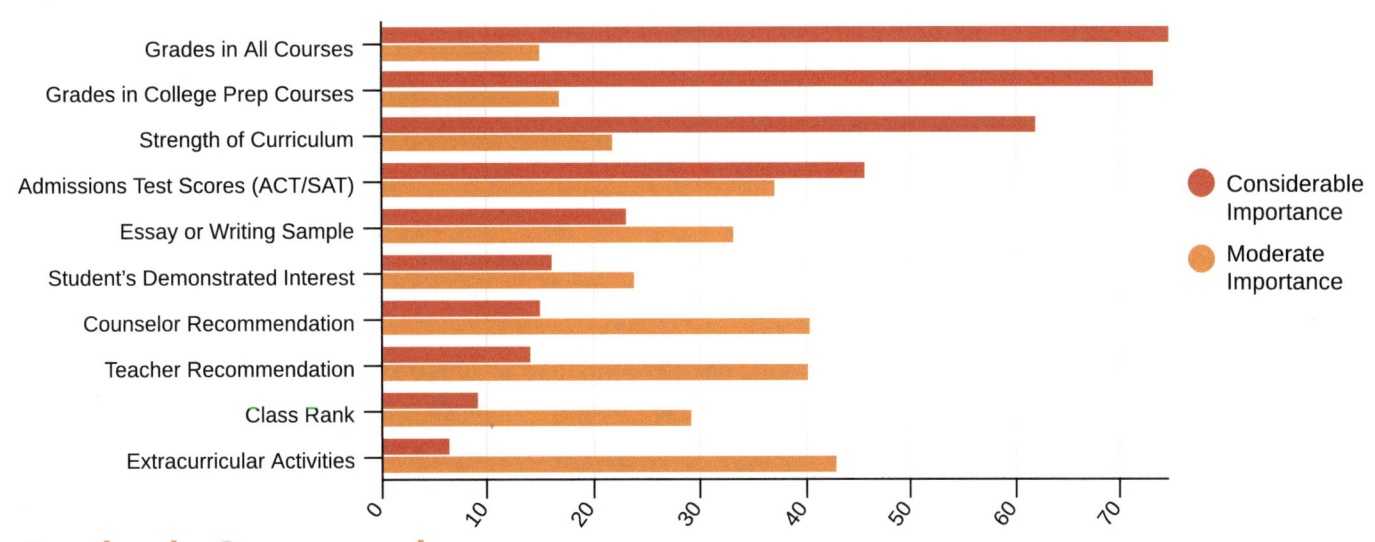

Bar chart showing factors in admission decisions by Considerable Importance (red) and Moderate Importance (orange):

- Grades in All Courses
- Grades in College Prep Courses
- Strength of Curriculum
- Admissions Test Scores (ACT/SAT)
- Essay or Writing Sample
- Student's Demonstrated Interest
- Counselor Recommendation
- Teacher Recommendation
- Class Rank
- Extracurricular Activities

Academic Coursework

High schools offer a range of programs, from which you decide what courses are best for you. While there are courses required for high school graduation and college admissions, the type, and level of courses you choose to take will determine the strength of your program of study. You will also have the opportunity to explore different subjects through, for example, electives and extracurricular activities. Some coursework can lead to an industry credential or college credit. The decisions you make about the classes you take in high school can also give you a chance to try out different Career Pathways - a topic we will cover in Chapter 3.

In most school districts, there are a variety of different academic courses and programs you can choose from. Even in small schools with fewer choices, there are programs that you and your parents may not be aware of. It is important to know the right questions to ask about all that is available to you. Knowing the names of programs and what is available at your high school, off-campus, and online can be instrumental in planning your high school curriculum. The earlier you start this planning process, the better. You do not want to say at the end of high school "I did not know I had that opportunity." High schools offer a wide array of coursework to allow you to specialize in areas you are interested in and excel. If you are interested in being in the medical field, your transcript should showcase courses such as Biology, Chemistry, Anatomy and Physiology, and advanced level Mathematics. Taking on advanced coursework in a specific field shows you are willing to stretch yourself to meet future career goals. Often there are four ways you can broaden and deepen your academic coursework:

Figure 2.2

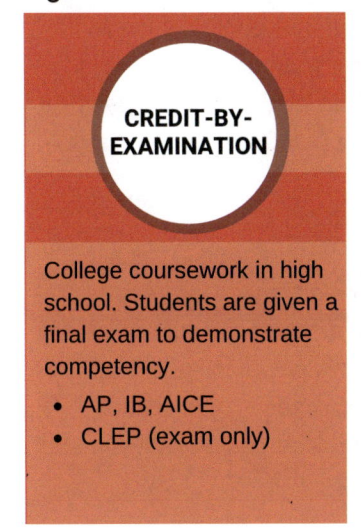

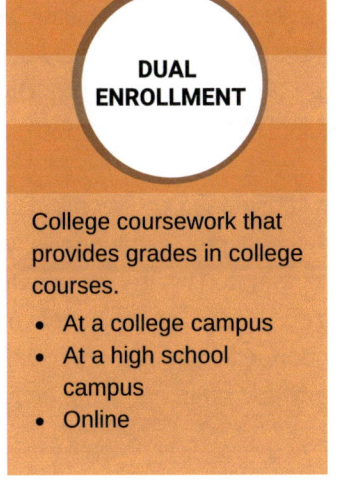

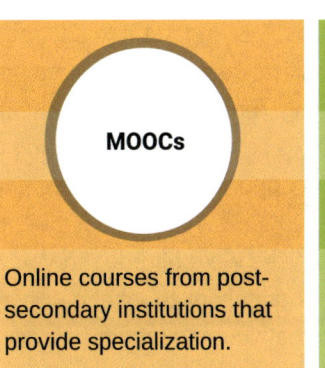

CREDIT-BY-EXAMINATION
College coursework in high school. Students are given a final exam to demonstrate competency.
- AP, IB, AICE
- CLEP (exam only)

DUAL ENROLLMENT
College coursework that provides grades in college courses.
- At a college campus
- At a high school campus
- Online

MOOCs
Online courses from post-secondary institutions that provide specialization.
- Coursera, Khan Academy, FutureLearn, Udacity, Kadenza, and Udemy

INDUSTRY CERTIFICATION
Career and technical programs through the high school or local college focused on a specific career skill set.
- CNA, welding, HVAC, dental hygiene, and more

CHAPTER 2: ACADEMIC FACTOR

Credit-by-Examination: Credit-by-examination courses are college-level courses taught by high school teachers that provide students with the opportunity to take on more rigorous coursework. At the end of the course, students are given a standardized test. The score earned on the test can could provide college credit. Examples of credit-by-examination are [Advanced Placement](#), [International Baccalaureate](#), [Cambridge Advanced International Certificate of Education (AICE)](#), and [College-Level Examination Program (CLEP)](#).

Dual Enrollment: Dual enrollment is when a high school student takes actual college courses, either at their high school through concurrent enrollment or through a local college or university. These courses are taught by college credentialed teachers or college professors. Dual enrollment courses enable students to begin building their college transcript.

Massive Open Online Courses (MOOCs): MOOCs are often free but may not provide high school credit. They are courses taught by experts at universities like MIT, Berkeley, and Harvard on a range of topics like coding, medical neuroscience, business, fitness, and psychology. These courses can provide some of the specialized content that you might not find at your school and allow you to explore your specific interests, which integrates your You Factor with your Academic Factor. Even if a MOOC you take does not show up on your high school transcript, it can still enhance your college application through your college essay and recommendation letters from your counselor or teachers about your expertise and motivation. Some MOOC sites and their focus are listed below.

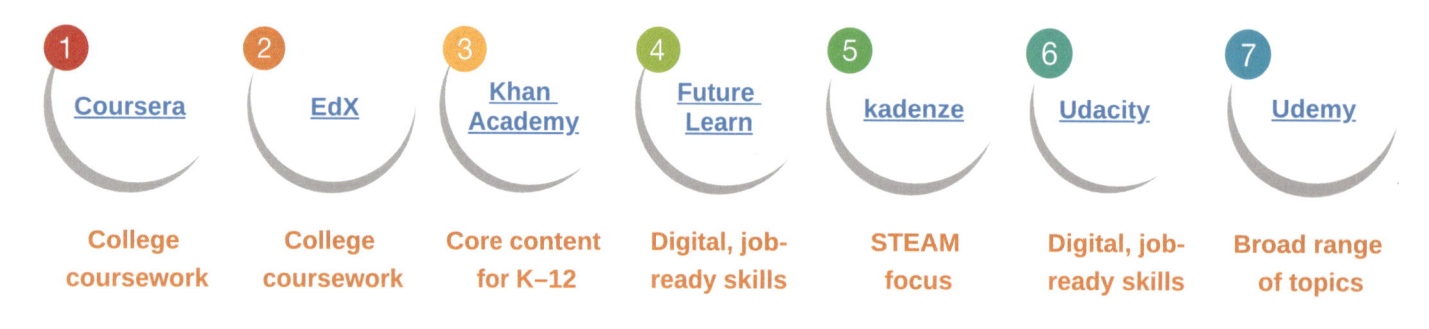

1	2	3	4	5	6	7
Coursera	EdX	Khan Academy	Future Learn	kadenze	Udacity	Udemy
College coursework	College coursework	Core content for K–12	Digital, job-ready skills	STEAM focus	Digital, job-ready skills	Broad range of topics

Industry Certification: Career and technical programs can provide students with hands-on experience in a specific field, often leading to an industry certification or micro-credential that leads directly to employment. Common programs are certified nursing assistant (CNA), veterinarian technician, welding, and many others. Industry certification can bolster your college application, but you should carefully consider how doing so strengthens your high school curriculum in the eyes of college admission counselors. The case of José starting on page 24 will illustrate this.

Besides core academic courses, it is important to choose electives that help you build on your 8 Strengths, such as Knowing Yourself, Having Positive Beliefs, and Becoming a Successful Student. Customizing your schedule to include some courses that are engaging, fun, and focused on your "T"-shape can be extremely beneficial. Elective courses like Band, Choir, Fine Arts, Junior Reserve Officers' Training Corps (JROTC), Engineering, Computer Science, Business, Health, and more can open up opportunities for career exploration and academic growth.

Colleges look at what opportunities were afforded to you when considering your application for admission. Typically, when you apply to a college, your school counselor will send a school profile that details what advanced courses are available, average admission test scores and other academic offerings. This is important for all students, but particularly so for students in high schools that do not have many specialized classes, as the school profile provides important context for admissions officers to consider. There are many opportunities to take advanced courses in high school, online, or through dual enrollment. We recommend you ask early and often about the opportunities available to you and build a strong high school course of study.

Grades

The grades you earn in high school courses are the most important factor admission counselors consider when reviewing your college application – nearly 9 out of every 10 admission directors view grades as moderately or considerably important. With many colleges and universities going test-optional since COVID-19, grades may become even more important to the college admissions process. Research has shown that grades in high school are the number one predictor of college success, even more so than test scores (Allensworth & Clark, 2020).

However, what many students and parents do not realize is that not all grades are created equal. Colleges and universities look at your grade point average differently than your high school. For example, many colleges recalculate a student's GPA to help them compare students from different high schools. Look at the example below and key terms to understand the different ways GPA can be calculated by high schools and colleges.

Figure 2.3

Class	Grade	Percentage	Unweighted	Weighted	Recalculated	College Credits
AP English	B	85%	3.0	4.0	4.0	3.0*
AP Biology	B	89%	3.0	4.0	4.0	3.0*
U.S. History	A	92%	4.0	4.0	4.0	0
Algebra 2 (Honors)	C	77%	2.0	2.5	2.5	0
Spanish 2	B	85%	3.0	3.0	3.0	0
Band	A	95%	4.0	4.0	N/A	0
Weightlifting	A	98%	4.0	4.0	N/A	0
Average		88%	3.28	3.64	3.5	6.0*

*Possible credits based on AP exam score and the college's requirements for awarding credit based on the exam score.

Key terms

Unweighted: This simply means that when an unweighted GPA is calculated, it does not receive any extra points for more rigorous courses like honors, dual enrollment, Advanced Placement, and so forth. For example, an A in Weightlifting counts as much towards the unweighted GPA as AP English.

Weighted: A weighted GPA accounts for the level of coursework taken. More points are awarded for more rigorous courses. For example, Algebra II Honors has a lower weight than AP English, and most electives and lower-level academic classes are not weighted at all. Class rankings are often determined from this.

Recalculated GPA: The recalculated GPA is a method colleges use to review a high school transcript based on their own grading criteria. It is often a weighted GPA based on academic core subjects (English, Social Studies, Mathematics, Sciences, and Foreign Language) and excludes electives such as weightlifting, band, and art.

Choosing courses that are appropriate for you and while balancing the difficulty of the courses with your ability to maintain good grades is important to consider as you plan your courses in high school. For example, it may be better for your recalculated and weighted GPA to take Honors English over the non-honors English as long as you are able to keep your grades up.

CHAPTER 2: ACADEMIC FACTOR

What if my grades are not where I want them to be?

Getting help early on in your middle and high school years to improve basic reading, math, writing, and study skills can go a long way in improving your academic profile. If you are not performing at the level you need to reach your educational and career goals, you can improve. You can assess your weaknesses by taking a frequent look at how you approach your learning – things such as your study habits, actively listening to classroom lectures, improving your notetaking, participating in lessons, preparing for exams, and getting enough sleep. These are small, everyday choices you have control over, and can make, that can improve your academic success. You can also use your College Support Network (teachers, counselors, parents, extended family, etc.) to help you learn new strategies to succeed in areas that have you given difficulty in the past.

College Admissions Testing (ACT/SAT)

Students and parents have a lot of questions regarding college admission tests–what they are, when it is best to take them, and what they mean for college admissions. While a select group of colleges are moving away from using the ACT and SAT at what are known as "test-optional" schools, at most colleges these college admission tests are still an important consideration. Not only are admission decisions connected to your test scores, but oftentimes your eligibility for scholarships, honors programs, and specific majors are tied to your admission test scores as well. In this section, we will introduce you to the key things you need to know and do to successfully navigate the admission test piece of the college-going maze.

What You Should Know

As discussed earlier, students are evaluated on many factors in college admissions. The ACT and SAT are standardized, norm-referenced tests colleges use to compare students and make admissions decisions. Research has shown both tests predict future college grades to some extent. However, these college entrance exams have not been shown to predict future career success. While these admissions tests are important for gaining entrance to college, they do not define who you are or what you will become. For example, there are many students who score low on college admission tests who do very well in college. Effort and developing your 8 Strengths are what is key to your success.

Below are basic facts about the SAT and ACT you should know.

Figure 2.4

ACT
Top Score: 36
National Average: 20

- Grammar and usage, math, reading, science reasoning, and writing (optional)
- Straightforward, questions may be long but are usually less difficult to decipher
- Costs $60.00 for each test. Vouchers are available for qualifying students
- For more information or to sign up, visit www.actstudent.org

SAT
Top Score: 1600
National Average: 1060

- Reading, relevant words in context, math, grammar and usage
- Questions are evidence and context-based and focus on real-world situations and multi-step problem-solving
- Costs $55.00 for each test. Vouchers are available for qualifying students
- Will be digital starting in 2024
- For more information or to sign up, visit www.collegeboard.org

What You Should Do

The first thing you should do is determine which test is best for you, as they focus on different thinking strategies and content knowledge. Typically, students gravitate to one test over another. By taking practice tests on each test's website or through Khan Academy (www.khanacademy.org), you can get a sense early on of which test is best for you.

After that, like any big exam you must take, you should prepare. There are a number of different ways to prepare but knowing the best way for you to study and learn is what matters. First, determine what you need to be successful: do you need to brush up on math, reading, or writing skills first, or learn strategies to tackle the different areas of the test? The earlier you study up on your academics, the easier it is for you to focus on the strategies. One of the biggest challenges of these tests is knowing what to expect. You want to feel comfortable walking in on test day knowing how they are going to structure the questions, what they are looking for in an answer, and the way to determine your answer quickly. A great way to determine your needs is by taking a full-length timed diagnostic test, often found on each test's websites, in test-like conditions that will give you a breakdown of your performance in each section and help you identify needed skills.

Test preparation can improve your performance. There are test preparation options for every type of learner, including individual study, one-on-one tutoring, group class instruction, or a combination. There are several good websites that can give you diagnostic tests, flashcards, practice tests, and overall guidance if you feel comfortable studying on your own. If you decide you want tutoring, make sure that your tutor is legitimate, or employed by a reputable tutoring center. Group classes can be the most cost-effective for getting what you need. Make sure that you choose a small group class with a maximum of 10 students so you can have individual attention from your teacher.

It is helpful to know how test-taking can fit into your four-year high school plan. You should develop a timeline for when you will take these tests. Below is an example of a typical timeline that works for most students.

Figure 2.5

1. 8th–9th
Testing is not a focus, but some academic summer programs might require testing.

2. Fall 10th
Many schools offer Pre-ACT or PSAT in the fall of the 10th grade year to begin practicing and getting a baseline. Be sure to watch for dates and sign up.

3. Spring 10th
This is a great time to plan taking tests if you may be interested in dual enrollment or other college-level programs while in high school.

4. Fall 11th
The 11th grade PSAT is used for multiple scholarships, such as National Merit Scholarships. Also, fee waivers can be used for both the ACT and SAT.

5. Spring 11th
This is a key time to start taking college admission tests. Most experts suggest taking both the ACT and SAT and see which score is highest.

6. Fall 12th
Some seniors use this as their last testing time for college admissions. Most colleges have a priority deadline of November 1st.

7. Spring 12th
Many seniors use this time to reach for a higher score.

CHAPTER 2: ACADEMIC FACTOR

Activity 2.1: Your Test Scores

You can use the chart below to keep track of your scores and what is known as a superscore, which is when colleges take the highest score from each section of different test attempts to create the highest composite scores. Superscores cannot be across the ACT and SAT, but only within each test across multiple attempts.

	Date Taken	Reading	English	Math	Science (ACT)	Composite
PSAT or Practice						
PreACT or Practice						
ACT						
SAT						

Step 2: Case Study – José

José is about to begin his junior year in high school. José has developed an interest in pursuing a medical career. During his sophomore year, he started visiting a nursing home to see his grandfather. During these visits, he found himself intrigued by the medical treatments provided to his grandfather by the nursing staff, as well as the machines they used. He only saw women doing this work, which led him to wrongly believe that nursing was a field only for women. Then on one visit, José was very surprised to find a male nurse taking care of his grandfather. The male nurse could see that José was interested in what he was doing and began mentoring him. Because of this relationship, José decided to volunteer at the nursing home this past summer. This experience was so positive that José met with his school counselor to enroll in the certified nursing assistant (CNA) training through his high school's Medical Academy, which helps students learn about various healthcare careers while earning an industry-recognized credential. Completing CNA training would allow him to work part-time at the nursing home while still in high school, as CNAs are in high demand. José's Individualized Academic Plan (IAP) is presented below.

	8th	9th	10th	11th	12th
English		English 1 Honors	English 2 Honors	English 3 Honors	Literature
Mathematics	Algebra 1	Geometry	Algebra 2	Pre-Calculus	Calculus
Science		Physical Science	Biology Honors	AP Biology*	Anatomy & Physiology (DE)*
Social Studies		World History	AP Human Geography*	AP US History*	Government (DE)*/ Economics (DE)*
Foreign Language	Spanish 1	Spanish 2	Spanish 3	AP Spanish*	
Elective		Physical Education	Computer Programming	Medical Academy	Medical Academy
Elective			Intro to Marketing	Medical Academy	Medical Academy
College Credits			3*	9*	9*

*Possible college credits earned based on AP exam score and the college's requirements for awarding credit based on the exam score or passing the college course.

> José has set out a rigorous and demanding schedule of courses for his last two years in high school. He aspires to enter a competitive four-year college the fall semester after he graduates. José expects to one day earn a graduate degree somewhere in the medical Career Pathway. Right now, he is exploring what a college major would look like if he wanted to become either a nurse practitioner or a medical doctor. When developing this plan, José discussed his thoughts and feelings with his family, school counselor, favorite teachers, trusted friends, and his mentor.
>
> José is eager to start his junior year in high school. He knows his grades in these demanding courses will have a large impact on college admissions, as 11th grade will be the final full year of coursework and grades college admissions officers will have to evaluate his application. So far, his grade point average is very good (3.7 out of 4.0, unweighted). He has gotten As and high Bs in all his science and math courses. He is planning to take both the SAT and ACT tests at least once during 11th grade. He is very motivated to get high grades over the next two years to qualify for as many scholarships as possible, as well as qualify for admission to more selective and competitive colleges. José would like to choose between several good college options.

How Well Developed Are José's 8 Strengths?

Agency: José has discovered an educational direction that connects his last two years of high school to what he might want to study in college. The rigorous course work in his Individualized Academic Plan, including earning a CNA certificate through the Medical Academy, demonstrates he is challenging himself academically. His IAP also shows how meaningful and important this direction is to him.

Positive Beliefs: José is demonstrating the needed self-confidence to challenge stereotypes that limit exploration about what careers are for what people. He is determined not to let destructive beliefs about gender or race rob him of opportunities he knows he can do well in and enjoy. He has the grit to persevere through whatever adversity might be thrown his way.

Effective Goals: Going to college is an aspiration firmly embedded in Jose's identity. José's educational goals to succeed in college and go to graduate school complement his identity of being someone who will one day graduate from college. College-going aspirations and well-developed goals to succeed in postsecondary education help high school students to get into college and persist to graduation. This is especially important given the fact that only about half of all full-time students who enter a four-year college graduate in four years.

Knowing Yourself: José has discovered that helping others is important to who he wants to become and what he wants to do in his work life. He also likes science and wants to use technology to help sick people get better. It is clear to José that working in the medical Career Pathway could be a very good match for his interests, skills, values, and personality. His rigorous coursework, including the Medical Academy, will help him further these explorations and grow in self-understanding.

Becoming a Successful Student: José is taking responsibility and ownership for becoming an effective student. This coming year he will be taking three AP classes and start the Medical Academy. In his senior year, he will take dual enrollment classes in Anatomy and Physiology, Government, and Economics. José has the potential to earn 21 college credits before graduating high school. His commitment to his own academic development and the strength of his rigorous coursework in high school will help José to become a successful college student, an effective lifelong learner, and demonstrate to admissions counselors that he is ready for challenging, college-level coursework.

CHAPTER 2: ACADEMIC FACTOR

Character for Workplace Success: José consistently exhibits, at school and when volunteering at the nursing home, the kind of character strengths that will make him college and workforce-ready. He gets along very well with his classmates, teachers, and supervisors at the nursing home. He is dependable, shows good judgment, and follows through on assigned work tasks. In addition, his mood is positive, upbeat, and optimistic. He will be able to get letters of recommendation for his college applications from key people who will attest to these critical, success-promoting traits.

College Knowledge: José shows that he is beginning to build a fund of knowledge that will help him understand how to get into college and succeed once there. As a beginning high school junior, he is now focusing on critical pieces of college information. For example, he understands the importance of taking rigorous and difficult courses, and having a high GPA, and is preparing himself to take the SAT or ACT test. He is starting to track the type of college he wants to get into and how he can put himself in the best possible position to earn scholarships and gain needed financial aid. His junior year will provide a good opportunity for José to begin to fill in needed college knowledge facts and ideas that will help him when he applies to college in his senior year.

College Support Network: Over this past summer, José gained a mentor. This is someone who can provide both the emotional and instrumental support José will need as he tries to figure out and finalize his plans to pursue postsecondary education in the medical Career Pathway. His mentor can support him emotionally by talking through the ups and downs of pursuing such an academic and Career Pathway. His mentor can educate José about what college study in the healthcare sciences will be like and can also help him to learn more about the wide variety of careers in the medical field. For example, how in the nursing field a CNA is related to an LPN degree, an RN degree, and eventually to a nurse practitioner. José is establishing a network of people (e.g., family, teachers, school counselor, friends, and now a mentor) who will actively support him as he completes his last two years of high school and begins his college studies.

Step 3: Developing Your Academic Factor

Now it is your turn to create an Individualized Academic Plan that focuses on both your high school and graduation requirements, as well as building your You and Academic Factors. This plan helps you conceptualize how you can intermix different program options to meet your needs. The first step is to review your school's course of study and talk to people in your support network to help find the answers to these questions, which help you become aware of the opportunities available to you.

Activity 2.2: Individualized Academic Plan (IAP)

1. **What programs does the school have that can help me reach my college and career goals?**
   - Credit-by-Examination:
   - Dual Enrollment:
   - Industry Certifications / Academies:
   - Other:

2. **What college credit can I earn in high school, and how would I do that?**

3. **Are there any special considerations with your high school graduation requirements, such as NCAA eligibility?**

COLLEGE UNMAZED

Now that you are aware of the opportunities available to you, complete the Individualized Academic Plan below and discuss it with your College Support Network.

First: List all courses you have already taken in the designated areas.
Second: Using the information you found about your school programs, complete the chart for your remaining years in high school. Note, as you learn more, this may change. Reviewing this every academic year is important for your success.

	9th	10th	11th	12th
English				
Mathematics				
Science				
Social Studies				
Foreign Language				
Elective				
Elective				

Chapter 2 Summary

In Chapter 2, you explored how you can build your Academic Factor. You looked at the three criteria colleges look at in determining college admissions; your academic coursework, your grades, and your scores on college admissions tests. The key takeaway from this chapter is that you can start building your Academic Factor now by asking good questions about the various course offerings and specialty programs that can earn you high school credit, and potentially college credit or industry certification. In addition, you are continuing to build and explore your You Factor and 8 Strengths.

At-Home Discussion

After discussing what academic opportunities are available at your school, show your family your Individualized Academic Plan. Discuss with them which opportunities they think would suit you and your career goals best. Write their answers below.

Review the High School Planning Checklist in Resources on page 133. What are some next action steps that you need to take in the next month, six months, and year?

CHAPTER 3
Career Factor

Enhance Your Career Knowledge and College and Career Decision-Making

You Factor — Academic Factor — **Career Factor** — Money Factor — Developing a List — Exploring Colleges — Applying to Colleges — Deciding on a College — Succeeding in College

In this chapter, you will continue to explore the key components that make up your unique identity based on your You Factor, Academic Factor, and now your Career Factor. You will learn what makes up your Career Factor and how to cultivate it through high school, college, and beyond.

The Career Factor is an important part of the college choice process, as it provides the foundation to help you find the kinds of colleges that are a good fit for you. By building and developing your Career Factor, you will learn a process for making good career decisions. In the short term, your career decision will be focused on finding college majors to explore, but the same skills we will teach you in this book can help you make effective and satisfying decisions about the kinds of work you do and where you do it for years to come. For most students approaching high school graduation, conversations often go something like this:

>Them: "Hey, you're almost done with high school, congratulations! What are you going to do after graduation?"
>You: "Thanks, it feels pretty good to almost be done. I'm planning on going to college."
>Them: "Oh that's a good idea. What are you going to major in?"
>You: "Ummm…"

In our opinion, expecting high school students to make this kind of decision is hard, as there are so many possible directions your future could head in – and you are likely unaware of many of them because you have not yet had the life experiences as a young adult to meaningfully expose you to the wide range of choices available. The Career Factor helps you with this. Each of us writing this book would have never dreamed of having the jobs we have today when we were high school students, and we bet that if you asked your parents what they wanted to do for work when they were your age, their answers may surprise you.

Your Career Factor Steps

1. Understanding the Career Factor. You will expand your knowledge about occupations and your own self-understanding about how different career options and majors fit you. You will be shown how to link knowledge of the world of work to self-understanding in order to make more informed occupational decisions.
2. Exploring Career Pathways. You will learn about Career Pathways and how your interests, abilities, and personal values match up to different fields of employment and college majors.
3. Case Study – Alex. Through a case study example, you will be shown how the 8 Strengths (used in both Chapters 1 and 2) enhance the Career Factor.
4. Developing Your Career Factor. As part of these activities, you will enhance the development of your Career Factor. You will complete a career exploration activity and write a résumé you will be proud of.

Step 1: The Career Factor

Your Career Factor is really a process you can learn and use to make good career decisions over the course of your working life. Once you have developed knowledge of yourself (self-knowledge) and knowledge of the world of work (occupational knowledge), you can then make informed career-related decisions. As we noted earlier, high school students are often lacking in both areas, and our primary goal in this chapter is to help you improve both your self-knowledge and occupational knowledge.

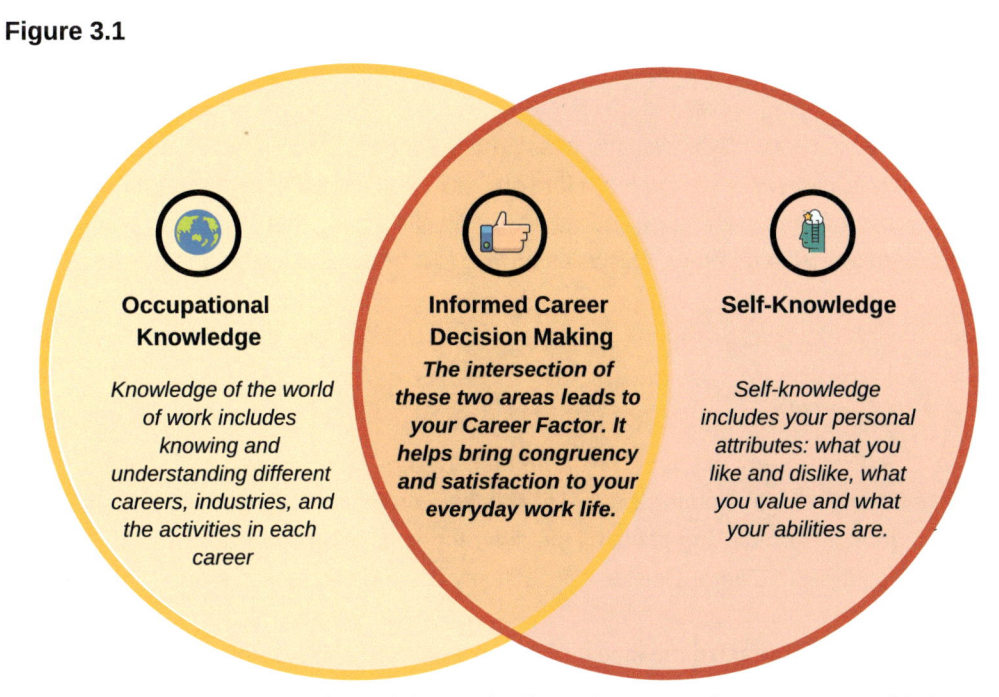

Figure 3.1

Occupational Knowledge
Knowledge of the world of work includes knowing and understanding different careers, industries, and the activities in each career

Informed Career Decision Making
The intersection of these two areas leads to your Career Factor. It helps bring congruency and satisfaction to your everyday work life.

Self-Knowledge
Self-knowledge includes your personal attributes: what you like and dislike, what you value and what your abilities are.

Both self-knowledge and occupational knowledge are constantly evolving and will continue to evolve across your lifetime. As you gain new experiences in the classes you take, part-time work, volunteering, etc., you learn more about yourself AND the world of work, and what you like and dislike about the work activities and work environment. One key challenge facing young people today that was not as problematic for your parents is related to technology; the rapid changes in technology have led to correspondingly rapid changes in where and how people work, and what they do. For example, jobs like data scientist, data engineer, and social media specialist did not even exist just a few years ago, and the number of employees able to work remotely from their homes instead of in traditional office buildings are due to changes in technology.

People are changing jobs faster and more frequently than at any time in our history. According to the Bureau of Labor Statistics, the average worker currently holds ten different jobs before age forty, and your generation is projected at twelve to fifteen jobs in your lifetime! It is hard to know what kind of work you will be doing in 10 or 20 years, but you can be confident in knowing that you can make a more informed decision if you reflect on both your self-knowledge and your occupational knowledge.

The focus you get from developing the Career Factor can save you and your family time and money by helping you understand Career Pathways and related college majors. Unfortunately, many college students do not graduate from college on time. While students are entering college at the highest rate ever, only 49% graduate within four years (Digest of Education Statistics, 2020)! In other words, only just over 4 out of every 10 students graduate college in four years. Framed another way, that means that almost 6 out of every 10 do not! Shockingly, the six-year graduation rate is only 58%, meaning that about 16% of the students who did not graduate in four years do earn a degree at some point over the next two years, and the remaining 42% of those students who started college and did not graduate in four or six years take longer than six years or do not finish at all. That is a lot of precious time and hard-earned money gone.

Who starts college with a 6- or 7-year plan to finish? Not many people. Far too many young people who take longer than four years to finish their degree face unexpected costs—not only in terms of money, as financial aid and scholarships stop, but also in terms of time and frustration. Why do so many students not graduate within four years? For many, one reason is that they change their major in college, which affects prerequisite courses and course sequencing, making it more difficult to graduate on time. For example, it was found that students at four-year colleges accumulate more credits than are required, as many as 16 credits for a Bachelor's degree and 22 credits for an Associate's degree. If a family is paying tuition, room, and board, this could be at least an additional $50,000 in lost wages and tuition for each extra year of college – for the same degree (Complete College America, 2017)!

Do not be dismayed! By diving into your Career Factor you will begin to develop needed occupational knowledge about what career pathways are out there for you. Next, you will be able to determine what degree or certificates you need for each job, while also assessing your abilities and skills to do that job. In the end, you will explore your values and what is important to you in a career. This will lead you to a better understanding of who you are and who you want to become.

Step 2: Exploring Career Pathways

Developing Occupational Knowledge

The U.S. Department of Labor lists more than 13,000 different jobs in the Dictionary of Occupational Titles. That might make finding the right job for you feel like finding a needle in a haystack. Fortunately, there are a few ways we can help you organize your thinking about all the different occupations available to you. One of the most widely used ways is grouping jobs into Career Clusters – effectively helping you look in smaller haystacks to find the needle.

Career Clusters organize the thousands of jobs available into 16 distinct Career Pathways, with each pathway containing hundreds of jobs. The 16 Career Clusters defined by the National Career Clusters Framework are described below, with 5 example occupations in each cluster. While we have only listed 80 jobs – that's just the tip of the iceberg! You have many choices available to you. We don't want you to miss any opportunities to learn about occupations you might be very interested in and successful in. To keep this from happening, we have an activity for you to explore Career Pathways a little later in this chapter.

Figure 3.2

Agricultural, Food & Natural Resources
Fiber engineers, biochemists, botanists, GPS technicians, ecologists park managers

Architecture & Construction
Architect, construction manager, civil engineer, solar energy installer, electrician

Arts, A/V Technology & Communications
Photographer, journalist, producer & director, fashion designer, writer/author

Business, Management & Administration
Entrepreneur, public relations manager, small business owner, human resources, logistics manager

Education & Training
Teacher, librarian & media collection specialist, education administrator, curator, language interpreter

Finance
Financial manager, personal financial advisor, budget analyst, insurance agent, loan officer

Government & Public Administration
Aviation inspectors, coroners, Special Forces, agricultural inspectors, appraisers

Health & Science
Physician, nurse, dentist, pharmacist, biomedical engineer

Hospitality & Tourism
Chef, food service manager, recreation worker, tour guide, hotel manager

Human Services
Psychologist, social worker, funeral home manager, credit counselor, clergy

Information Technology
Computer programmer, web developer, video game designer, web administrator, business intelligence analyst

Law, Public Safety, Corrections & Security
Lawyer, police officer, paramedic, intelligence analyst, private detective

COLLEGE UNMAZED

Manufacturing
Robotics technician, mechanical drafter, aerospace engineer, industrial machinery mechanic, medical equipment repairer

Marketing
Account managers, sales engineers, brokers, store managers, copywriters

Science, Technology, Engineering & Mathematics
Engineers, astronomers, biostatisticians, economists, urban and regional planners

Transportation, Distribution & Logistics
Pilot, air traffic controller, recycling coordinator, logistics analyst, fleet manager

Degrees

People often do not realize that specific jobs within each Career Pathway reflect a wide range of educational qualifications. Some occupations require advanced degrees, such as medical doctors and lawyers, but many jobs require a lot less postsecondary education than that. For example, if you recall the case of José from Chapter 2, you will see that nursing is one such Career Pathway that can have multiple certificates and degree levels. Higher salaries are often related to greater levels of postsecondary education. If José chooses to stay in the nursing field, he can continue his education through different degree programs. As the chart below shows, increasing his knowledge and expertise by furthering his education will also help him substantially increase his salary.

Figure 3.3

	$20,000	$40,000	$60,000	$80,000	$100,000+
Certified Nursing Assistant (CNA), 4-12 weeks	███				
Licensed Practical Nurse (LPN), 12-18 months	██████████				
Registered Nurse (ADN) 2 years		██████████			
Registered Nurse (RN/ BSN) 4 years		████████████████			
Advanced Practice Registered Nurse (APRN), 2 years (post-graduate)		████████████████████			

Across the 16 Career Pathways, there are many different degree options available to you, and it can be confusing. The chart on the next page shows a brief description of the postsecondary certificate and degree programs that are available. Several of them can build on themselves, meaning you can earn a certificate, complete a two-year Associate's degree, and then finish a Bachelor's degree. However, many do not allow this flexibility. So, it is always best to find out ahead of time if credits from a certificate program would transfer into an Associate's degree, and/or if credits from an Associate's degree would transfer into a Bachelor's degree program. Often colleges call these kinds of transfer options articulation agreements. Figure 3.4 is an overview of postsecondary degree options and how they related to each other.

Employers are looking to hire people with a skill set and knowledge base so they can do the assigned job. One way to acquire these skills and knowledge is by attending some form of postsecondary training. Some occupations have specific certificate/degree requirements to legally do the job, such as a nurse, physician, accountant, teacher, welder, firefighter, architect, and lawyer. Without the proper training and credentials, you simply cannot do these jobs. Other occupations may require or expect people in the job to have a college degree of some sort, but do not require a specific major. This is because the knowledge and skills you learn in college regardless of what your major is are valued by employers, such as time management, being able to set and achieve goals, logical reasoning, and critical thinking. In the next section, you will learn more about yourself and which of the 16 Career Pathways fit you.

CHAPTER 3: CAREER FACTOR

Figure 3.4

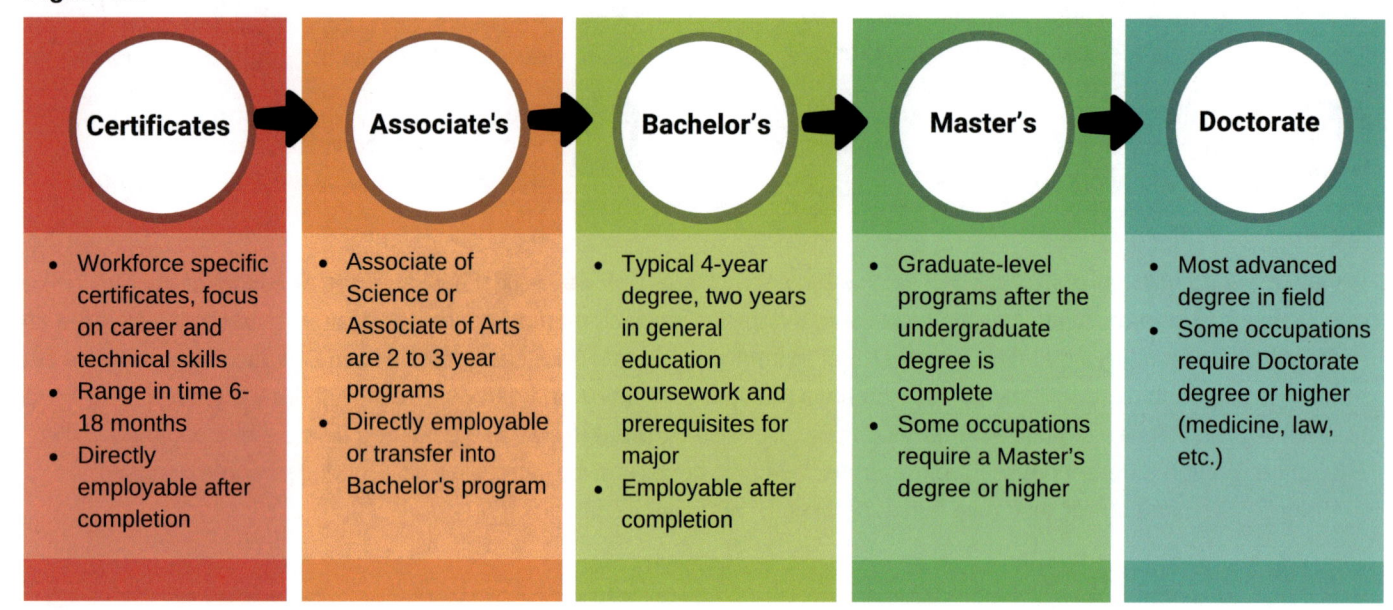

Certificates	Associate's	Bachelor's	Master's	Doctorate
• Workforce specific certificates, focus on career and technical skills • Range in time 6-18 months • Directly employable after completion	• Associate of Science or Associate of Arts are 2 to 3 year programs • Directly employable or transfer into Bachelor's program	• Typical 4-year degree, two years in general education coursework and prerequisites for major • Employable after completion	• Graduate-level programs after the undergraduate degree is complete • Some occupations require a Master's degree or higher	• Most advanced degree in field • Some occupations require Doctorate degree or higher (medicine, law, etc.)

Developing Self-Knowledge

Now that you have a beginning understanding of what the world of work looks like (the 16 Career Pathways), it is time to think about how your interests, abilities, and work values (self-knowledge) can help you identify which Career Pathways fit you best. By developing your self-knowledge and connecting it to your occupational knowledge, you will be well-positioned to identify a targeted range of careers to explore. As illustrated in the "Informed Decision Making" (Figure 3.1) infographic at the beginning of the chapter, informed decision-making occurs at the intersection of occupational knowledge and self-knowledge.

Your Interests

An important part of developing self-knowledge is to understand the kinds of work tasks you like and dislike. A common way of organizing your likes and dislikes (your interests) is through categories developed by John Holland's Theory of Careers (O*Net Interests). Holland's theory suggests that people's interests can be categorized into six broad types – Realistic, Investigative, Artistic, Social, Enterprising, and Conventional (RIASEC), described on the next page.

Holland's Theory of Careers helps students, like you, to search for careers that will let you use your skills and abilities, and to also express your attitudes and values. For example, Realistic careers are those that involve working with tools or machinery (e.g., carpenter, mechanic, or airline pilot). Students who are in Social careers enjoy helping others in a cooperative environment (e.g., teaching, coaching, social work, or hospitality). The next few pages and activities will help you understand and communicate some of your unique Career Factor traits that can guide you to future occupations.

Activity 3.1: Career Pathways Mapping

Holland's Theory of Careers was developed not only to describe people's interests but also work environments. As you can see in the Career Pathways map on the next page, we have related the 16 Career Pathways to the 6 Holland categories to help you see how your interests map onto a smaller, more targeted range of careers to explore. What career paths most closely match your interests?

Please take a few moments to read the descriptions, and then put a 1 in the circle next to the name of the category you are most interested in, a 2 in the next category you are interested in, and then a 3 in the third category you are interested in.

COLLEGE UNMAZED

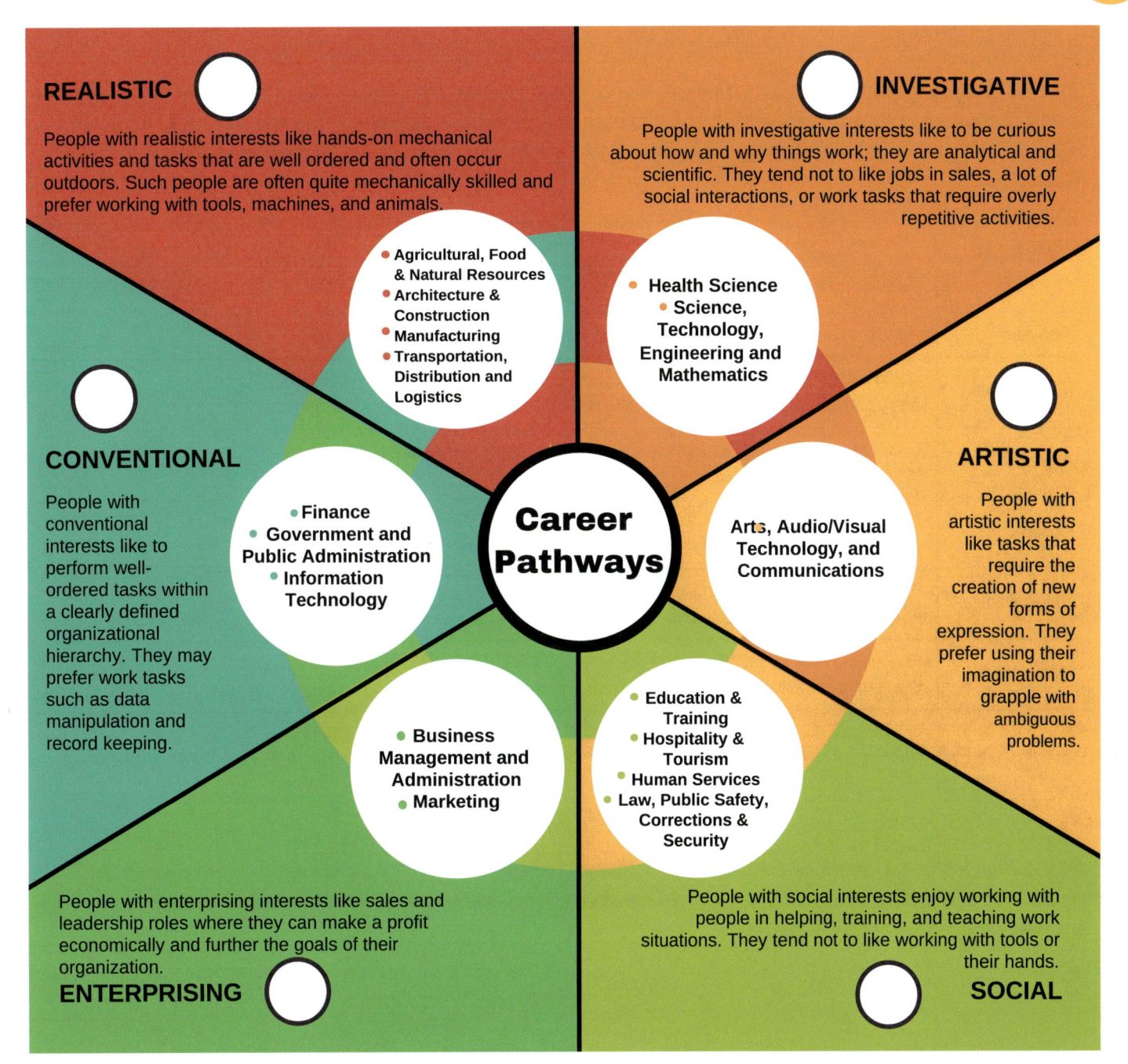

Career Pathways

REALISTIC
People with realistic interests like hands-on mechanical activities and tasks that are well ordered and often occur outdoors. Such people are often quite mechanically skilled and prefer working with tools, machines, and animals.

- Agricultural, Food & Natural Resources
- Architecture & Construction
- Manufacturing
- Transportation, Distribution and Logistics

INVESTIGATIVE
People with investigative interests like to be curious about how and why things work; they are analytical and scientific. They tend not to like jobs in sales, a lot of social interactions, or work tasks that require overly repetitive activities.

- Health Science
- Science, Technology, Engineering and Mathematics

CONVENTIONAL
People with conventional interests like to perform well-ordered tasks within a clearly defined organizational hierarchy. They may prefer work tasks such as data manipulation and record keeping.

- Finance
- Government and Public Administration
- Information Technology

ARTISTIC
People with artistic interests like tasks that require the creation of new forms of expression. They prefer using their imagination to grapple with ambiguous problems.

- Arts, Audio/Visual Technology, and Communications

ENTERPRISING
People with enterprising interests like sales and leadership roles where they can make a profit economically and further the goals of their organization.

- Business Management and Administration
- Marketing

SOCIAL
People with social interests enjoy working with people in helping, training, and teaching work situations. They tend not to like working with tools or their hands.

- Education & Training
- Hospitality & Tourism
- Human Services
- Law, Public Safety, Corrections & Security

Your Abilities

Another important part of developing self-knowledge is beginning to understand your abilities and skills, and how they connect to Career Pathways. This is a difficult thing to do because high school students have generally not had enough life experience to really know what their work-related abilities are. For example, young women may think they are not good at math and science. These are often inaccurate perceptions of ability that lead these young women away from the Science, Technology, Engineering, and Mathematics Career Pathway. In high school, these young women may not seek out or have the needed experiences provided to them to develop their math and science abilities and talents.

Your abilities and talents are not fixed. You are still growing and developing – in fact, your brain will continue to develop into your 20's. Further, the skills needed to succeed in a variety of occupations are continuously evolving. For example, developing a website used to require serious coding while today you can develop an app or website without a single line of code. You have a wide range of abilities that can be strengthened and developed. While you can't develop every single ability, you can be intentional about which ones you want to put the effort in to strengthen and more fully develop.

CHAPTER 3: CAREER FACTOR

Activity 3.2: Rate Your Abilities

Understanding your abilities and recognizing where you want to focus your efforts is a critical developmental task. Below is a list of common work tasks and abilities typical of each Holland type. Please read these and place a 1 next to the Holland type you think you have the highest ability in right now, a 2 next to the second-highest, and a 3 next to the third highest.

Holland Type	Work Tasks	Your Ability Ranking
Realistic	Hands-on and outdoor activities; working with tools, machines, and animals	
Investigative	Using scientific methods to understand how and why things work; gathering and analyzing information and data; dealing with abstract problems and concepts	
Artistic	Creative activities such as expressive and visual arts; developing or designing new ideas and forms of expression	
Social	Helping others to promote their growth and development through teaching, training, and counseling; communication skills; caring for and informing others	
Enterprising	Persuading and sales; leadership; motivating others; providing direction; entrepreneurship; business and financial management	
Conventional	Organizing data by recording, storing, and maintaining facts and records; following directions; compiling, categorizing, auditing, and verifying information	

Now, look back at the Career Pathways Map. What career paths most closely match your abilities? Answer below.

What Career Pathways are aligned with both your interests and abilities, if any? Answer below. If your interests and abilities do not overlap at this point, that's OK! Remember, you are still learning, growing, and developing your interests and abilities.

Your Values

A third important part of developing self-knowledge is beginning to understand your work values and preferred working conditions. This is a particularly important thing to do because the personal values you bring to your career and college decisions will greatly shape what you end up doing with your interests and abilities. Some people pursue a specific Career Pathway because they feel it is a calling, and it is an important part of their identity. Other people pursue a specific Career Pathway less because it is a calling and more because it helps them have the kind of lifestyle they seek. For example, many teachers who work in K-12 schools chose the Education Career Pathway over careers in science or math-related fields with higher earning potential because being a teacher fit with their values – they could help others and have time off in the summer to be with family.

Activity 3.3: Rate Your Career Values

On the next page is a list of work-related values and preferred working conditions. Please review this list and pick at least 3 but not more than 5 of your highest work values.

COLLEGE UNMAZED

Value	Rank	Value	Rank	Value	Rank
Earning a high income	1	Having an opportunity to be creative	3	Helping others	
Earning recognition or prestige	5	Being able to work independently	1	Being a leader and making decisions	
Having flexibility in work hours	2	Having a variety of work tasks to do	5	Being curious and solving problems	
Working indoors or outdoors	7	Using your hands and doing physical things in your work	6	Being your own boss	
Having autonomy to exercise some personal control over the work tasks and problems that are the focus of your work energy	3	Taking risks and being adventurous either physically (e.g., special forces in military), in intellectual problems, or economic ventures	2	Entering a career that requires a long training time after high school (e.g., Bachelor's, Master's or Doctorate degrees)	
Enter a career that requires a relatively shorter training time after high school (e.g., 1 or 2 year industry certification programs)	4	Earning advancements in one's career	4	Working with specific tools, technologies, animals, plants, people or ideas	
Achieving economic security	6	Being compatible with your religious orientation	7	Working in an organization as part of a work team	

Now, look back at the Career Pathways you identified in relation to your interests and abilities. Which Career Pathways do you think are also aligned with your work values? Answer below.

Step 3: Case Study – Alex

Alex is a senior attending a rigorous college preparatory magnet school that offers a wide range of Advanced Placement courses along with the AP Capstone Diploma, which requires four AP exams, and two courses called AP Research and AP Seminar. Alex has always been interested in science. After volunteering for a local science camp and joining his high school's Science Olympiad team, his interest in science was strengthened even further. He eventually became the team's Vice President and helped the team win 1st place in Robotics and 2nd place in Chemistry and Engineering at regional competitions. His dedication to the team led him to take every AP math and science course available at his high school, including Chemistry, Biology, Physics, and AP Calculus BC. Alex also obtained a part-time job he likes at a local math tutoring center, helping younger students with their math skills. He also joined his school's Model United Nations (MUN) club and was surprised that he really enjoyed thinking about how to help people from other countries and cultures. Around his home, Alex likes figuring out how to fix and maintain things – bicycles, the computer, and Wi-Fi, and changing the oil in the family's car.

When starting to think about his future, Alex knew he wanted to attend a prestigious, selective college but was still unsure of what he wanted to do for a career focus as he could not seem to figure out how to merge science and politics - his two favorite areas of study. Unfortunately, in Alex's junior year of high school, his mother was

CHAPTER 3: CAREER FACTOR

diagnosed with breast cancer. The doctors believed it had been caught early and that through chemotherapy and surgery she could make a full recovery. Tragically, his mother suffered a stroke due to an error in the implantation of the medical port by the doctor. Not only did Alex's mother have to combat breast cancer, but she now had to learn to walk and talk again. To this day his mother still has lingering, negative effects.

Alex is quite shy, and while the MUN club gave him much-needed confidence in public speaking, he could not see it as a career option he wanted to pursue. He had not talked to many people about his mother's ongoing health issues. But when he started thinking of his career options and talking things through with his high school counselor and his favorite AP Physics teacher, Mrs. Johnson, Alex realized that he was deeply passionate about improving medical technology to help people like his mother. He realized through these conversations with his teacher and counselor that, through engineering, he could combine his love of science and creativity, while simultaneously allowing him to tackle practical problems. Still unsure of what specific field of engineering he wanted to pursue he began looking at colleges that allowed him to explore biomedical engineering or medical engineering related to medicine and biology for healthcare purposes.

Alex's Career Map

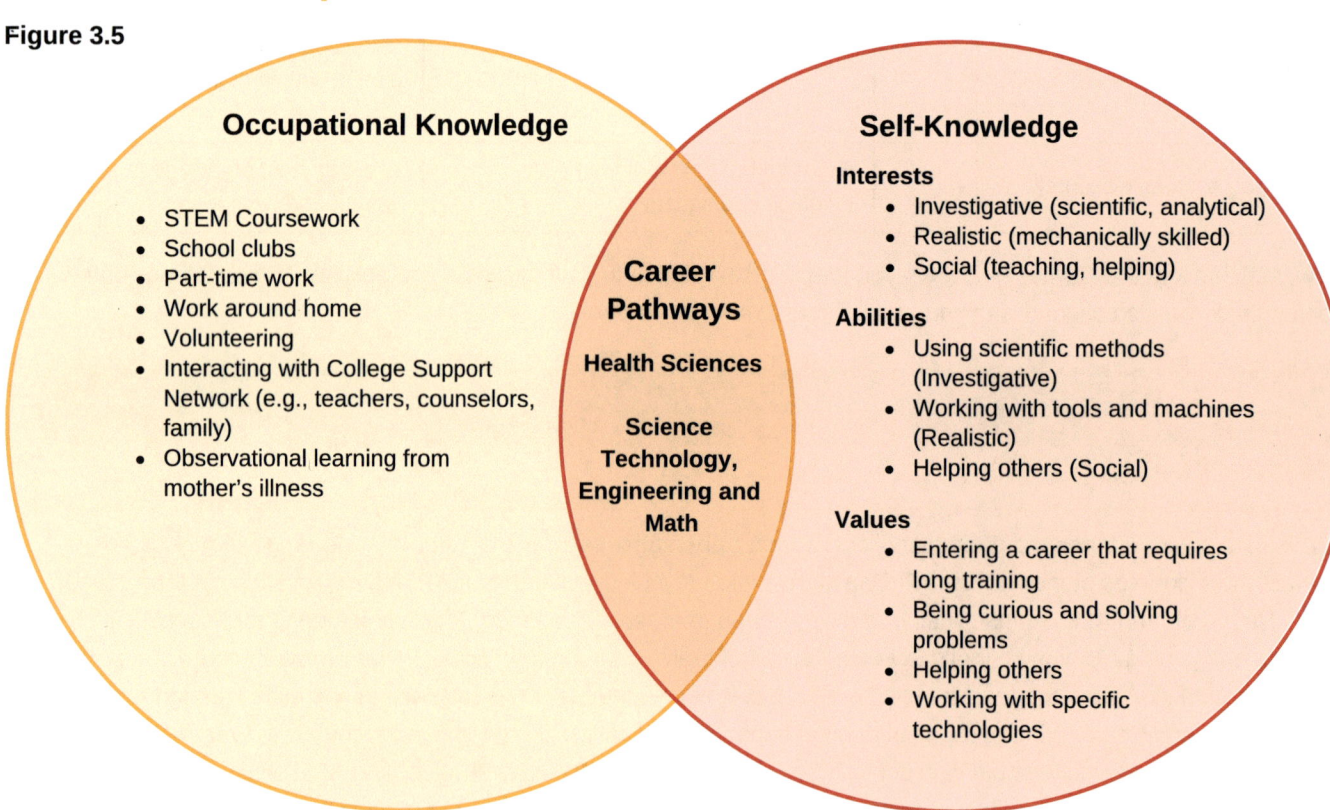

Figure 3.5

Occupational Knowledge
- STEM Coursework
- School clubs
- Part-time work
- Work around home
- Volunteering
- Interacting with College Support Network (e.g., teachers, counselors, family)
- Observational learning from mother's illness

Career Pathways

Health Sciences

Science Technology, Engineering and Math

Self-Knowledge

Interests
- Investigative (scientific, analytical)
- Realistic (mechanically skilled)
- Social (teaching, helping)

Abilities
- Using scientific methods (Investigative)
- Working with tools and machines (Realistic)
- Helping others (Social)

Values
- Entering a career that requires long training
- Being curious and solving problems
- Helping others
- Working with specific technologies

The chart above illustrates how your Career Factor is a process you can use to make good career decisions. For Alex, he developed occupational knowledge and self-knowledge from his experiences at home, at school, part-time work, and conversations with his College Support Network. The intersection of Alex's occupational knowledge and self-knowledge have helped him identify two Career Pathways that may be a good match for him to further explore. Given where Alex's development is right now, beginning his career exploration by focusing on the Health Sciences and STEM Career Pathways allows him to focus his efforts on just two of the sixteen Career Pathways. Right now, these two Career Pathways are the most highly related to his interests, abilities, values, and life experience.

How Well Developed are Alex's 8 Strengths?

Agency: Alex realizes that he can use his strong academic skills to help others. Having his own personal experience with his mother's illness created an even stronger sense of direction in making his career decisions.

Positive Beliefs: While his mother's illness was a very hard experience for his whole family, Alex developed the confidence to believe that through his talents and skills he could help people like his mother with better medical technology.

Effective Goals: While Alex was unsure of his exact career path, he made a commitment to pursue goals that require specialized technical training after high school. He took rigorous coursework that supported the attainment of these goals.

Knowing Yourself: Alex's experiences in and out of school have helped him identify a range of Career Pathways that may fit him well. Talking with his College Support Network, his teacher, and his counselor helped him develop and understand his occupational and self-knowledge.

Becoming a Successful Student: Alex took advantage of the opportunities to pursue rigorous courses. He also actively engaged in extracurricular activities and school clubs to further his knowledge in areas of interest.

Character for Workplace Success: Alex has demonstrated the ability to get along with others in school clubs and at work, dependability in completing rigorous coursework, flexible problem-solving in helping the Science Olympiads win first place, and positively cope with his mother's illness. He may want to work on areas of vulnerability, like public speaking, that could be of real value to him in his future career.

College Knowledge: Alex is taking the kinds of rigorous courses he needs to gain admission to and be successful in college. His emerging focus in health science and STEM will help him to identify a range of college majors that fit his interests, abilities, and values. This information will be valuable in helping him make an informed decision about which college to attend.

College Support Network: Alex was grateful for having caring teachers and a school counselor for emotional support while his mother was sick He has developed a strong College Support Network that will not only provide emotional support but also instrumental support as he navigates the college application and decision-making process. For example, he has several teachers and his counselor from whom he can obtain effective and detailed recommendation letters.

Step 4: Developing Your Career Factor

There are two steps we would like you to complete to explore your Career Factor in more depth. The first step is to summarize your occupational knowledge, self-knowledge, and the career pathways you identified earlier in the diagram on the next page. This will illustrate how your occupational knowledge and self-knowledge work together to help you discover the Career Pathways that fit you best.

The second step is to gather more information about the Career Pathways you have identified as a good fit. O*Net Online, sponsored by the U.S. Department of Labor, is an excellent source of career information. Identify the Career Pathway you feel the strongest connection to considering your current interests, abilities, and values. Visit https://www.onetonline.org/find/career and select a Career Pathway (known as a Career Cluster on O*Net) from the list provided and complete the chart below to identify three specific occupations of interest within your selected Career Pathway. We have provided Alex's case as an example of what to do.

CHAPTER 3: CAREER FACTOR

Activity 3.4: Career Exploration

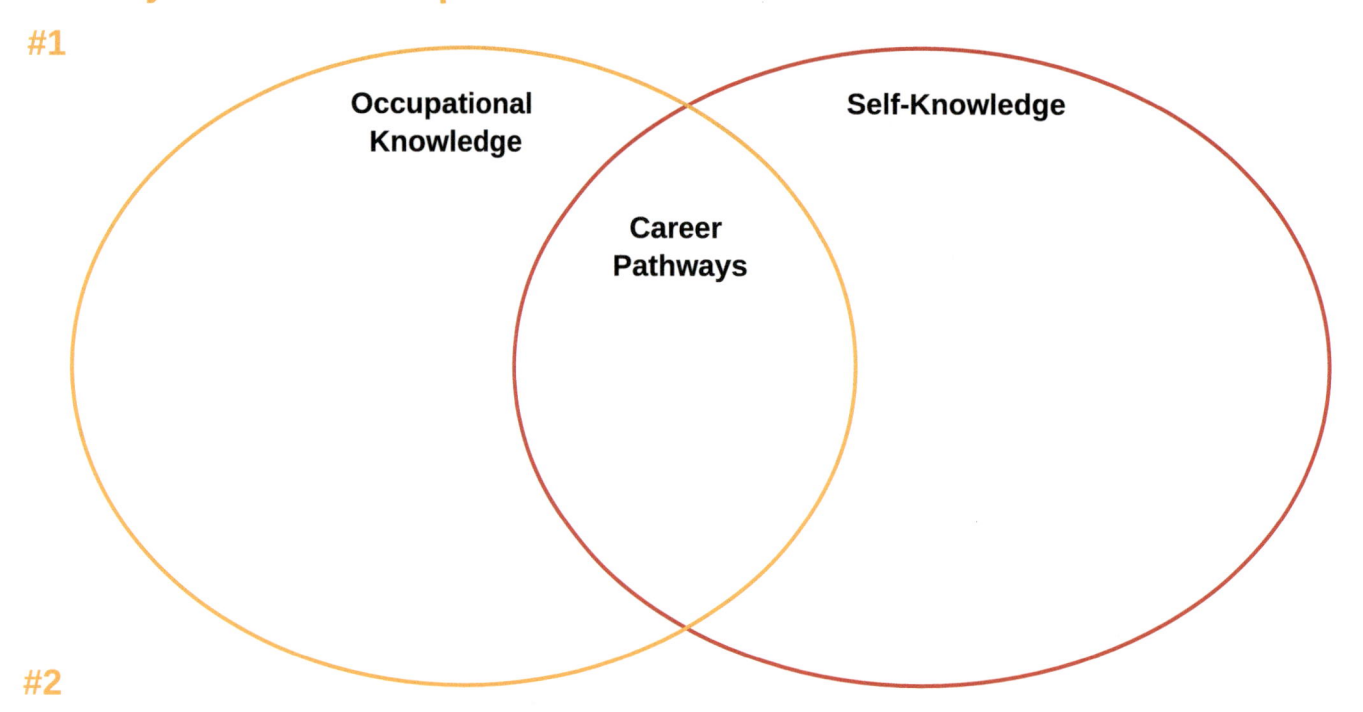

#1

Occupational Knowledge ⬭ **Self-Knowledge**

Career Pathways (intersection)

#2

	Occupation 1	Occupation 2	Occupation 3	Alex's Occupation (Biomedical Engineering)
What is the most common education level? (Education)				Bachelor's Degree (53%), Master's Degree (7%)
What is the median annual salary in the United States? (Wages & Employment)				US- $91,140,
What is the median annual salary in your state, if available? (Wages & Employment)				Florida- $81,410
What is the projected growth in the United States? (Wages & Employment)				Bright Outlook, 5-7%
What is the projected growth in your state, if available? (Wages & Employment)				11% growth
List one related occupation. (Related Occupations)				Logistics, Chemical & Photonics Engineers
Review the Tasks, Knowledge, Technology Skills, and Work Context areas of O*Net, and rate your level of interest (1 = not interesting to 5 = interesting)				5

Building Your Résumé

Building your Career Factor takes time, as you will need to learn from experiences and sharpen your knowledge of your interests, abilities, and values. Your career knowledge will also grow and develop as you begin to interact with the world of work through exploration and opportunities. A great way to fully assess where you are right now and see your career factor is will be to build a résumé. There are three reasons why you should start writing your résumé now:

1. A résumé can guide your high school experience to majors and Career Pathways you are interested in. By adding information as you go, it will be easier to have a clear picture of what your interests are, and fill in holes where your experience might be lacking.
2. By starting your résumé early, you do not forget all of the things you have done while in high school.
3. Your résumé is part of the college application process. Instead of writing out all your activities on every single application, your résumé helps you organize your information and put the best activities and information forward. This is a KEY part of the application process, discussed further in Chapter 7: Apply. Use your College Support Network to help you edit your résumé so you are putting your best foot forward on every application. You will also want to give a copy of your résumé to each person you ask to write a recommendation letter.

Résumés are as unique as the people who write them, but certain conventions should be followed. Here is a checklist of what to include:

Objective or summary: The objective describes what are you trying to achieve in terms of major/minor fields of study, current career objective, or the type of college you are seeking to attend.

Summary of skills/ qualifications: Summarize your skills and achievements to highlight them 'front and center' on your résumé. For example, describe any foreign language skills you may have (e.g., fluent, conversational, intermediate, etc.), computer and coding skills, and softer skills such as leadership and communication.

Education information: This includes the name and address of your high school, your GPA, and your class rank if available. Advanced coursework and any other unique academic experiences can also go in this section if you have any.

Activities: These can be in or out of school—for example, marching band, intramural basketball, or youth group at your church or temple, in addition to any clubs or other school-related activities. It is particularly important to note any leadership roles you may have had.

Work experience: If you have any part-time work experience, describe with some details – particularly if it is related to your intended field of study. When possible and appropriate, use outcome-oriented statements to describe accomplishments and outcomes related to your work experience. For example, instead of saying "worked part-time as cashier", say "responsible for approximately $5,000 in sales each shift." If you earned any accolades, such as Employee of the Month, be sure to describe that as well.

Volunteer experience: Participation in a fundraiser, walk to raise cancer awareness, or contribution to a science fair are all pertinent details. As with work experience, try to focus on outcome-oriented descriptions and accomplishments. Instead of saying 'participated in a fundraiser for Alzheimer's disease' say 'raised $1,000 to support Alzheimer's research.

Awards/ Certificates: Academic awards or awards in extracurricular competition – state wrestling champion or member of the top-ranked marching band in the region, for example.

Anything else that makes you shine: A résumé is an excellent way to tell college recruiters about you. If something makes you unique and interesting include it.

CHAPTER 3: CAREER FACTOR

Figure 3.6

Student Name

Senior at XYZ High School

KEYS TO SUCCESS	
	## OBJECTIVE
An objective keeps your résumé on track and gives an overview of your short- and long-term goals.	Earn acceptance and merit scholarships to top-tier universities in the state of Pennsylvania to pursue a degree in Biomedical Engineering.
	## SUMMARY
Write down what you believe are your overall strengths.	- AP Scholar with Distinction - President of the Math Team and Key Club - Intermediate language skills in written and spoken Spanish - Proven ability to organize time and resources to meet goals - Active, engaged member of the community
	## EDUCATION
Having your academic statistics is helpful for recommenders that know you through extra-curriculars.	XYZ HIGH SCHOOL, 2018-2022 School Address & CEEB Number - Unweighted GPA: 3.92, Weighted GPA: 5.12, Ranked 2nd in class - #1 ranked high school in the state - This is a STEM college preparatory magnet high school - ACT Composite: 33 - SAT Composite: 1480
	## ACTIVITIES & EXPERIENCES
This is how the Common Application asks for your student information to be entered. Begin writing this information down as early as 9th-grade year. Keeping track of how long and how frequently you do the activity will help with your college applications later on, as well as for volunteer purposes.	**Student Activity Name** **Type:** Club/ Organization/ Work/ Academic Activity/ Volunteer/ Sports **Description:** keep under 150 characters **Grades Participated in:** 9, 10, 11, 12 (still participating) **Weeks Per Year:** **Hours Per Week:** **Key Club,** Academic Activity, 9, 10, 11, 12 (still participating) 3 hours per week, 28 weeks per year As president of Key Club I seek to improve the community through different projects including, but not limited to canned food drives, building houses for the financially needy, and participating in STEM-related activities with elementary age students. **Math Team,** Academic Activity, 10, 11, 12 (still participating) 2 hours per week, 10 weeks per year I competed against other students in my area, through timed math tests and working in groups with my peers to solve problems as a team. As team captain, I was able to earn 5th in Statistics at the Penn College Math Competition.

ACTIVITIES & EXPERIENCES

Karate, Sports, 6,7,8,9,10,11, 12 (still participating)
9 hours per week, 51 weeks per year
I joined karate when I finished elementary school and continued with it until my senior year. It taught me the values of hard work, discipline, and commitment. I received my second-degree black belt.

Students Against Melanoma, Club/ Organization, 9, 10, 11, 12 (still participating)
2-3 hours per week, 25 weeks per year
Having spent the majority of my life outdoors, I feel very fortunate as the president and Director of Social Media of the XYZ High School SAM Club, to lead the effort to educate students about the dangers of melanoma and ways to prevent it.

Mathnasium, Work, 11, 12 (still participating)
8-10 hours per week, 52 weeks per year
I tutor middle and high school students on their math skills in a professional manner. Provide small group and one-on-one assistance on standardized tests and math concepts.

Williamsport Hospital, Volunteer, 10, 11
8-10 hours per week, 10 weeks per year
I interacted with and served patients by providing essential supplies like water and blankets. I contributed to the efficient functioning of the hospital by performing errands for the nurses, and I learned about how the hospital functions.

Boys' Varsity Tennis, Sports, 9, 10, 11, 12 (still participating)
15 hours per week, 30 weeks per year
I compete in matches across the state. This season, I was chosen to be captain, leading my teammates and friends on and off the field. We have been historically successful, winning the District Championship in the 2021 season, and competing as semifinalists every season since. In 2020, I was selected to receive the Sportsmanship Award.

> Every application is different, but expect 8-10 spots for extra-curricular activities, including volunteering, school clubs, and sports. You may need to be very selective and condense multiple items together.

> Carefully organize based on involvement, passions, longevity, and leadership.

> Admission counselors will read them in the order you put them, so more important activities that tell your story should go first, less important activities, go last.

HONORS & DISTINCTIONS

National Honors Society
Grade Received: 10, 11, 12

AP Scholar with Distinction
Grade Received: 11, 12

Tennis Team Captain & Leadership Award
Grade Received: 11, 12

> Use your space wisely. Use section to highlight awards and achievements that you won or received.

COURSEWORK

High School Transcript of Courses Taken
- List of courses with grades, term, and type (AP, ADV/Honors, IB, Dual Enrollment, etc.).

> This is a great time to check your transcript to make sure it is accurate.

CHAPTER 3: CAREER FACTOR

Activity 3.5: Build Your Résumé

Take some time and complete your résumé. For now, focus on writing down all the activities you have done. You will need to do several revisions to narrow it down to exactly what you want and need. However, once you do so, your college and scholarship application process will be much easier. Right now, you are working on developing your 'master' résumé. You will likely develop several versions of your resume to tailor it to a specific objective. For example, if you are applying to a college where community service is emphasized, you will want to revise your résumé to ensure your community service experience is as close to the top of your résumé as possible.

Through a web search, you can easily find a template to help you organize and format your résumé. Microsoft Word comes with several templates built-in.

In looking at this list of résumé words, circle which ones describe you best and then integrate them into your résumé.

Balanced	Enthusiastic	Innovative	Passionate	Scientific
Bold	Explorer	Involved	Proactive	Self-starter
Challenger	Genuine	Knowledgeable	Purposeful	Strategic
Committed	Goal oriented	Leader	Reliable	Successful
Determined	Hard working	Logical	Researcher	Team player
Developed	Imaginative	Opportunity	Resourceful	Thoughtful
Diverse	Independent	Optimistic	Responsible	Visionary

Chapter Summary

Answering the tough questions, Who am I? and Where do I want my life to lead?, have only just begun for most high school students. It takes time to have the life experiences needed to really know what kind of an educational and career pathway you should pursue. For most of us, finding a career direction that fits us takes time and slowly evolves from an accumulation of life experience. These experiences combined with your academic courses (Academic Factor) and your personal identity (You Factor) will start providing you with information about future career opportunities and begin developing your Career Factor. Combining your self-knowledge with occupational knowledge helps you identify a range of Career Pathways where you are likely to find success and satisfaction. Your résumé is the place where you can pull your experiences together to highlight three of your key Factors – You, Academic, and Career – for your college applications.

At-Home Discussion

Discuss with your family and others in your College Support Network the 3 occupations you researched. Ask them what they think about each of these careers, and their thoughts on your Career Pathway(s). Write their thoughts below.

Create your résumé using word processing software and share it with your family and others in your College Support Network. Brainstorm about other activities you might have forgotten or would like to add to the document.

Review the High School Planning Checklist in Resources on page 133. What are some next action steps that you need to take in the next month, six months, and year?

CHAPTER 4
The Money Factor

Become Financially Literate and Savvy to Pay for College

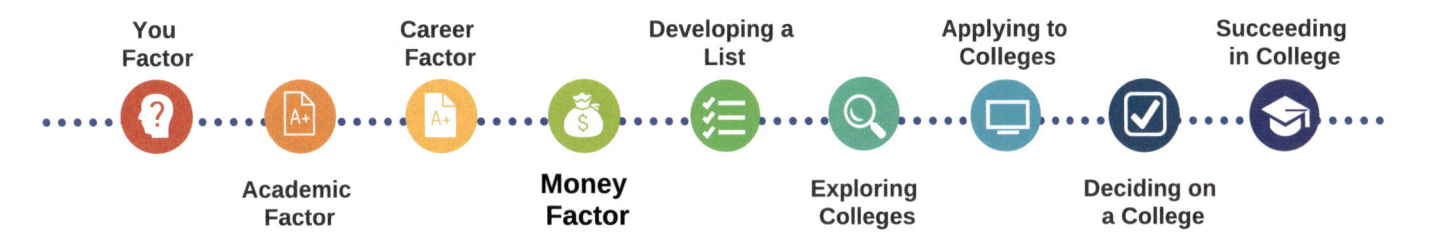

You Factor · Academic Factor · Career Factor · **Money Factor** · Developing a List · Exploring Colleges · Applying to Colleges · Deciding on a College · Succeeding in College

The Money Factor will help you manage the cost of college so that paying for college doesn't manage you. While it is true that college is expensive and student loan debt is a very real problem, you and your family can prepare you to navigate these challenges successfully. This chapter will introduce you to the following key concepts that will help you manage the costs of college: federal financial aid, including the FAFSA and determining financial need; the real cost of attending college; ways to get "free" money to pay for college, such as gift aid from colleges, states, and the federal government; loans for students and parents; and work-study aid. There is a lot to know about the Money Factor and this chapter is an introduction to help you get started. We will expand on the Money Factor in the second half of the book with more detailed information when it comes to making an informed decision about which colleges to apply to and ultimately attend.

There is a lot of misinformation and myths about the costs of attending college. For example, many people do not recognize there is very often a sizeable difference between the advertised cost of a college (also known as the *sticker price*) and what students actually pay to attend. For example, a private college in the northeastern United States lists a sticker price of about $40,000, but 95% of the students attending that college, on average, get a $20,000 scholarship from the institution. In other words, nearly every student who attends this college gets a big discount on the tuition, and they only pay, on average, $20,000 for tuition and fees – only 5% of the students who attend this college pay the full sticker price.

This kind of 'discounting' of tuition is fairly common among private colleges and can make the actual cost of attending a private college less expensive than a public college. Public colleges provide tuition discounts as well, although the dollar amounts are often lower because of the lower cost of tuition and smaller endowments. Endowments are money donated to a college, usually from alumni and businesses, and can help the college provide scholarships.

Every year, Sallie Mae (a banking institution that provides student loans across the United States) produces a report titled "How America Pays for College." Some of 2020's key findings include: only 52% of families have a plan to pay for college; 44% of the cost of college is covered by parent income and savings; 25% covered by scholarships and grants (gift aid); and 13% covered by student borrowing.

CHAPTER 4: MONEY FACTOR

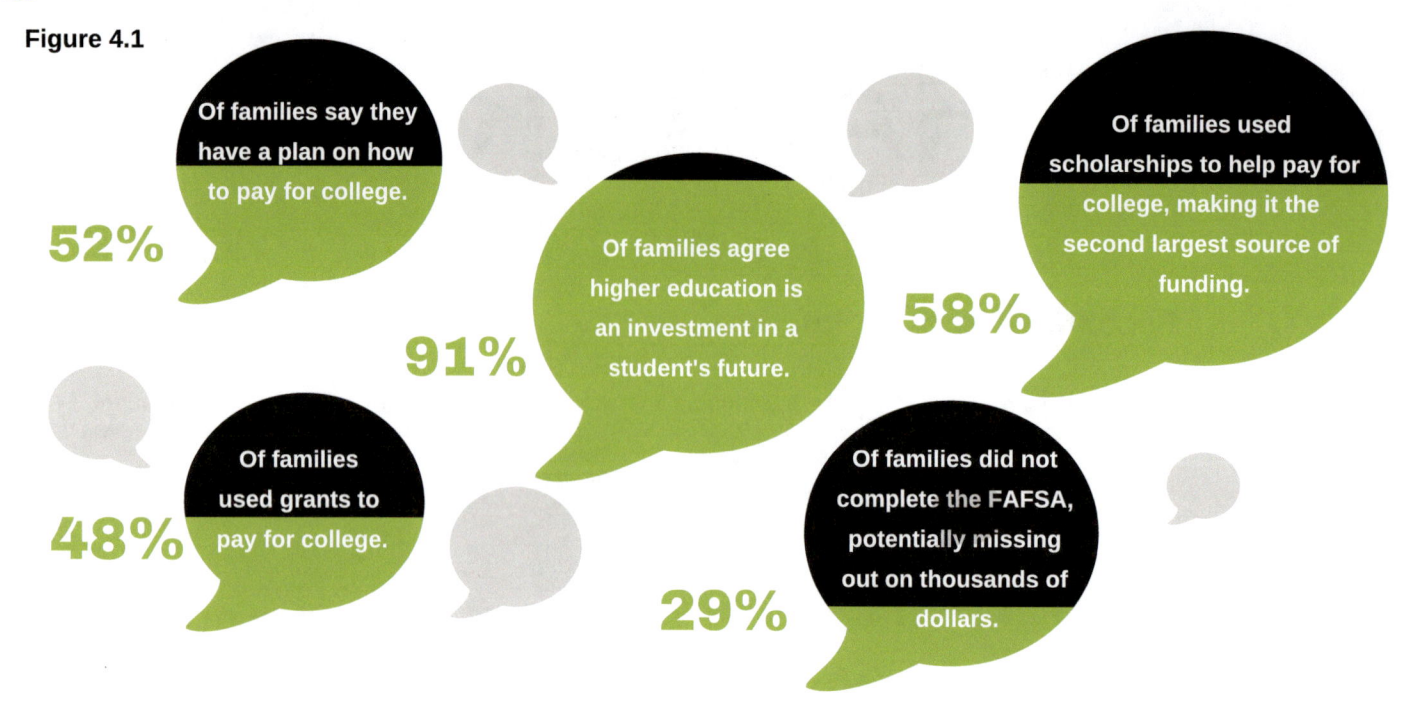

Figure 4.1

- **52%** Of families say they have a plan on how to pay for college.
- **91%** Of families agree higher education is an investment in a student's future.
- **58%** Of families used scholarships to help pay for college, making it the second largest source of funding.
- **48%** Of families used grants to pay for college.
- **29%** Of families did not complete the FAFSA, potentially missing out on thousands of dollars.

Research we conducted with high school seniors regarding their plans to pay for college (all students in good academic standing who had been accepted and planned to attend college in the Fall) found remarkably similar results to Sallie Mae. Half of all the graduating seniors in our study had limited plans to pay for college. However, the first-generation students in our study planned to get money to pay for college from a variety of sources (e.g., parents, scholarships, loans, and work-study) – they were willing to get money from anywhere they could. The amount of debt you accumulate to pay for college is a critical issue for all students. As debt increases, a student's chances of graduating decreases – and this is particularly true for first-generation students.

This chapter will help you become aware of the many sources of financial aid available to pay for college. In Section 2 of this book, we will help you choose a college that is right for you – a college that matches you and your finances.

Your Money Factor Steps

1. Managing the Costs of College. You will be assisted in planning how to pay for college. You will be shown strategies to help you navigate this challenge.
2. Understand Key College Finance Terms. You will learn about critical components of financing college. For example, you will be introduced to details about college costs and how to finance your education – federal aid, state aid, and aid provided by colleges, the FAFSA, loans, scholarships, and work-study.
3. Case Study – Sholondo. Through a case example, you will be shown how the 8 Strengths (used in Chapters 1, 2 and 3) promote the development of the Money Factor.
4. Understand Net Price. You will be helped to distinguish between the *sticker price* and the real price you will pay at each college – the *net price*. You will better understand how colleges discount tuition costs to make the cost of attending their college more affordable. It is important not to eliminate a college from consideration based on its sticker price – the net price is a more accurate cost estimator.

We realize the monumental importance the Money factor can have on a student's decisions to attend a college or not. Before we dive into the actual college admissions process in Section 2, we want to make sure you know some of the basics about how to pay for college and even start reducing your college costs today. In this chapter, we will provide an overview of the costs of college and the types of financial aid available to you to help you be one of the 52% of families that has a solid plan to finance your postsecondary education.

Step 1: Managing the Costs of College

The average tuition and fees at in-state, public universities across the United States have increased 212% in the last 20 years. In addition to higher tuition prices, housing, food, transportation, books, and other school-related fees have also increased, adding thousands of dollars to college expenses. The average cost to attend college in the United States is $32,889 per student, per year. The chart below shows averages for both public and private institutions, including nonprofit and for-profit.

Figure 4.2

Institution Type	Institution	Cost of Tuition & Fees	Additional Expenses	Cost of Attendance
Public (4-year)	In-state	$9,580	$16,284	$25,864
Public (4-year)	Out-of-state	$27,437	$16,284	$43,721
Public (2-year)	In-state	$3,372	$12,665	$16,037
Private (4-year nonprofit)	In-state or out-of-state	$37,200	$16,749	$53,949
Private (4-year for-profit)	In-state or out-of-state	$13,475	$21,073	$34,548
Private (2-year nonprofit)	In-state or out-of-state	$17,294	$17,262	$34,556
Private (2-year for-profit)	In-state or out-of-state	$15,974	$13,984	$29.958

Data taken from the Education Data Initiative

When you look at the above numbers, you can see that some colleges are significantly less expensive than others. A public 2-year college's tuition, the amount you pay to take courses, is around $3,372 while a 4-year private college is $37,200 per year. While these numbers may look intimidating, keep in mind that the tuition costs listed in the table above are *sticker prices* – the price you see is not always the price you pay. It is important to understand the Cost of Attendance and the Net Price.

Cost of attendance (COA) is the total estimated price of direct costs like tuition, fees, and room and board, and indirect costs, like books, supplies, transportation, loan fees, and other miscellaneous expenses. On most college websites they provide the COA. For many students and parents seeing the COA for some colleges can be frightening – but it has been found that only 14% of students do not receive any type of aid (Education Data Initiative).

This means about 9 out of every 10, 86% of families pay a reduced amount. This is called the net price. A college's net price is an estimate of the actual cost families pay to attend a particular college for one year and is the college's COA minus any federal grants or institutional scholarships you may qualify for. In other words, the net price of a college is the discounted cost to attend the college. You can find a Net Price Calculator to estimate your costs on nearly every college's website. You can search for any college's Net Price Calculator at https://collegecost.ed.gov/net-price.

Figure 4.3

Total Cost of Attendance **minus** **Gift Aid**
- Institutional gift aid (grants/scholarships)
- Federal gift aid (grants)
- State gift aid (grants/scholarships)
- Athletic scholarships
- Gift aid from external sources

equals Net Price

CHAPTER 4: MONEY FACTOR

Step 2: Understand Key College Finance Terms

Gift Aid

Gift aid is money that is given to students that does not need to be paid back, such as scholarships and grants. Gift aid comes from many different sources to reduce the cost of college. Knowing the sources of gift aid can help you tap into several different streams of funding to lower your cost of attending college. The most common gift aid comes from colleges, individual states, the federal government, national and local scholarships, and college-bound programs. Many of these are stackable, meaning you can receive money from multiple sources and use them to drastically reduce your costs.

While there are thousands of scholarships available to students, not all parents and students know where to start the process. Listed below are the 6 main money sources for college for students.

Figure 4.4

Institutional
Institutional scholarships come from the university to bring down the price of tuition, room, and board. Sometimes, because of test scores, grades, and your student demographics, you just receive them - other times you must apply! Be sure to ask the college's Office of Financial Aid for help.

Local
Local scholarships come from the community where students live. While these scholarships are often smaller in value than national scholarships, fewer people are applying for them making them very accessible.

National
National scholarships are from large corporations like Coca-Cola, the American Council of the Blind, Siemens Corporation, Don't Text and Drive, and more. These usually have larger monetary value, but more people apply. typically, an essay, letter of recommendation, and/or other information needs to be included when you apply.

Federal
While not necessarily a scholarship, filling out the Free Application for Federal Student Aid (FAFSA) can provide grants, loans, and access to scholarships that otherwise could not have been received.

State
Many states have scholarship options to entice their high achieving students to stay in-state. These scholarships are often based on GPA, class rank and/or standardized test scores.

Programs
Students can access different programs that help fund a college education. Programs such as the U.S. military, AmeriCorps, Learn and Serve, Teach for American and National Health Service Corps provide both tuition reimbursement and career skills.

Institutional Gift Aid: Institutional gift aid, also known as institutional scholarships, is the money a specific college will provide a student to lower the Cost of Attendance at the college. While many families often hear about full-ride scholarships, most do not know that universities give millions of dollars every year to all types of students. Institutional Gift Aid can come in several different forms and is often focused on your 3 Factors- You, Academic, and Career Factors, such as:

- **Merit:** Based on a student's academic standing, including college admissions test scores and grade point average.
- **Special talents & abilities:** Given to those students who are seeking to participate in the college's activities and programs, such as sports, dance, music, art, theatre, etc. programs.
- **Major/program of choice:** Focused on specific majors or programs, often to increase participation from certain a particular demographic of students.
- **Ethnicity & background:** A college is looking to increase the diversity of its student body may provide gift aid to students with certain demographic characteristics, like out-of-state, first-generation, low-income, or ethnicity.

Every college is different in how they disperse gift aid. Often, private institutions have the most flexibility in how aid is distributed and have larger endowments, but the already lower costs of public institutions keep them an affordable option. The data in the graph below are from three selected universities and shows how gift aid affects the net price.

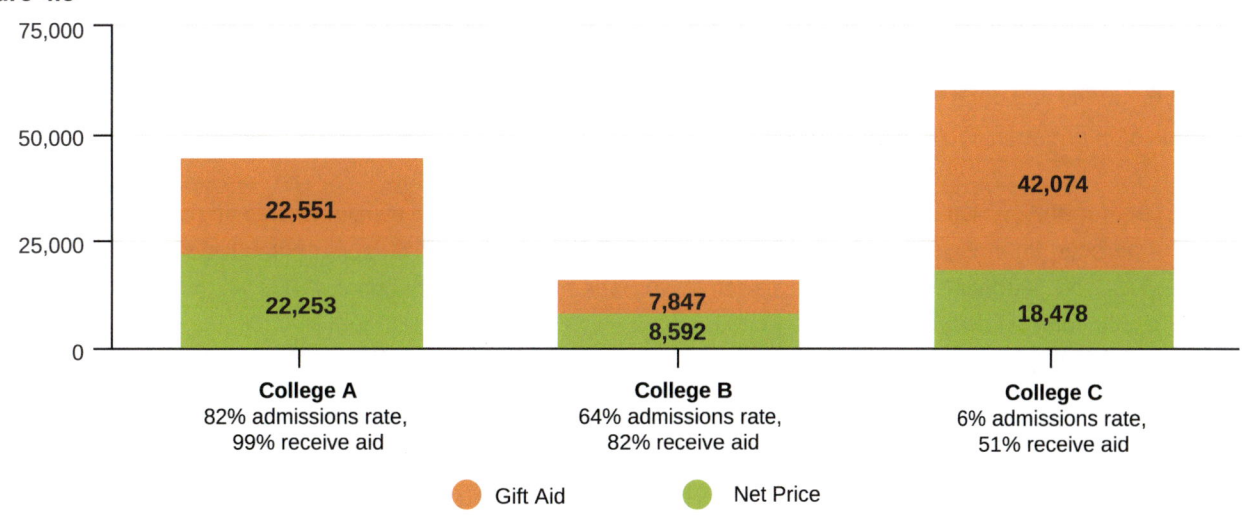

Figure 4.5

College	Gift Aid	Net Price
College A (82% admissions rate, 99% receive aid)	22,551	22,253
College B (64% admissions rate, 82% receive aid)	7,847	8,592
College C (6% admissions rate, 51% receive aid)	42,074	18,478

● Gift Aid   ● Net Price

College A is a moderately selective private college with a sticker price (tuition only) of $45,074, but 99% of the students who attend this college get $22,521 in institutional gift aid (on average). This reduces the actual cost to attend College A to half of its sticker price. College B is a selective public university with an in-state sticker price of $16,439, but 82% of the students who attend here get $7,847 in institutional gift aid. This reduces the actual average cost to attend College B to $8,592. College C is a highly selective private university with a sticker price of $60,552, but 51% of the students who attend get $42,074 in institutional gift aid. This reduces the average cost to attend College C by 69% to $18,478 for those who qualify.

As you can see in the graph above, there can be a lot of variability in how much institutional gift aid colleges provide, and how many students qualify for it. Also, colleges use different approaches to allocate the money they put aside to help students and families reduce the cost of attendance. For example, colleges like College A, where nearly every student qualifies for institutional gift aid, distribute most of their money in a merit-based fashion to attract who they consider the most academically qualified students they can. College C, on the other hand, is an example of a college that distributes its institutional gift aid in a need-based manner. If you qualify for admission to College C and demonstrate financial need, they will provide substantial amounts of money to help cover the cost of attendance – enough to make the cost of attending a highly selective private university comparable with a public university.

CHAPTER 4: MONEY FACTOR

Remember, the graph on the last page (Figure 4.5) shows you the average net price and gift aid amounts for all students at each college. Some students can receive enough gift aid to cover the entire cost of their college education, while others are paying the full cost of attendance (i.e., the sticker price). It all depends on some of the decisions you start making today. Knowing how much gift aid students at a particular college typically qualify for, and how many qualify for it, can help you see how much the college's sticker price may differ from the actual price for you.

State Gift Aid: Some states have designated scholarship programs that are often based on merit attributes such as standardized test scores. For example, Florida has a statewide program based on college admissions tests and recalculated GPAs that provides a 100% or 75% scholarship discount to attend any state college or state university. Over 4 years, that is a cost savings of around $28,000 for top scholars. Every state is different, and you should find out what kind of gift aid may be available to you and how to qualify for it.

Federal Gift Aid: Financial aid is provided by the federal government to help pay for college. The office of Federal Student Aid awarded $120 billion to students in 2020. Unfortunately, many students and families simply do not complete the Free Application for Federal Student Aid (FAFSA) – leaving over $2.6 billion on the table every year!

Completing the FAFSA is required to qualify for and receive federal financial aid and is the single most important thing you and your family should do each year you are in college. Completing the FAFSA requires you and your parents to provide detailed information about who you are and your finances (e.g., number of siblings in college, income as reported on your federal taxes, non-retirement assets, education savings account(s), and marital status). To learn more about the FAFSA and the steps you need to take, visit https://studentaid.gov/help/fafsa-worksheet to see a practice FAFSA form and the kinds of information you need to provide.

Families can earn grants, which is a form of financial aid that doesn't have to be repaid. Grants are often determined by the income of parents, but not always. Common grants are Pell Grants, Federal Supplemental Educational Opportunity Grants (FSEOG), and Teacher Education Assistance for College and Higher Education (TEACH) Grants. Families who earn less annual income often qualify for greater amounts of aid. The current maximum Pell Grant award for the 2021-2022 academic year is $6,495.

The FAFSA is used to determine the Expected Family Contribution (EFC), which is an estimate of how much money you and your family can pay for one year of college. The EFC is used by the federal government, state governments, and colleges to determine how much need-based financial aid you qualify for. After you submit the FAFSA, you receive a Student Aid Report that tells you what your EFC is and which types of federal financial aid you qualify for. You can calculate your EFC on the College Board's Big Future website (CollegeBoard). In 2023, the EFC will be renamed the Student Aid Index (SAI).

External Aid: Outside of government and postsecondary institutions, you can earn a host of other scholarship and financial aid opportunities from external sources.
- **National Scholarships:** National scholarships are plentiful! It is estimated that sites like www.fastweb.com offers over 1.5 million scholarships totaling $3.4 billion dollars. Other popular websites include www.scholarships.com and www.cappex.com.
- **Local Scholarships:** Local scholarships are typically available through local school districts, activities (science fairs and art shows), and non-profit groups (Kiwanis Club, Boys Scouts). While smaller, local scholarships are often stackable and easier to earn as fewer people apply.
- **Program-Based Scholarships:** Program-based scholarships are based on a program you may do alongside your postsecondary education, such as the military, AmeriCorps, Learn and Serve, Teach for America, and National Health Service Corps.

Activity 4.1: Raise.Me

You can start earning scholarship money today. One national scholarship program, called Raise.Me (www.raise.me), allows students to earn micro-scholarships. By putting in your Individualized Academic Plan from Chapter 2 and your résumé from Chapter 3, colleges across the nation will provide you small micro-scholarships for your different activities, like volunteering, campus visits, good grades, and college admissions test scores. What is helpful is it gives you an early look to see if you are on track for earning scholarships, what you are earning, and what colleges might be interested in giving you institutional aid.

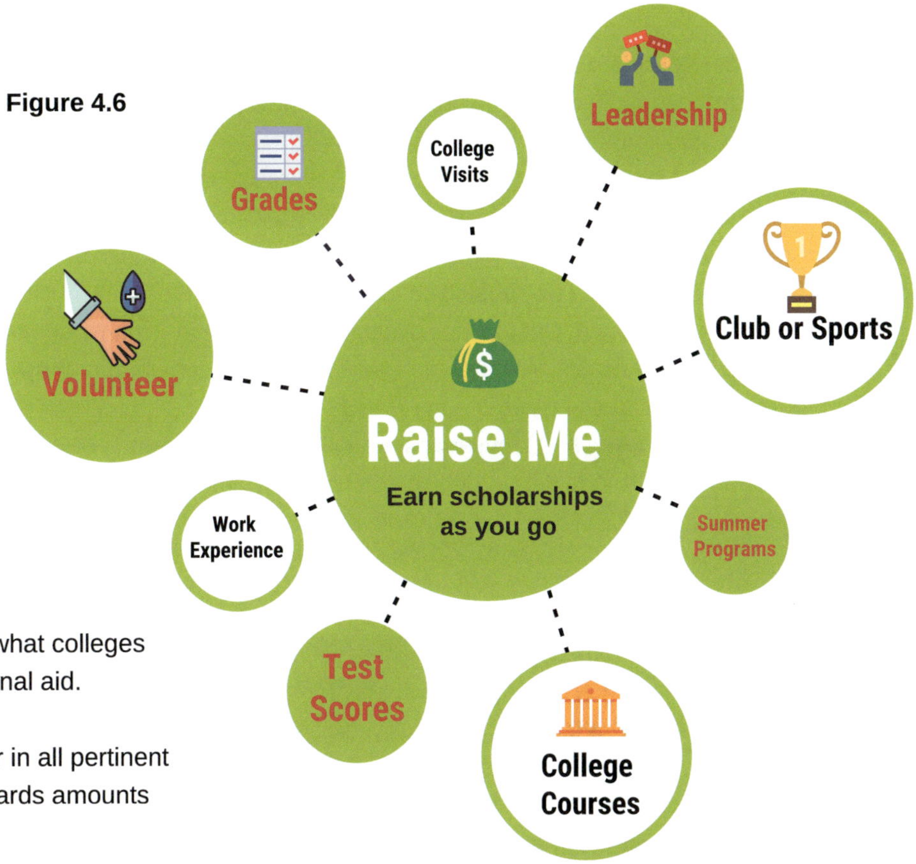

Make an account on www.raise.me. Enter in all pertinent information. Write down some of your awards amounts below.

Figure 4.6

Institution Name	Type of Institution	Location	Raise.Me Annual Amount	Raise.Me Total Amount

Self Help Aid

While gift aid is preferred, because it does not have to be repaid, loans and work-study are other ways to reduce the cost of attending college. Loans, in particular, can have both short- and long-term consequences that you should be aware of.

Loan aid is when you borrow money to attend a college. As we have discussed, student loan debt is the second largest debt held by Americans today. You must repay the loan, as well as the interest that accrues. It is important you understand your repayment options so you can successfully manage your loans. Your loan can either be through the federal government (if you complete the FAFSA) or through private lenders. Please note – students and parents do not have to accept loans that are offered by the college as part of an award package. This will be discussed further in Section 2.

CHAPTER 4: MONEY FACTOR

Some common loans that may be offered by the college you are considering are:

Federal Loans: There are three types of federal loan programs available: Subsidized, Unsubsidized, and Direct Plus loans for parents. These federal loan programs do not require a credit check for students. The FAFSA is required and determines the maximum amount you may borrow.
- **Subsidized Loan:** Subsidized loans are student loans that the federal government pays interest on until after you have graduated from college, which you will then start paying after you graduate. The college determines the amount you can borrow, and the amount may not exceed your financial need. Only students with demonstrated financial need qualify for subsidized loans.
- **Unsubsidized Loan:** Unsubsidized loans are also student loans, but your interest starts accruing from day one, and without deferment, you also start paying them from day one. These loans do not require a family to demonstrate financial need, but the FAFSA is required.
- **Direct Plus Loan:** Direct Plus loans are loans made to parents on behalf of the student. The loan amount cannot exceed the COA, and the parents' credit history is considered when determining eligibility.

Private Loans: Private loans are offered through banks and credit unions to help you cover the costs of college not paid for by scholarships, grants, and/or federal student loans. While federal student loans are all fixed interest rate loans, private student loans can be fixed-rate or variable rates. This is a very important issue to consider; fixed-rate loans provide predictable repayment plans, while the interest rate on variable rate loans can change, potentially increasing your college debt. The FAFSA is not required to apply for a private loan, but your credit history is considered. Having a co-signer (someone who also takes responsibility for loan repayment) may increase your chances of qualifying for a private loan.

Work-Study Aid: Work-Study aid is another opportunity for students to help reduce the cost of college by working for the college they are attending. The Federal Work-Study program allows you to earn money to pay for school by working part-time, often for the college, you are attending. By working with the financial aid office at the college, you can earn a job working at the dining center or in a computer lab, or choose from a host of other occupations. Work-study eligibility is determined by completing your FAFSA.

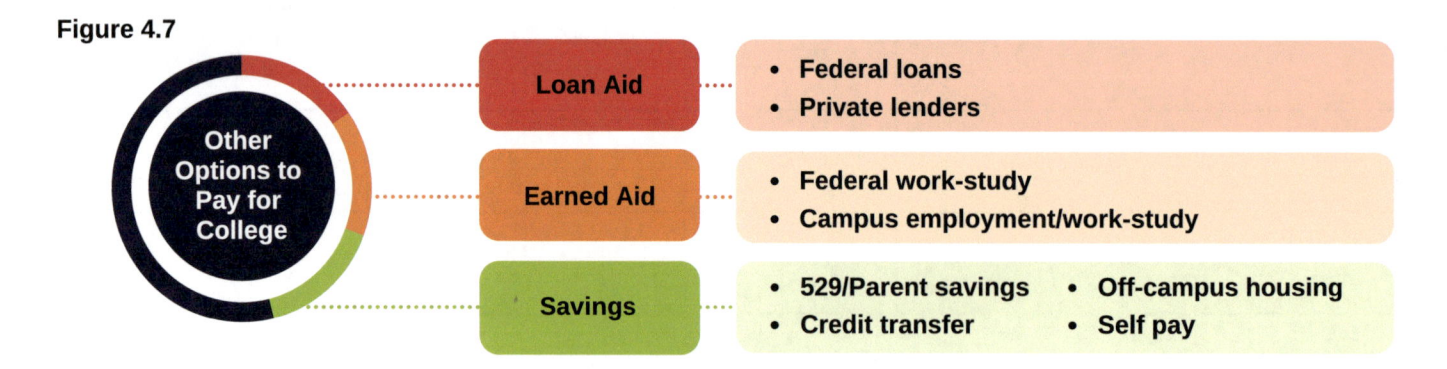

Figure 4.7

Other Options to Pay for College:
- **Loan Aid**
  - Federal loans
  - Private lenders
- **Earned Aid**
  - Federal work-study
  - Campus employment/work-study
- **Savings**
  - 529/Parent savings
  - Credit transfer
  - Off-campus housing
  - Self pay

Step 3: Case Study – Sholondo

> Sholondo lives in southwest Florida and needs to reduce his college costs as he plans on earning both a Bachelor of Accounting and a Master of Business Administration to achieve his career goal of working in a leadership position as a business executive. Both his parents are teachers with salaries of $48,134 (median salary rate), so a combined income of $96,268. His sister currently attends Florida Atlantic University in their Honors Program. Sholondo has a part-time job at Panera Bread and made $4,120 last year. They have some savings, but not much. He is looking into all opportunities to reduce his costs to go to college.

Sholondo took part in his high school's AP program and took some dual enrollment (DE) courses his senior year. He found out from his sister, who recently met with her college academic advisor, that the courses he is taking at his high school through AP and DE can count towards his general education courses he would take at any college. His state has it clearly articulated how his credit-by-exam credits will transfer. His 2 AP exams (AP English Language and AP Biology) along with his 3 DE courses (Composition II, College Algebra, and Microeconomics) will earn him 15 college credits saving him in tuition alone: $1,650 (15 x $110) at a state/community college, $3,300 (15 x $220) at a state university, or up to $14,970 (15 x $998) at a private university.

Sholondo has been working hard on his GPA and college admissions test scores as it could earn him 75% to 100% free tuition for up to 4 years through the state's scholarship program called Bright Futures. He also found that his local community has a scholarship foundation that provides over 85 scholarships to local students, ranging from $500 to $10,000 for up to 4 years. His school counselor let him know that only 435 students applied last year, so he could have a great chance of earning a scholarship. Unbeknownst to him, the baseball scholarship he was interested in only had two applicants!

While Sholondo has yet to start the application process, he sat with his parents, school counselor, and his sister to discuss how he can reduce the cost of college by starting early in his high school career. By having a plan and a general budget, he knows approximately how much money he needs to save and some ways he can reduce the cost.

How Well Developed are Sholondo's 8 Strengths?

Agency: Sholondo is taking charge of his educational and career future. He already knows that he wants to go to graduate school so it will be particularly important for him to reduce the cost of his undergraduate education. He is acting in proactive ways to follow a direction he has set for himself. He is using all the resources around him to make early, informed decisions.

Positive Beliefs: Sholondo strongly believes in his ability to manage the costs of college so that it does not manage him. He is willing to persevere to find affordable ways to pay for the education he needs to reach his career goals. By focusing on how he will pay for college now, Sholondo hopes to concentrate on his studies and build his résumé while in college. The time and attention he gives to funding his education now will pay off for him in the future.

Effective Goals: Sholondo has both long-term and short-term goals. He knows he would like to go to graduate school to earn an MBA (a long-term goal). To achieve that goal, Sholondo has set several short-term goals to reduce his undergraduate costs by qualifying for his state's scholarship program and available community scholarships.

Knowing Yourself: While Sholondo has clear goals for his future, he is still unsure of which specific college he might attend. He is exploring all options and is being proactive. He is looking at colleges that would give him gift aid (merit and/or need-based aid) and explore college environments he would flourish in academically and socially. He realizes that the skills he will acquire in both his undergraduate and graduate degree programs will help him achieve his goal of working as a business executive.

Becoming a Successful Student: Sholondo realizes the importance of his hard work in and out of the classroom. He is earning college credit while in high school through rigorous dual enrollment and AP courses, and his performance in these classes will demonstrate to admissions counselors that he is able to succeed academically at the college level. He is focused on achieving a strong high school GPA and the test scores needed for admission to college and as much merit-based gift aid as possible.

CHAPTER 4: MONEY FACTOR

Character for Workplace Success: Sholondo's part-time job has helped him develop the ability to get along with others, work as part of a team, demonstrate initiative, follow rules, and be flexible and dependable. Working part-time while in high school demonstrates to college admission counselors that he has organizational and time management skills to achieve both academically and in the workplace.

College Knowledge: Sholondo is improving his awareness of ways to finance his postsecondary education (e.g. by taking AP and DE courses, identifying several community scholarships to apply for as well as state scholarships). He understands how his college education can help him achieve his career goals, how undergraduate and graduate education are related and has a firm idea of what he wants to pursue as a college major. It will be helpful for Sholondo to improve his college knowledge in the areas of college culture and life on campus so he can identify the learning environment he will fit best.

College Support Network: Sholondo has a strong College Support Network. His parents are supportive of his educational and career aspirations. Both are college graduates and are well-positioned to support his success in the transition to college. His sister is a successful undergraduate herself and is an active source of support for Sholondo. He has a good working relationship with his high school counselor, who has helped him identify scholarships he has a good chance of qualifying for. His College Support Network is providing the emotional and instrumental support he needs to successfully navigate the process of applying to and paying for college.

Step 4: Understand Net Price

Activity 4.2: Calculating Net Price

Use the website https://collegenavigator.gov and search by college name. Choose four colleges you have heard of or might be interested in. Use the site to review and research these colleges by completing the chart below. This activity is to begin to show you how to look for critical information about each college and the average cost of attendance (COA) and net price. As a reminder, there are a variety of ways to pay for college and a variety of ways colleges reduce the cost of attending their college. What you list below are reported averages for each college.

1. Use the formula to add the costs (tuition, books and supplies, and room and board) to get the COA.
2. Subtract institutional grants or scholarships from COA to determine the net price.

Institution Name	In-State/Out-of-State Tuition*	Books & Supplies	On-Campus Room & Board	Cost of Attendance	Institutional Grants or Scholarships	Net Price
Tennessee State University	22,284	1,600	10,120	0	0	34,004
Georgia State University	23,709	2,600	16,328	0	0	41,537
Florida A and M uni	17,725	569	3,840 + 1,475	0	0	23,609
Clark Atlanta	24,730	1,900	7,630 + 4,516	0	0	38,829

* For public universities, choose in-state or out-of-state tuition based on if you live in the state of the college (in-state tuition) or live in a different state (out-of-state tuition). Private universities are the same price whether you live in the state or not.

COLLEGE UNMAZED

Summary

There are many ways that you can pay for college. Learning and understanding all the options will help you and your family make a well-informed decision about your college options. In Section 2, you will look more closely at colleges you may be interested in and assess what your financial options are.

At-Home Discussion

While it is tough to talk finances as a family, this is the time to sit down and find out what everyone's expectations are for your college future, especially your finances. Even with scholarships and financial aid, there may be some gaps of funding that has to come from somewhere. Paying for college is a team effort, and everyone must be on the same page. Having this discussion early and often is key to reducing costs. Complete the question-and-answer section below.

- **Determine your Expected Family Contribution (EFC).** Use an EFC Calculator at https://bigfuture.collegeboard.org/pay-for-college/paying-your-share/expected-family-contribution-calculator to prepare an estimate on how much you and your family are expected to contribute to the cost of college along with possible grant money. What is your EFC?

    EFC is around 10-15000 $ dollars TBD.

- **Set clear expectations.** Discuss the additional costs of college, such as room and board, transportation, personal expenses, books, etc. Who will be responsible for paying what costs? Are there other ways to reduce costs?

    My parents would be responsible for paying the cost of these things, but I will sign up for finical aid and try at different scholarships.

- **Discuss the pros and cons of borrowing.** Student loans can be difficult to understand. Use a loan calculator so you understand exactly how much your monthly payments would be. Use the estimated net price on the last page minus your EFC to determine an estimated loan payment. Use https://smartasset.com/student-loans/student-loan-calculator.

    3,000 $ will be my estimated loan price. but TBD.

- **The scholarship process can be a team effort.** Senior year is a busy time but earning a few scholarships can make a large impact on reducing your college expenses. Pursuing scholarship opportunities is easier when it is a family effort. Everyone can help in locating scholarships and keeping track of deadlines. Write down a few scholarship sources in your state or local community.
    - *Niche 50,000 "no essay" scholarship*
    - *C.W. and Frances Aneshansley Scholarship*
    - *Amelia D. Davis and Elizabeth J. Davis Lawere Scholarship*
    - *Bob Little Pastoral musicians scholarship*

- **Discuss opportunities at community colleges and through accelerated credit (dual enrollment and credit-by-exams).** With many states having clearly defined transferability of credits, it can make transferring credit easy and colleges less expensive. Starting at a community college or taking credit-by-exams can save time and money. For the colleges on the preceding page, use their website to find out how credits you earned while in high school may transfer.

    - *I plan on going to a community college first then transfer to a university (GRCC)*
    - *My Dual enrollment credits will transfer to GRCC.*

- **Learn how to budget and save.** As you transition into college, you need to understand financial responsibility. This includes setting up a bank account, budgeting, and savings. Many banks have programs set up that can help you learn how to stay on track financially. Check your bank to see what is available.

    Yes it is available, I bank with Huntington and I also have a savings account

Review the High School Planning Checklist in Resources on page 133. What are some next action steps that you need to take in the next month, six months, and year?

Apply for scholarships and put in more college applications and stay focused (:

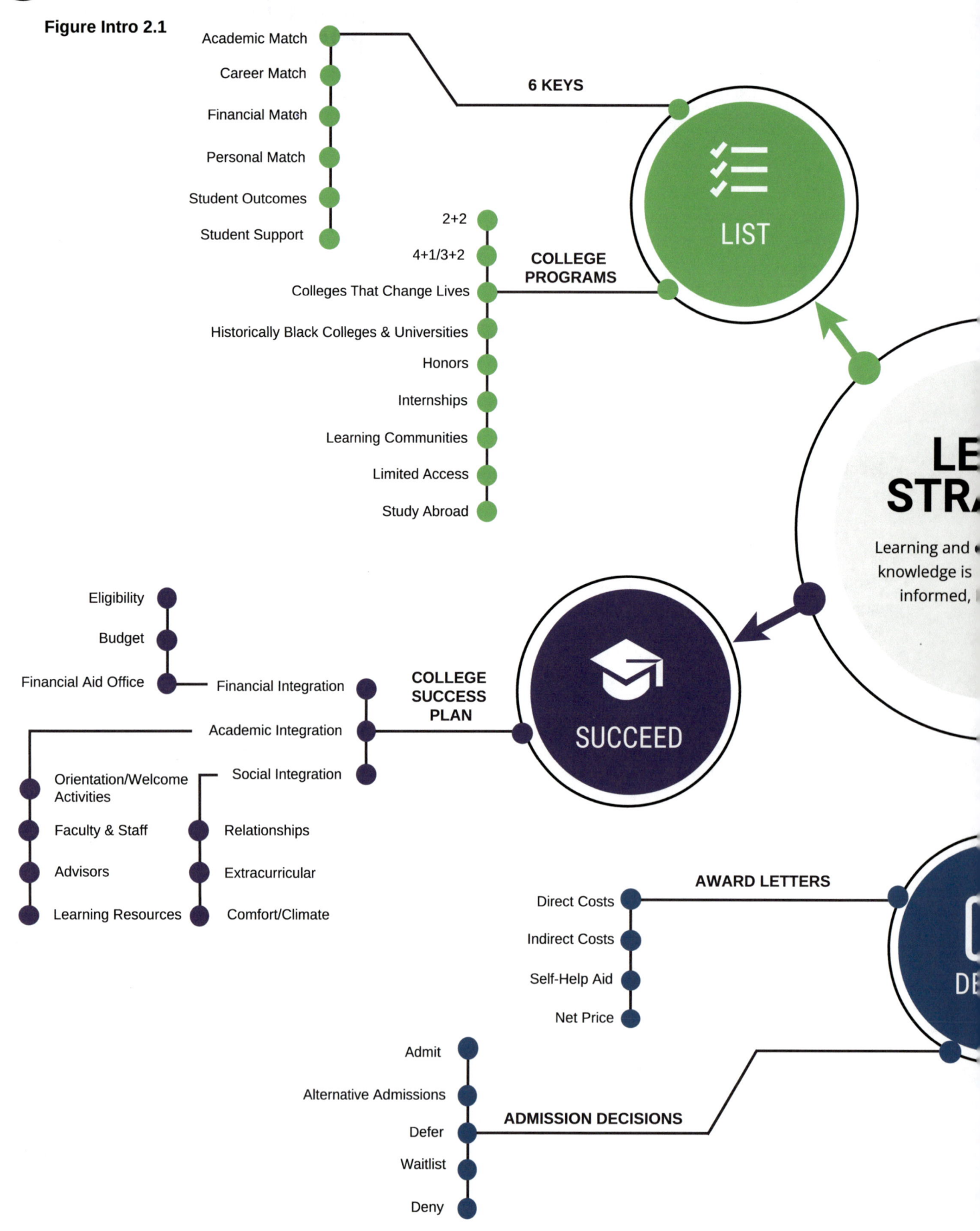

INTRODUCTION - SECTION 2

Figure Intro 2.1

6 KEYS
- Academic Match
- Career Match
- Financial Match
- Personal Match
- Student Outcomes
- Student Support

COLLEGE PROGRAMS
- 2+2
- 4+1/3+2
- Colleges That Change Lives
- Historically Black Colleges & Universities
- Honors
- Internships
- Learning Communities
- Limited Access
- Study Abroad

LIST

LE
STRA

Learning and
knowledge is
informed,

COLLEGE SUCCESS PLAN

Financial Integration
- Eligibility
- Budget
- Financial Aid Office

Academic Integration
- Orientation/Welcome Activities
- Faculty & Staff
- Advisors
- Learning Resources

Social Integration
- Relationships
- Extracurricular
- Comfort/Climate

SUCCEED

AWARD LETTERS
- Direct Costs
- Indirect Costs
- Self-Help Aid
- Net Price

ADMISSION DECISIONS
- Admit
- Alternative Admissions
- Defer
- Waitlist
- Deny

54

COLLEGE UNMAZED

EXPLORE

ADMISSION TYPES
- Open Access
- Competitive
- Selective
- Highly Selective

VISITS
- Formal
- Informal
- Fly-ins
- High School Visits
- College Fairs
- Virtual Fairs

ACADEMIC & NON-ACADEMIC FACTORS
- Rigor
- Class Rank
- GPA
- ACT/SAT
- Essay
- Recommendations
- Talent/Ability
- Interview
- Character/Personal
- Extracurriculars
- Volunteer Work
- Work Experience
- Level of Applicant Interest
- First-Generation
- Alumni Relation
- Geographical Residence
- State Residency
- Religious Affiliation/Commitment
- Racial/Ethnic Status

APPLY

DOCUMENTS
- Résumé
- Essay
- Letters of Recommendation
- ACT/SAT
- Transcript
- FAFSA/CSS Profile

APPLICATIONS
- Common App
- Coalition App
- Institutional Application

ALTERNATIVE ADMISSIONS
- Support Programs
- Online
- Alternative Programs
- Alternative Term

DEADLINES
- Early Decision
- Early Action
- Priority Deadline
- Regular Decision
- Rolling Admissions

INFORMED DECISION
- Create
- Evaluate
- Analyze
- Apply
- Understand
- Remember

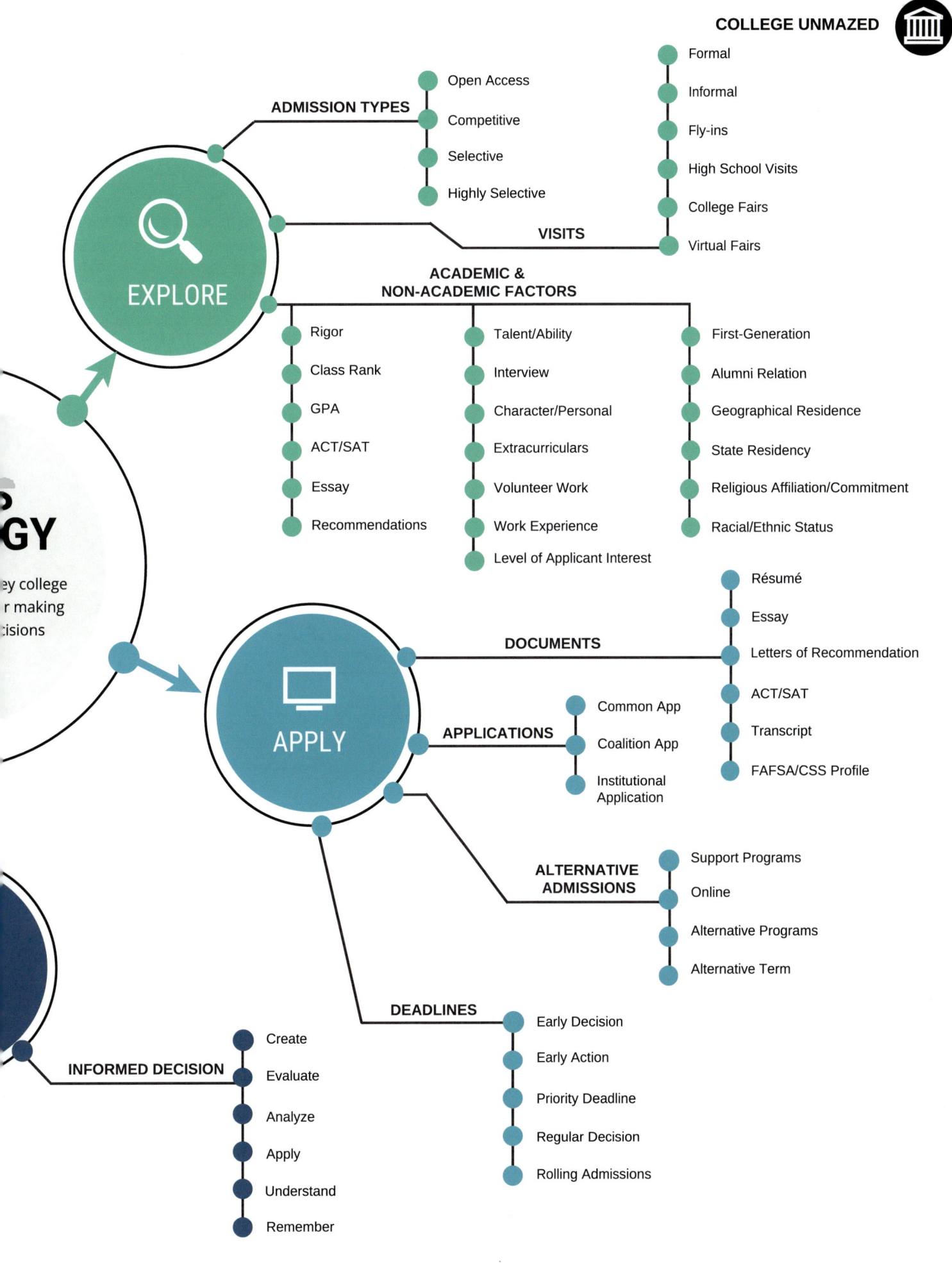

55

INTRODUCTION - SECTION 2

You will learn a higher-order thinking strategy (LEADS) to make a more informed college decision in Section 2 of this book. In Section 1, you strengthened your college and career readiness. Now, you will build on this foundation to identify a list of colleges you may be interested in, explore these colleges in-depth, narrow your list down to those colleges where you will apply, make a final decision on which college you will attend, and then take steps to be successful during your college years and beyond. To accomplish this, we are going to teach you a step-by-step process using examples and activities. The figure (Figure I2.2) and discussion below provide an overview of the LEADS strategy for making informed college decisions. You are introduced to the 6 Keys of College Fit that will enable you to assess the fit between you and each college you are considering. Effectively using these 6 Keys will guide you through the maze that is college decision making.

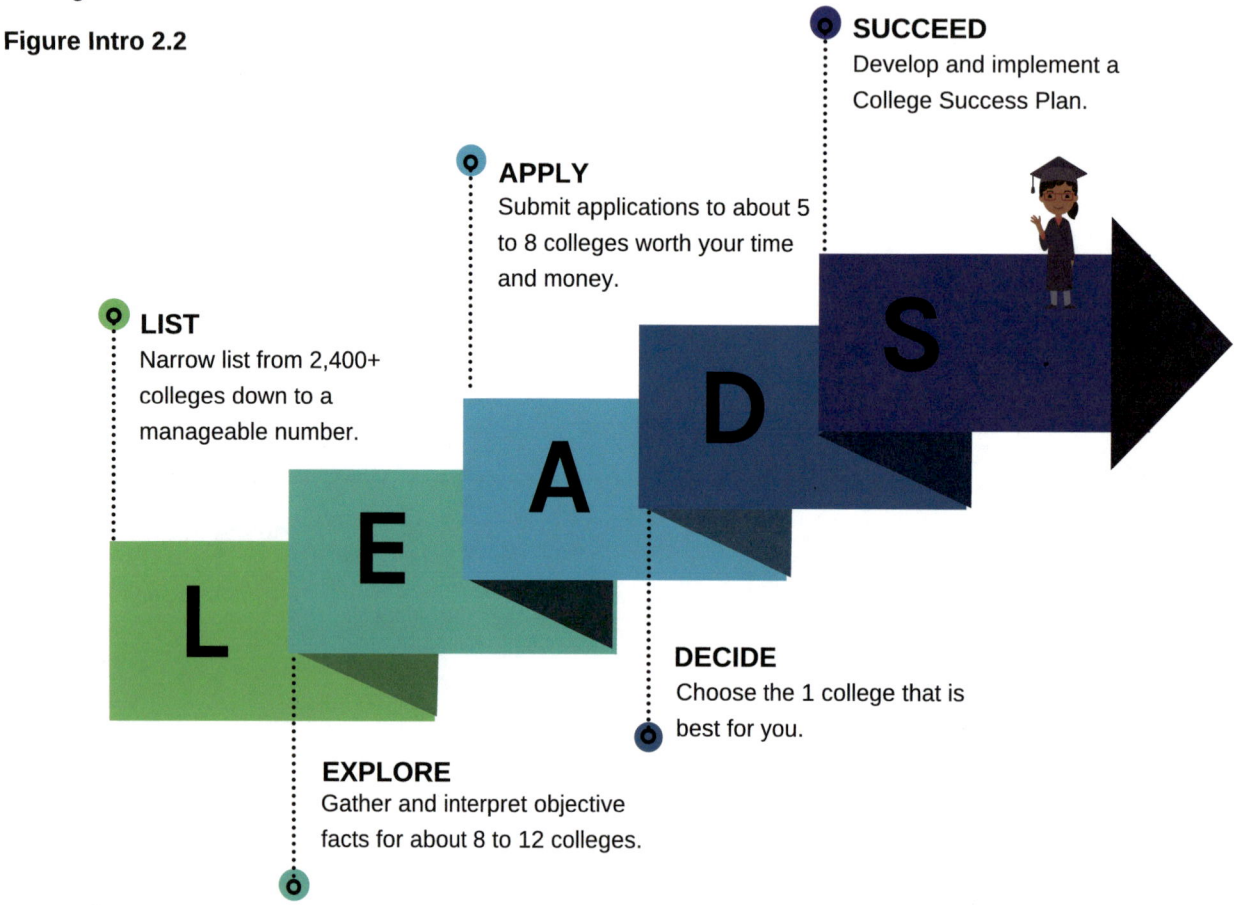

Figure Intro 2.2

SUCCEED — Develop and implement a College Success Plan.

APPLY — Submit applications to about 5 to 8 colleges worth your time and money.

DECIDE — Choose the 1 college that is best for you.

EXPLORE — Gather and interpret objective facts for about 8 to 12 colleges.

LIST — Narrow list from 2,400+ colleges down to a manageable number.

LEADS is a strategy you can use to make better college decisions. Making a more informed college decision requires perseverance and effort to progress through a predictable 5 step sequence. There are more than 2,400+, public and private, four-year colleges to choose from in the United States alone. The good news is that there are many good choices for you. However, what is a good choice for you may, in fact, be a bad choice for other family members and friends, and a great choice for your friend could be a terrible choice for you. LEADS will help you find those colleges that fit you best to send applications to, and then help you decide on the one college you will attend. You will go through the entire LEADS process in Section 2 to determine the best college for you.

You might be asking yourself, Why do I need to use a college decision-making process like LEADS? Using the LEADS process does several things to help you through the college choice process that will pay off for you in the long run. LEADS puts you in control by helping you learn what to pay attention to, thus reducing your stress levels. Given the high cost of college and the fact that far too many people do not make it to graduation, the LEADS process helps to improve your match and fit with colleges. Improved match and fit are connected to success and satisfaction in college.

6 Keys of College Fit

What do you see in the picture to the right? Do you see two people facing each other? Or, do you see an ornate vase? If you focus on the black space in the middle of the picture, you will see a vase. However, if you focus on the white spaces, you will see two heads facing each other. In Gestalt Psychology, this demonstrates the power of perspective. Depending on what you choose to look at, that becomes the focus of what you perceive. When you are able to look at something from multiple perspectives, you will have a more complete understanding of what it is you are actually looking at. Informed college decision-making is exactly the same. When you understand a college from 6 key perspectives, you are better able to see the whole picture and visualize how it may or may not fit you.

Figure Intro 2.3

The 6 Keys of College Fit will allow you to focus on important aspects of each college you may be considering.

1. Academic Match: Understanding how your academic profile compares to students attending the college, and how the college's learning environment fits you. Your academic profile includes things such as high school GPA and admission test scores. A college's learning environment consists of things such as class size and types of classes offered (e.g., large lecture halls, smaller seminars, and field-based experiences), student to faculty ratio, and writing-intensive requirements.

2. Career Match: Ensuring the college aligns with your career aspirations and with majors available to help you reach your career goals. Being able to pursue a major that fits within a Career Pathway consistent with your interests, abilities, and values provides direction towards satisfying work in the future.

3. Financial Match: Knowing what a college will actually cost you and your family. Being aware of all the sources of financial aid such as grants, scholarships, and loans will help you more fully understand the affordability of each college.

4. Personal Match: Assessing how the college matches your personal preferences to design the lifestyle you want, and how ready you are to be successful at the college. Considering characteristics like distance from home, size of the college, and diversity of the student body and faculty will help you feel more connected and that you belong at the college. Further, having the right attitude, skills, and behaviors will support your success at college.

5. Student Outcomes: Colleges use marketing and branding to recruit students they view as desirable. In the competitive world of college admissions, colleges highlight selected information to entice students to attend their school. You can balance off the marketing and branding colleges employ with factual information about student success such as retention rates, graduation rates, and alumni earnings.

6. Student Support: Identifying the formal institutional supports available to you at the college. To help meet your individualized needs, investigate the student support services available to you at the college (e.g., advising, tutoring, counseling, writing support, disability services, career and alumni services).

INTRODUCTION - SECTION 2

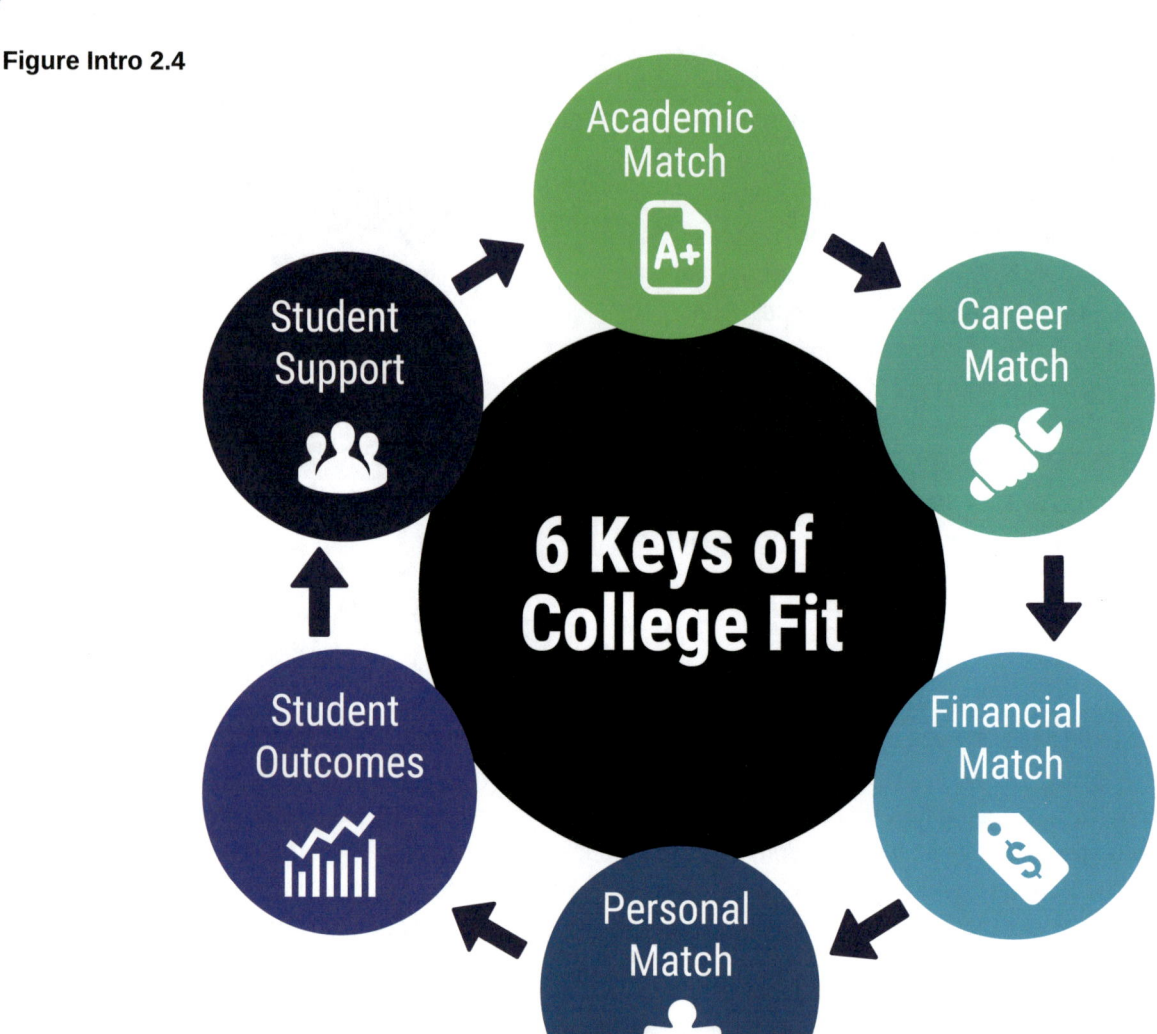

Figure Intro 2.4

Diagram: 6 Keys of College Fit — Academic Match, Career Match, Financial Match, Personal Match, Student Outcomes, Student Support

As you will learn, the LEADS strategy embeds the 6 Keys in a higher-order thinking sequence. This will become very clear to you in both the Apply and Decide steps. However, in different ways, the 6 Keys have a role to play in each step of the LEADS process. For example, in the List step, you will focus on the Academic, Career, and Personal Match Keys. These critical perspectives will help you to identify a group of colleges to explore more fully. While some students go straight to comparing costs, this is a misplaced step, as the actual cost of attending a particular college can be obscured and difficult to find early in the college search process. You will investigate costs later, in the Explore step, so you don't miss out on learning more about colleges that might fit you very well. In other words, we don't want you to get hung up on the sticker price before you have a good sense of the net price. In the Explore step, you will consider all 6 Keys to decide on which colleges to submit applications to. In Apply, you will review all the information you collected in Explore and will learn how to create a great application to increase your chances of admission and scholarships. Next, the Decide stage will allow you, once admissions decisions are released, to make a fully informed decision about where to attend college! Finally, in the Succeed step, you will mainly use Cost, Academic Match, Personal Match, and Student Support to transition from being a high school student to a successful college student as you create your own College Success Plan. In the following chapters, we will walk you through the LEADS process and show you how to do this for yourself.

Let's begin!

CHAPTER 5
List

Identifying Colleges & Gathering Information

You Factor · Academic Factor · Career Factor · Money Factor · **Developing a List** · Exploring Colleges · Applying to Colleges · Deciding on a College · Succeeding in College

The first step on your journey towards making an informed college decision starts with developing an initial List of colleges to consider. With more than 2,400 4-year colleges and 1,100 2-year colleges in the United States alone, there are a lot of choices! The primary goal of this chapter is to help you develop your List. By the end of this chapter, you will have a manageable number of colleges to explore further in the next chapter. Your List should not have too many colleges, making it overwhelming. At the same time, your List should be extensive enough so that you don't prematurely rule out colleges that could be a good fit for you. Completing the Progress Check at the end of this chapter will help you determine if you are ready for the next phase of Explore.

Your List Steps

1. Use Online Resources. Explore useful, high-quality resources that provide you with reliable college information.
2. Learn about College Attributes. Begin understanding how the 6 Keys relates to your soon-to-be-made college decision while exploring unique college programs that could make a big difference for you.
3. Review Case Study – Alex. Through a case study, you will be shown how to start building your college list.
4. Develop Your Own List. Begin creating a college list that matches your 6 academic, personal and career goals.

How many colleges should be on your List? How many colleges should you eventually apply to? Well, it depends; the number can vary a great deal from one student to the next, and from one family to the next. Organizations like the College Board, for example, suggest applying to 5 to 8 colleges. However, depending on who you are and what part of the country you live in, this number can change quite a bit. For example, in some parts of the country, there will be many 4-year colleges within a two-hour drive of your home. In other parts, you may only have a couple of colleges to choose from and you may not be able to find 5 to 8 colleges to consider unless you are willing to travel very far from home. You have probably heard stories of how some young people might go too far and apply to dozens of colleges, while other students only apply to one or two. We will help you find the right balance that matches your personal circumstances. With that said, and generally speaking, we think having somewhere between 10 to 15 colleges on your initial List is a good starting point – but you might have a few more or less!

Step 1: Use Online Resources

To help you get started, we will use an internet-based tool called the College Navigator (https://collegenavigator.gov). There are plenty of websites on the internet that will help you get information about colleges, but we are using the College Navigator here for two reasons. First, because it is a website sponsored and run by the U.S. Government's National

CHAPTER 5: LIST

Center for Education Statistics, it is an unbiased source of college information. The second reason we use the College Navigator is that it uses most of the same information that all the other websites use – a treasure trove of information about colleges known as the Integrated Postsecondary Education Data System (IPEDS).

You will be using the College Navigator both here and in the next few chapters – so if you are not familiar with it, we will walk with you step-by-step through how to use it efficiently and effectively. If you would prefer to use another college information and search tool (e.g., College Board, Naviance), you can adapt the LEADS process to be used with any of the other tools available – just note that they might emphasize different information, and how you find information in another system is likely to differ.

Great Websites to Explore

1. College Navigator: National Center for Education Statistics
As part of the Department of Education, the College Navigator's information is independent and unbiased.

2. CollegeBoard Big Future
Run by the organization that publishes the SAT, this site provides a wealth of information from a great search function to each college's information and data.

3. Cappex
Cappex contains a great deal of information about colleges, scholarships, and majors. There are good articles on the website, and they report the average GPA of admitted students.

4. College GreenLight
College GreenLight connects first generation and underrepresented students to caring colleges, generous scholarships, and mentors.

5. Niche
Niche develops college lists by rankings, acceptance rates, test scores, and net price. It provides a report card for each college and additional detailed information.

6. Princeton Review
Known for their test prep workbooks, The Princeton Review has a robust college search site with easy charts to compare colleges.

Activity 5.1: What Colleges Do You Already Have in Mind?

Do you already have colleges you know about and want to be included on your List? If so, write down their names, and why you are considering them. Don't be hesitant about stating your reasons; if you are including a college on your List because you like their football team, that's OK – there are colleges that provide access to both a good education and a good football team!

College Name	Reason I Am Considering

Step 2: Learn about College Attributes

Academic Match

- Online/distance learning options
- Availability of weekend classes
- Credit for life experience
- Available degrees (certificates, Associate, Bachelor's)
- Type of college, 2- or 4-year
- Public or private

Career Match

- Majors & programs offered

Personal Match

- Location
- Distance from home
- Size of campus (small, medium, large)
- Sports teams
- Religious affiliation
- Special mission (HBCU, tribal, single sex)

When developing a List using internet-based tools, the kind of information you will get related to each Key is very general and perhaps, sometimes, even superficial. But, as you move through the LEADS process, you will gather much more specific and detailed information that will help you reduce the number of colleges you have explored down to a shorter list of colleges where you will apply. At the beginning of the process, however, it is helpful to list colleges in terms of the general characteristics provided by these online information systems, to make sure you do not miss good options.

You will use 3 of the 6 Keys of College Fit to generate your List - **Academic Match, Career Match, and Personal Match**. You will think about and gather information related to each of these 3 Keys to help you figure out what is important to you, and then use that information to find colleges that meet your preferences and needs. The specific characteristics of colleges related to these 3 Keys are available on College Navigator.

The aspects of Academic Match on College Navigator include thinking about college learning environments, the type of degree you are looking for, and the type of institution. We do not recommend limiting your List, such as selecting only public or only private colleges, as doing so can be misleading at this point. You will attend to Career Match while developing your List by examining whether or not a college offers majors you are interested in exploring further. If you did not complete the activities in the Career Factor (Chapter 3) yet, please do so to help get a sense of the kinds of majors you might consider exploring. Even if you are undecided about a specific major, you should still have a general idea about Career Pathways that you may be interested in, and make sure that related majors are available to you at colleges you are considering.

The pieces of Personal Match you will examine to make your List are what most college search programs on the internet use. A common thread among these Personal Match characteristics is that none of them have anything to do with the quality of the education you will receive. So, as you consider how important these things are to helping find the right college for you, take some time to really think about how these things benefit your educational experience. For example, some people say they want to attend a small college because they attended a large high school and want a more personalized college experience. The fact is that small, personalized learning communities can be found on large college campuses as well – but if you leave large colleges off your List from the start, you will never have the opportunity to learn about them.

Other important aspects of Personal Match you may consider in the List stage include the mission of a college. Gender specific colleges, tribal colleges, and historically black colleges and universities (HBCUs), as well as colleges with a particular religious affiliation, are often designed to serve and support a specific segment of the college-going population.

For many students and families, cost is a primary consideration – so why aren't we including it here? The fact is that including cost at this stage of your college search process is premature and may lead you to exclude colleges that are not only a good fit for you, but also very affordable. Remember, as we discussed in Chapter 4: Money Factor, a college's sticker price is very often not its actual price. You will explore cost deeply in the Explore, Apply, and Decide stages.

CHAPTER 5: LIST

Figure 5.1

9 College Programs That You Should Know

2+2 Programs

Many colleges, including community colleges, state universities, and even selective liberal arts colleges, offer 2+2 programs where you start at one college (typically a community college) and are guaranteed admission into a more selective college or program. These programs offer benefits to students such as lower cost and different admission standards.

4+1/3+2 Programs

Some colleges offer accelerated degree programs that combine a Bachelor's degree and a Master's degree in as little as five years. Common programs include MBA, Education, Hospitality, Communications, and Engineering. 3+2 programs are common at liberal arts colleges and lead to 2 Bachelor's degrees – one in a liberal arts major, and the second degree in a field like engineering from a different college.

Colleges That Change Lives

A program that consists of more than 40 colleges dedicated to the advancement and support of a student-centered college. These colleges have a goal for each student to develop a lifelong love of learning that provides the foundation for a successful and fulfilling life beyond college.

Historically Black Colleges & Universities

HBCUs are institutions of higher education in the United States that were established before 1964 with the intention of serving the black community. There are more than 100 HBCUs today, including public and private, 2- and 4-year institutions, medical schools, and community colleges. Almost all are in former slave states.

Honors Programs

An honors program allows students with high academic achievement to be placed in courses designed to thoroughly explore topics and further develop critical thinking skills. Honors programs typically have smaller class sizes and offer extra-curricular activities. Admission requirements of honors programs vary by institution but typically emphasize scores on the SAT or ACT, high school class rank, or GPA. Sometimes a supplemental application is required.

Internships

Internships provide students with real-world, hands-on experience in a field they wish to pursue. To be competitive when you graduate, having an internship can help you make the connections and gain the experience you need to get hired. Some colleges make experiential learning, such as internships, a central feature of their programs.

Learning Communities

Learning communities may look very different from one institution to the next, but they often refer to a situation in which the same students are registered for two or more courses that are, in some way, linked. Students may also be divided within classes and/or residential living into specialized groups with a common theme, such as a major, interest, program, or even where you are from (out-of-state/international).

Limited Access

A college program that has additional admission and program requirements before entering. Oftentimes space is limited, and they are incredibly competitive in nature. College admission does not guarantee acceptance to a limited access program. However, some colleges offer direct entry programs that will allow you to avoid additional applications and enter directly into your chosen major. Typically found in nursing, architecture, and other competitive programs.

Study Abroad

Studying abroad affords students an opportunity to travel and live outside of the United States, explore other cultures, and speak other languages. Most colleges provide short-term (as short as one week over spring break) to whole semester and year-long options.

Step 3: Review Case Study – Alex

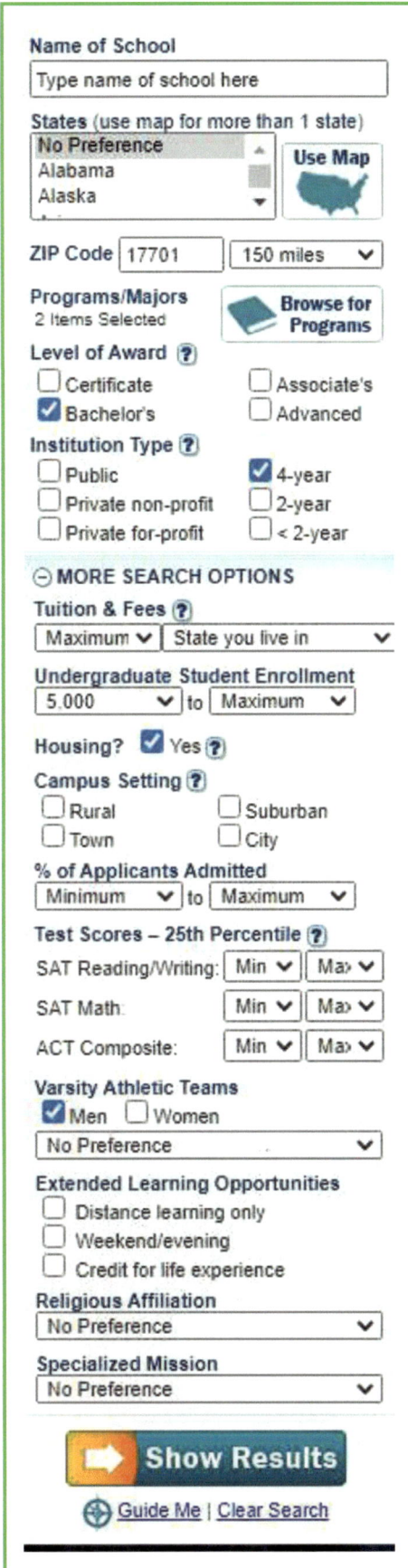

Please recall Alex from Chapter 3 (Career Factor), who is interested in exploring Biomedical or Medical Engineering. He reviewed his Academic, Career, and Personal Match Keys and rank-ordered his priorities, described below in order of importance (1 is most important):

1. Career Pathways (Bioengineering and Biomedical Engineering)
2. Housing available on or near campus
3. Distance from home (about 150 miles)
4. School size (does not want to be at small college, wants at least 5,000 undergrad students)
5. Varsity athletic teams (likes the idea of rooting for the football team)
6. Institution type (wants to attend 4-year colleges)
7. Level of award (wants a Bachelor's degree)

Alex lives in Williamsport, Pennsylvania (ZIP code 17701). In the College Navigator (as shown on the left) he added "Biological/Biosystems Engineering" and "Bioengineering and Biomedical Engineering" in the Programs/Majors section, selected 150 miles from his ZIP code, and placed a check next to Housing to indicate on or near-campus living arrangements are required, and left everything else blank. Identifying colleges using his top 3 priorities resulted in a list with 23 colleges on it.

As Alex studied his list, there were colleges he had heard of and was familiar with, and others he hadn't heard of. He felt that 23 colleges were too many. To reduce his list a little further, he went to his 4th priority (school size). He then set the Undergraduate Student Enrollment minimum to 5,000, which narrowed his List down to 16 colleges. This still seemed a bit too many. So, Alex reflected more on his priorities and concluded that he really did like the idea of rooting for a college's football team (5th priority). This narrowed his initial list of colleges down to 13, shown below. Each college on his List matches his top 5 priorities.

- The Pennsylvania State University — University Park, Pennsylvania | Distance from ZIP 17701: 49.9 miles
- Cornell University — Ithaca, New York | Distance from ZIP 17701: 87.0 miles
- Lehigh University — Bethlehem, Pennsylvania | Distance from ZIP 17701: 97.0 miles
- West Chester University of Pennsylvania — West Chester, Pennsylvania | Distance from ZIP 17701: 115.8 miles
- University of Delaware — Newark, Delaware | Distance from ZIP 17701: 125.4 miles
- University of Pennsylvania — Philadelphia, Pennsylvania | Distance from ZIP 17701: 130.5 miles
- Temple University — Philadelphia, Pennsylvania | Distance from ZIP 17701: 131.8 miles
- Syracuse University — Syracuse, New York | Distance from ZIP 17701: 131.9 miles
- The College of New Jersey — Ewing, New Jersey | Distance from ZIP 17701: 133.4 miles
- University of Rochester — Rochester, New York | Distance from ZIP 17701: 133.9 miles
- Johns Hopkins University — Baltimore, Maryland | Distance from ZIP 17701: 134.5 miles
- Rutgers University-New Brunswick — New Brunswick, New Jersey | Distance from ZIP 17701: 144.2 miles
- Rowan University — Glassboro, New Jersey | Distance from ZIP 17701: 146.4 miles

In reviewing the list, he became a little anxious because he was worried that his chances of getting accepted to some of these colleges were pretty low. However, his school counselor reassured him that this was a good starting list, and that he would soon be learning more about each of these colleges to see how he might fit in with them, and how they might fit his needs and preferences.

CHAPTER 5: LIST

Step 4: Develop Your Own List

Now, it is time to make a List for yourself! As we saw with Alex, his initial search produced too many colleges, so he could be more specific and narrow down his list by using his priority rankings. If Alex's initial list of colleges only had 2 colleges on it, he would have needed to revisit his priorities and modify them. For example, instead of limiting his search to colleges within 150 miles, he could expand it to 200 miles. He could also change his preference for specific majors by adding more majors to the list in College Navigator. You can start building your List, like Alex did, by using your top priority rankings, and then adding or removing priorities to expand or narrow your list.

Activity 5.2: My List Priorities

Before you dig into the College Navigator, first consider what is important to you. Below are the Academic, Career, and Personal Match characteristics you will use in College Navigator to make your List. Review them carefully, and then rank at least 5 of them using the space provided below, with 1 being the most important. You can rank all 11 characteristics if you'd like.

Key Perspective	College Characteristic	How Important to You?
Academic Match	Extended learning opportunities are available (e.g., distance learning, weekend classes)	
	Institution type (e.g., public, private, 2-year, 4-year)	
	Level of award (e.g., Certificate, Associate, Bachelor's)	
Career Match	The college offers Career Pathways you are interested in	
Personal Match	Undergraduate student enrollment (a school's size)	
	Housing is available on or near campus	
	Campus setting (e.g., located in city or in rural area)	
	The college has varsity athletic teams	
	The college has a religious affiliation	
	The college has a specialized mission (e.g., HBCU, single sex)	
	Distance from home	

With your List priorities in hand, go to the College Navigator (https://collegenavigator.gov), and use your rank ordering to help you develop your List. Be sure to click on "More Search Options" to see all of the college characteristics you can search for. Remember, there are things we are leaving blank for now that we will consider a little later – things such as cost and selectivity are very important, but we are going to focus on your List priorities right now.

TIPS: You can save your results by clicking the SAVE button at the top of the College Navigator, just enter your email address. If you are not going to enter a specific program/major, be sure you indicate what Level of Award you are seeking and enter an institution type (2-year and/or 4-year) to avoid getting an overwhelming number of institutions in your results list.

Remember, this is YOUR list, and you need to be satisfied with it. Tools like the College Navigator can be very useful in helping you sift through and filter a lot of college information, but you should not let a computer make decisions for you. Earlier in this chapter, we asked you to name schools you had heard of and are interested in – are they on the List you developed in the College Navigator? If they are not, consider why that might be. What priorities do you have that are preventing them from showing up? It could be, for example, the college is a little further away than you thought it was, the school's size is a little smaller or larger than what you specified, or perhaps they do not offer the major you specified. Finally, also remember that you may revisit the List phase again in the future. As you progress in the college-choice process, you will inevitably learn more about colleges and what is important to you – and your priorities may change. If that happens to you, that's OK – it just means you are learning and growing!

Activity 5.3: My List

Take a moment and review your list. Write down the name of the colleges you wish to continue exploring more in-depth in the chart below.

Name of College	Name of College
1.	9.
2.	10.
3.	11.
4.	12.
5.	13.
6.	14.
7.	15.
8.	16.

Progress Check

You will know you are ready to move onto the next step (Explore) of the LEADS process if the colleges on your List:
- are not too large or too small a number (about 10 to 15)
- fit your priorities
- give you choices you are interested in and excited about

Chapter Summary

Developing an initial List of colleges to more fully explore is the first step of the LEADS process to make more informed college decisions. The colleges on your List are ones that meet your priorities. You can always come back to this chapter and redo the activities you completed to develop your List as your knowledge and/or priorities change.

At-Home Discussion

Ask your parent(s) or guardian(s) to complete the List Priorities activity (Activity 5.2) on page 64. Review what their priorities are alongside your priorities to identify and discuss areas where you agree, and where you do not agree.

Review the High School Planning Checklist in Resources on page 134. What are some next action steps that you need to take in the next month, six months, and year?

CHAPTER 6
Explore
Gathering & Analyzing Information

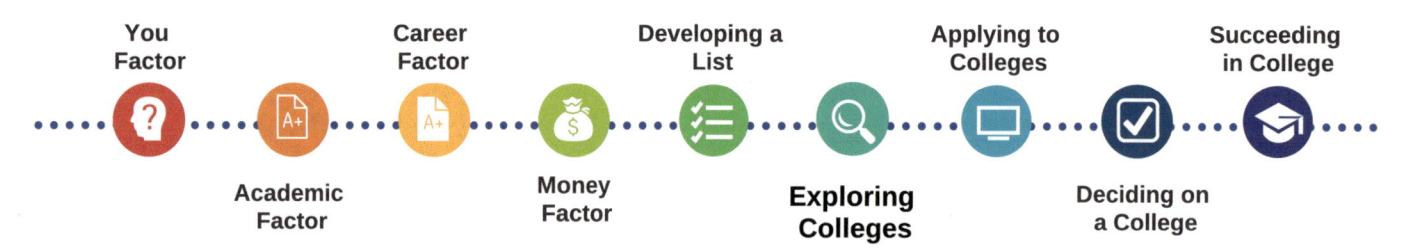

| You Factor | Career Factor | Developing a List | Applying to Colleges | Succeeding in College |
| Academic Factor | Money Factor | **Exploring Colleges** | Deciding on a College | |

This chapter helps you reduce your list of colleges down to approximately 8 to 12 top choices. These are the colleges you will bring with you to the Apply stage of LEADS (Chapter 7). There are 4 ways you will now narrow and focus your list – using the 6 Keys of College Fit to assess specific characteristics of which college's fit you best, understanding what college admissions officers are looking for and your chances of acceptance, effectively investigating colleges by making in-person and virtual visits, and considering whether or not each college is a school you would value attending. This chapter shows you how to take charge collecting a wide range of invaluable information as you complete Explore and move to Apply.

As you explore each college on your list and deepen your thinking about what is important to you, you may find colleges on your list that do not fit you and want to cross them off and then add more colleges – that is OK and is part of the LEADS strategy! In other words, you may bounce back and forth between building your List (Chapter 5) and Exploring colleges (Chapter 6) as you figure out which colleges fit you best. This chapter concludes with a Progress Check to make sure you are ready to move on to the Apply phase.

We recommend that before you move on to the Apply stage you have about 8 to 12 colleges, as this is a good number for most people as it ensures you have enough good options to consider, but not so many that you are overwhelmed. As noted previously, the number of colleges you finally end up with on your list depends on your personal circumstances – you may have a few more or a few less. As you will see, getting the information you need to complete Explore will take some time and effort, so if you have a lot of colleges to explore just be sure you also have the time to invest in getting to know each college better.

With so much information to explore, you will see that finding everything in one place is not possible. Most websites used by students only paint part of the picture. However, we have tried to simplify the process and will show you where and how to look! You will use several resources and strategies to gather information that can help you see how well you might fit at each college on your list. Take your time gathering information and learning more about each college, and move on when you are ready!

Your Explore Steps

1. Dig Deeper Using the 6 Keys of College Fit. Gather and analyze information about specific college characteristics that affect your chances of being admitted and then succeeding at each college on your list.

2. Explore Admission Factors. Investigate what each college on your list is looking for when they admit students and what that means to you.

3. Explore Your You Factor to Make the Most of College Visits. Learn about the different ways you can get more information about specific colleges through visits that are helpful and meaningful to you.

4. Review Case Study – Sholondo. Through a case study, you will be shown how to more deeply explore colleges and narrow your choices.

Step 1: Dig Deeper Using the 6 Keys of College Fit

The first step in building a college list is to dig deeper into the 6 Keys of College Fit. At this beginning stage, you will need to gather and analyze information about specific college characteristics that affect your chances of being admitted and then succeeding at each college on your list. There are several websites that you can use to find this information, such as the College Navigator (https://collegenavigator.gov/), the College Scorecard (https://collegescorecard.ed.gov/), and each college's website. This information helps you to better understand how each college on your list fits you personally and provides what you want and need in a college to be satisfied and successful. This information is spread out across several websites and some of it may require you to talk to college representatives and/or review their websites, e.g., how does each college's alumni network assist graduates to get jobs?

Anticipating this problem, we developed the College Data Organizer (CDO) to help you search out and organize much of the information you need to see how well you match up with each college on your list (www.collegeunmazed.com/downloads). Using the CDO will save you a great deal of time in locating and making sense of the factual information needed to make informed decisions about the colleges you are considering applying to and, ultimately, the one college you choose to attend.

Activity 6.1: Exploring Your List

Complete the College Data Organizer (CDO) by following these steps:

CDO STEP 1 — Review and understand the 6 Keys of College Fit characteristics, definitions, location of resources, and specific instructions for each Key.

CDO STEP 2 — In the CDO (www.collegeunmazed.com/downloads) identify up to 12 colleges from your list that you would like to learn more about. Information will then be automatically provided to you regarding things like graduation rates, net price, and acceptance rates for each college.

CDO STEP 3 — Gather additional information about each college from other sources, e.g., the College Scorecard and the Common Data Set report (see pps. 71-74), college websites, in-person and virtual college visits, and talking to college representatives.

CDO STEP 4 — Review information gathered and compare colleges on your list to each other. Then rate each college as to how well each one fits you on the 6 Keys of College Fit.

CHAPTER 6: EXPLORE

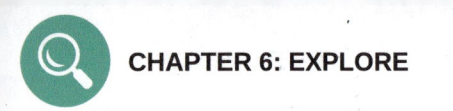

A description of Characteristics, Definition, and Where to Find this information for each of the 6 Keys is provided below.

Academic Match

- ACT/SAT Scores
- GPA
- Selectivity
- Student-to-faculty ratio
- Program size and availability

Academic Match helps you to see how your academic profile compares to students currently enrolled in each college. It also focuses on the learning environment specific to each college you are considering.

Characteristic	Definition	Where to Find
Student-to-faculty ratio	How many students there are for each full-time faculty member	College Data Organizer
Percent admitted	The percent of applicants the college chose to accept	College Data Organizer
Percent admitted who enroll	The percent of applicants who chose to accept the college's offer	College Data Organizer
SAT Reading & Math 25%/75%	This is the "middle 50%" of all admitted students – if your score falls between these numbers, you have moderate chance of getting accepted.	College Data Organizer
ACT composite 25%/75%	This is the "middle 50%" of all admitted students – if your score falls between these numbers, you have moderate chance of getting accepted.	College Data Organizer
High school GPA	The average high school GPA of admitted students	Common Data Set, College website
Number of graduates in field of study	The number of students with the specified major who graduated from the college the previous year	College Navigator: Programs/Majors
Website review for major(s) you are interested in. Rate based on your needs on scale from 1 to 5.	Learning more about potential majors on your visit and reviewing the college's website can help you gain additional information.	College website/visit

Student Outcomes

- Graduation rate
- Retention rate
- Alumni salary
- Loan default rate

Student Outcomes enable you to add into your decision-making critical fact-based information about each college such as retention and graduation rates, alumni earnings, students' ability to repay their college loans, and other markers of student growth and development. Factual information can also be used to balance out the marketing and branding efforts used by many colleges to 'sell' themselves.

Characteristic	Definition	Where to Find
Retention rate	This is the percentage of first time, full-time freshmen who were satisfied and supported enough to return as sophomores.	College Data Organizer
4-year/6-year grad rate	These are the percentages of first-time, full-time freshmen who persisted to graduation.	College Data Organizer

COLLEGE UNMAZED

Characteristic	Definition	Where to Find
Cohort default rate	This is the loan default rate, and it is an indicator of how financially stable students are after leaving the college, with or without a degree.	College Data Organizer
Median salary by field of study. If not available, use middle of range for the college	This is the median salary earned by graduates of this college within 2 years of graduation.	College Scorecard
Median debt by field of study. If not available, use the middle of the range for the college.	The median amount of loan debt graduates of this college have at graduation.	College Scorecard

Financial Match

- Sticker price
- Gift aid
- Net price
- Median debt

Financial Match allows you to estimate what you might pay at each college given the various sources of aid, as well as the median amount of debt graduates of a particular college have.

Characteristic	Definition	Where to Find
Tuition and fees	Tuition and fees. Choose in-state or out-of-state as appropriate.	College Data Organizer
Living arrangement – Room and board	Cost for room and board. Choose on campus, off-campus, or off-campus with family as appropriate.	College Data Organizer
Living arrangement – Other	Cost for other living expenses. Choose on campus, off-campus, or off-campus with Family as appropriate.	College Data Organizer
Average net price	This is the college's estimate of your actual cost, and it is the best way to assess your likely cost.	College Data Organizer

Career Match

- **Alumni network**
- **Mentoring**
- **Internships**
- **Career placement**

Career Match helps you to research the availability of support to help your career even after you graduate, such as alumni networking, mentoring, internships, and career placement. While it may not be feasible to thoroughly investigate each and every aspect of the career services available on every campus, be sure to learn about those you feel you may need.

Characteristic	Definition	Where to Find
Career services support. Rate based on your needs on scale from 1 to 5.	Most colleges have an office on campus to help students with their career development (e.g., choosing a major), internship placement, job placement, and/or alumni networking.	College website review/visit

69

CHAPTER 6: EXPLORE

Student Support

- Tutoring services
- Academic labs/tutoring centers
- Counseling centers
- Disability/Adaptive services
- Recreational and community service organizations

Student Support explores the invaluable resources that may, or may not, be available to you on each campus. College visits provide excellent opportunities for you to learn all you can about each college's student support services, e.g., writing, tutoring, counseling centers, disability services, alumni organizations, and recreational and community service organizations.

Characteristic	Definition	Where to Find
Academic supports available. Rate based on your needs on scale from 1 to 5.	Academic support includes tutoring centers that cover many academic subjects and study skills, and writing centers.	College website review/visit
Disability services. Rate based on your needs on scale from 1 to 5.	For students with disabilities, the disability services office can help them access needed resources and accommodations	College website review/visit

Personal Match

- Diversity
- Institution type
- Recreational options
- Living arrangements (dorms, food, etc.)

Personal Match helps you determine if the student demographics represent you as a student in relation to race, ethnicity, and diversity, as well as your preferences for degree level (e.g., Associate or Bachelor's) and institution type (public or private). It also considers your recreational options (e.g., workout center, intermural sports, clubs, sororities/fraternities) and living arrangements (e.g., dorm set-up, learning communities, meal options).

Characteristic	Definition	Where to Find
Diversity of enrolled students, recreation options, living arrangements, etc. Rate based on your needs on scale from 1 to 5.	Diversity can include any aspect of diversity that is important to you – racial/ethnic diversity, gender, religion, disability status, etc.	College Navigator: Enrollment, and/or College visit/website review

Other Considerations

In the Explore phase of the college-choice process, we want you to look at data about each college so you can be an informed consumer that uses critical and objective thinking skills. So, before you proceed to the next topic, it is important to briefly discuss three critical issues students face when trying to understand the extent to which a college matches them – prestige, marketing, and cost.

Prestige

Our perceptions of prestige are a powerful force in the kinds of colleges and careers we choose. A college's admission rate (the percent of students a college admits from their applicant pool) is often equated with its level of prestige. Generally speaking, most people believe that colleges that are harder to get into, or more selective, are better than other colleges, and therefore more desirable. This is not necessarily true. The fact is that a lot of successful people do not attend prestigious, highly selective colleges. How can that be? Because it is not the college that makes you successful, it is you who makes yourself successful. There are many colleges that can help you reach your goals – maybe some are more prestigious, maybe some are less prestigious, but many of them can help you reach your goals – even the less prestigious ones. We suggest that you focus on finding those colleges that really match the person you are, as well as what you want and need in a college. For example, in the United States, 2-year community colleges are often seen as being much less prestigious than 4-year colleges. However, the quality of education and very low cost of these community colleges make them an excellent place for many students to begin their postsecondary education journey.

Marketing

Think about a time you have wanted to purchase an item because of an influencer, an ad, or a commercial you saw. Something resonated with you enough for you to think, "I need to buy this!". Colleges are no different. If you visit any college website, chances are very good that people with expertise in marketing designed the website. The colors, the wording, and the images all are choreographed to be the best representation of what the college has to offer you. It is therefore important to understand colleges would love for you to feel they are your match and that you should submit an application to them. We want you to be a more informed consumer and look beyond the marketing techniques and see if the college really fits your individual desires and needs.

Cost

Cost is a critically important factor for many students and families. You will gather information from the College Navigator to move beyond advertised sticker prices and learn more about what students actually pay. This will help you see how the colleges on your List fit you financially. A myth many students and families believe is that public colleges are always cheaper than private colleges. With gift aid and other sources of financial aid, it is certainly possible for private colleges to compete on cost with publicly funded state universities. It is true that private college sticker prices are higher than public college sticker prices, but most private colleges also give a lot more gift aid.

Step 2: Explore Admission Factors

Colleges generally fit into one of the four selectivity categories described on the next page (Figure 6.1). It is important to understand that selectivity is just one of the admission factors for you to consider as you Explore which colleges fit you best.

Let us be clear and honest: there are absolutely no guarantees when it comes to being accepted at – or rejected by – a college. Every year, many highly qualified students are rejected by colleges where their academic achievements exceed those of students who are typically accepted at that college. However, the opposite is true as well – students get accepted to colleges where their academic qualifications, typically defined by their GPA and test scores, would suggest that they have very little chance of getting in. This happens because college admission decisions are based on a wide range of both academic and nonacademic factors (see Figure 6.2). These priorities can vary from college to college, as you will soon find out. While this may sound a little scary, the good news is that more than half of all students get into their first-choice college, and in fact, often have many choices.

Figure 6.1

Open Access	Competitive	Selective	Highly Selective
• Open access colleges are non-selective in their admissions criteria and admit all applicants with a high school diploma or equivalent. These are typically 2-year community colleges, but some 4-year colleges are open access as well.	• Competitive colleges often focus on a student's Academic Factor – standardized test scores and GPA – to help them make admissions decisions. Almost 500 4-year colleges accept more than 75 percent of applicants.	• Selective colleges often use a wider range of academic and non-academic factors to determine admissions by using a holistic review of the student's entire application. Moderately selective colleges accept 35% percent to 60 percent of all applicants.	• Fewer than 100 colleges in the U.S. are highly selective, which means they accept less than 35% of applicants. Sometimes referred to as "Ivy League" or "Ivy Like," admission to these colleges is very competitive.

CHAPTER 6: EXPLORE

Many colleges use a much wider range of criteria for determining admission than just test scores and high school GPA. If you remember Figure 2.1 in Chapter 2 (p. 19), we ranked the importance of various academic factors that college admissions directors consider when making decisions about an applicant. However, most students do not know how to explore what their chances of admission might be at various colleges beyond their test scores and high school GPA. While your test scores and GPA may be important sources of information for admission counselors, most colleges also consider nonacademic factors as well. Listed below are several malleable (things you can somewhat easily change) and less malleable (things that are harder to change) non-academic factors that colleges use to make admission decisions.

Figure 6.2

MALLEABLE NON-ACADEMIC FACTORS
- Talent/ability
- Interview
- Character/personal qualities
- Extracurricular activities
- Volunteer work
- Work experience
- Level of applicant interest

LESS MALLEABLE NON-ACADEMIC FACTORS
- First-generation
- Alumni relation
- Geographical residence
- State residency
- Religious affiliation/commitment
- Racial/ethnic status

Common Data Set

Finding the "real" admission information that each college looks at is going to take some work, but it will be well worth it in the end. An extremely helpful resource is the Common Data Set initiative (CDS), which is a voluntary program that a college may participate in to share information commonly requested from organizations like U.S. News & World Report, Peterson's and College Board. If a college on your List participates in the CDS initiative, you can see how important each of the academic and non-academic factors are to them when they make admissions decisions in section C7. You will also find a lot more information you may find useful about students who succeeded in gaining admission to the college, such as the class rank of admitted students (section C10) and the range of high school GPAs (section C11).

There is no single website where you will find every college's CDS report. If a college participates, you will find their report published on the college's website, and the easiest way to find it is by performing a web search on the college's website using the phrase "common data set" (without quote marks). If the college does not participate in the CDS initiative, reach out to an admissions representative to ask what they consider when reviewing applications, and what the most and least important academic and non-academic factors are.

Figure 6.3 shows an example of one of Sholondo's college's CDS reports.

The CDS information can be very helpful as you Explore and Apply to each college. For example, if you find that a college you are interested in uses demonstrated interest (listed as "level of applicant interest" on the CDS report), you should know that the college may use customer relationship

Figure 6.3

C7	Relative importance of each of the following academic and nonacademic factors in first-time, first-year, degree-seeking (freshman) admission decisions.				
C7		Very Important	Important	Considered	Not Considered
C7	**Academic**				
C7	Rigor of secondary school record	X			
C7	Class rank			X	
C7	Academic GPA	X			
C7	Standardized test scores	X			
C7	Application Essay				X
C7	Recommendation(s)				X
C7	**Nonacademic**				
C7	Interview				X
C7	Extracurricular activities			X	
C7	Talent/ability			X	
C7	Character/personal qualities				X
C7	First generation				X
C7	Alumni/ae relation				X
C7	Geographical residence				X
C7	State residency				X
C7	Religious affiliation/commitment				X
C7	Racial/ethnic status				X
C7	Volunteer work			X	
C7	Work experience				X
C7	Level of applicant's interest		X		

management (CRM) technology that can track contacts with each applicant. These contacts can occur by visiting the college's website, opening their email messages, and even clicking the links in email messages! So, if you are interested in a college that takes demonstrated interest into account in their decisions, be sure they know you are interested by visiting the college, paying attention to the email they send, and following them on social media.

At the college in Figure 6.3, demonstrated interest is the most important non-academic factor – and it is just as important as class rank (an academic factor). What are some things you could assume about this college and what they view as important in an applicant? Answer below.

One word of caution here before engaging with colleges: be sure to thoroughly look over your email address (is it professional sounding?) and social media accounts (is there anything inappropriate on there?). A 2021 Kaplan Test Prep survey ([Kaplan Survey](#)) found that 36% of college admissions officers review applicants' social media profiles, and 65% claimed social media accounts should be part of the application process. Of those who stated they viewed an applicant's profile, 58% said it had a negative impact. While not common, students have had admission offers rescinded due to inappropriate social media posts.

Activity 6.2: Your Common Data Set

Explore your List's CDS information. On each of the colleges' websites, search for "common data set" and look for the most current document. Information about the importance of academic and non-academic factors will be listed under section C7. As a reminder, not every college participates in the CDS initiative – if they do not participate, review the college's website and ask a representative of the college questions about their admissions priorities.

In your CDO, click on the tab at the bottom of the page labeled CDS. Under each college's name use the numbering system 1-3 to write in the importance of each factor to each college in the admission process.
Very Important = 3, Important = 2, Considered = 1. Leave blank if not considered.

For colleges you are considering that participate in the CDS initiative, reflect on the importance of the academic and non-academic factors each college values, and how that may impact your chances of acceptance. For colleges that do not participate in the CDS initiative, reach out to an admissions representative to see what they value when making admissions decisions. Once your chart is completed, use the space below to write down some of your specific thoughts about how each college views non-academic factors and how that might affect you.

College	Things to Note

73

CHAPTER 6: EXPLORE

Step 3: Explore Your You Factor to Make the Most of College Visits

You have Explored quite a bit about the colleges you are considering. However, there is a particularly important factor that needs to be discussed - YOU! In Chapter 1 of this book, you learned about the You Factor and the importance of having your own unique identity and personal strengths to become college and career-ready. Knowing Yourself is one of the 8 Strengths you can have as an ally in your journey to making an informed college decision. To Explore your List more deeply, you need to focus on You Factor assets like your interests, abilities, and values. Now is the time to reflect on what you really value in a college to make sure the college supports who you are and who you want to be on a personal level.

When narrowing down your list to those schools you will take with you into the Apply step, it is critical that you assess and make decisions about each college with respect to how important it is to you to attend that particular college. The question here is not if you can gain admission to the college. The question is: Do you value what they have to offer you? If your list doesn't include enough colleges that you really value, then the colleges you actually apply to will mean much less to you than if your college options really meant something to you. These valuing decisions are your own personal choices and vary from student to student. You should speak to your family and extended College Support Network so you can talk out loud about why you would value going to each school on your list. For example, a recent student stated her top value was being able to take her dog (a show dog that competes nationally) with her. However, many of the schools on her list require her to stay in the dormitories for the first two years and do not allow dogs to reside there. If that is her top value, then she should not consider applying to those colleges. Values can range from religious beliefs and preferred living location to unique curricula and programs, cost, and more.

Activity 6.3: Your Personal College Values

Consider what some of your values are in selecting a college. Circle some of the values that are most important to you. There is not a right or wrong answer, and you can select as many or as few as you wish.

- Campus environment
- Change and variety
- Clubs and activities
- Community
- Compassion
- Competition
- Connections
- Cost
- Creativity
- Curriculum structure
- Democracy
- Diversity
- Environmental stewardship

- Excellence
- Faculty engagement
- Financial gain
- Geographic location
- Global view
- Helping other people
- Instructional methods (online, in-person, etc.)
- Major/ minor degrees
- Mission-driven
- Off-campus recreation
- On-site services (medical, adaptive, etc.)

- Personal development
- Power and authority
- Recognition
- Recreation opportunities
- Reputation
- Research
- Security
- Size
- Spirituality
- Type of school
- Volunteering
- Work opportunities

Do you not see a value listed above that you find important to you? Write it down below.

Activity 6.4: Your College Visits

This is the point in the LEADS process where, we would recommend, you begin to visit colleges that you are exploring. There are several different ways to visit and interact with colleges, as shown on the next page (Figure 6.4). Visiting college campuses is often an important source of information – you should make every effort to visit each college you are seriously considering to get a sense of how it feels to be on campus and what it might be like to be a student there. You can make the most of your college visit by using the College Visit Checklist on page 77. Here are common ways college visits happen:

Figure 6.4

Formal Visits

A formal visit to a college typically includes signing up for a tour to see the campus and facilities with a tour guide and learn about their programs. You might even be able to sit in on a class or have lunch on campus. These structured tours are useful and highly recommended, but do keep in mind that the tour guides (usually current students) are trained to do their job and are largely following a prescribed script and path.

Informal Visits

Informally visiting a college is just as important as doing a formal visit. You can often do this after you have finished with the formal tour, so it does not necessarily mean you need to make another trip. It is your opportunity to get off the beaten path and see how you feel both on campus and in the surrounding community. Do you need a car to get around? Does it feel safe? Does it seem like a place you could see yourself living?

Fly-Ins

Some colleges offer fly-in opportunities at no cost to students. You usually need to apply for this type of program. If you are very interested in a college but cannot afford to go visit in person, ask an admissions representative if they offer any programs like this. These are traditionally for smaller, selective private colleges.

High School Visits

Admission representatives often come visit high schools, so you should try to meet the representatives from every college on your List that comes to your high school. These are usually the people who will read your application and who will answer your questions about the college and your application, so you really should get to know them – and they should get to know you.

College Fairs

College fairs are another great way to get information about colleges you are interested in, as they provide "one-stop shopping" with access to representatives from a number of different colleges. You should go into the college fair with a game plan to help you get the most out of the experience

Virtual Fairs

Since COVID-19, colleges have moved to providing virtual college fairs where students can still interact and meet college admissions representatives. Often the college will host live informational sessions or partner with organizations like CollegeBoard to host large regional fairs.

A word of caution about doing a college visit. College admission events are well designed and implemented. Your tour guide is usually led by a likable and knowledgeable student at the college. You get to see the nice landscaping and the new, fancy buildings. You should understand that you are a potential paying customer and the college is trying to get you to buy-in. As we already mentioned, colleges spend a lot of money on their marketing, branding, and advertising all aimed at getting you to feel that this is the best place possible for you. And, in fact, it might be. But a college visit is not the time to be a passive consumer; you should get yourself ready to ask questions that will enable you to better understand what that college is really all about. For example, if you have an IEP or a 504 Plan, you should visit and meet with the office that supports students with disabilities on campus. Be sure to explore writing and tutoring services, as well as academic and personal counseling services that are there to support you and help you be successful. You should also learn about alumni networks, mentoring support, and the career center to help you transition into the world of work after you graduate. Using the College Visit Questions (Activity 6.5), listed on the next page, on each of your visits will help you ask the kinds of questions to help you see if the college is a good fit for you. Use the College Visit Reflection (Activity 6.6) to write down some key answers you received.

CHAPTER 6: EXPLORE

Activity 6.5: College Visit Questions

Review the college visit questions below. Based on your needs, highlight what you would like to have answered on a formal college visit. Write college representative's responses and your reflections on the next page.

Academic Match

- How much time do students typically spend on homework?
- How much writing and reading are expected?
- What is the average class size of introductory classes?
- How widely used are teaching assistants on your campus?
- What is the average class size of upper-division courses?
- What opportunities are there for undergraduate research?
- How many students participate in undergraduate research?
- Is there a culminating senior year experience?
- Do you have an honors program or college?
- Do you have a learning community or other freshman experience?

Career Match

- What are the most popular majors for students here?
- How easy is it to have additional majors and minors?
- When do students have to declare a major?
- What is the process of seeing my college advisor for help with course selection?
- How does the college help me secure internships?
- When can I access internships, being a teacher assistant, or other experience-building opportunities?
- What types of career services does the college offer and how do I access them?
- Do alumni have access to career services after they graduate?

Financial Match

- What are the requirements to remain eligible for scholarships after the first year?
- What is the typical breakdown of loans versus grants?
- What percentage of financial need does your college typically meet?
- Do local scholarships affect how much financial aid I might receive from your college?
- What work-study opportunities are there?
- Have there been any changes in your financial aid policies recently?

Personal Match

- What kind of dorm choices are there?
- Are students required to live on campus? If so, for how many years?
- What percentage of students live on campus?
- How long are dorm accommodations guaranteed?
- Do most students go home on the weekend?
- What percentage of the student body belongs to a sorority or fraternity?
- What activities are offered to students?
- What clubs do you have on campus?

Student Outcomes

- What does your college do to help students graduate on time?
- What are some of the reasons you think students do not graduate in four years?
- What are some of the reasons students do not come back for sophomore year?

Student Support

- What type of tutoring program do you have?
- How do you provide academic advice to students?
- Do you have a writing center and if so, how do I access it?
- What kind of learning disability resources do you have?
- How can I access other mental and physical health programs on campus?

My Questions

_____
_____
_____
_____
_____
_____

COLLEGE UNMAZED

Activity 6.6: College Visit Reflection Form

College Name: Central Michigan University

Choose questions from the list of questions to ask college admissions representatives on your college visit. Write their responses and your reflections on each of the responses.

Question #1 Are there any Scholarships there?

Yes they have plenty of scholarships. They have a 2,000 "No Essay" Scholarships

Question #2 What Events do they have?

They have lots of events like Competitions, they have events to help students like therapy dogs at the park, They have alot of events for help.

Question #3 What apliances can we bring in the dorms?

fan, refridger, freezer, microwave, alarm clocks.

Question #4 Can we have cars there as a freshman in College.

Yes you can but you have to have a 100% digital parking permit.

Question #5 What is the undergraduate percentage.

71.45% is the undergraduate Percentage.

Question #6 how does the meal plans work?

All meal plans cost 3,068 per semester. You get 450 FLEX dollars per semester. Central give you 12 meal swipes per week in the dinning hall.

CHAPTER 6: EXPLORE

Step 4: Review Case Study – Sholondo

As you may recall from the case study in Chapter 4, Sholondo lives in southwest Florida (zip code 33901) and is looking for a college with an Accounting or Business Administration major. He completed high school with a 3.9 GPA and scored an 28 composite on his ACT. Cost is a primary consideration for Sholondo. He knows the most cost-effective path is most likely to live at home and attend a local college to get an Associate degree in liberal arts and then transfer to finish his Bachelor's degree, so he is considering a 2 + 2 program to do that. However, he wants to explore all of his options to see what might else be possible for him. Sholondo's initial list included 10 colleges. Nine are 4-year colleges and 1 is a 2-year community college. He completed 4 clear and distinct steps:

1. **Dig Deeper Using the 6 Keys of College Fit**. Sholondo reviewed the 6 Key matching data he recorded in his CDO. He highlighted the information he found to be most favorable in green and least favorable in yellow. By comparing and contrasting colleges based on this information, he more clearly understood that:

Positive (green): Saint Leo reported everyone attending their college received some type of institutional grants. The least expensive tuition was at his local community college, Florida SouthWestern State College (FSW). The University of Miami (U of M) and the University of South Florida (USF) both had much higher retention rates. He wondered how varying retention rates across colleges would impact his chances of returning for his second year and what he would need to do to make sure he was successful. Also, USF had the lowest cohort loan default rate which could indicate that their graduates were entering the workforce after graduation and were able to immediately start paying down their loans.

Average/blank (white): His Academic Match with Florida Gulf Coast University (FGCU) was white. This meant that other schools were either more difficult (U of M) or easier (Ava Maria, FAMU) to gain admission to. This put FGCU in the middle range of admission chances. He also noticed that some colleges had blank information. He learned that when information is blank, that means the college does not report that information. FSW, being a community college, does not require test scores and thus they don't report them.

Negative (yellow): Overall, Sholondo noticed that Hodges University showed that no one received institutional grants, and also had the lowest median salary by field of study and the lowest retention and graduation rates. He was also concerned about U of M having the highest average net price and lowest percent of applicants admitted. Saint Leo and Keiser both had the highest cohort loan default rate of all the colleges in his CDO list.

2. **Explore Admission Factors.** He then reviewed how each college uses academic and non-academic factors in admissions. He used the CDO and the Common Data Set to accomplish this. With the help of this information, he was better able to formulate his Chance of Admission to each college.

3. **Use Your You Factor to Make the Most of College Visits.** Sholondo visited colleges in-person and virtually, attended college fairs, spoke to college representatives, and gathered additional information to learn as much information as he could about each college on his List.

4. **Reviewed Case Study.** Lastly, he reviewed all the information he had gathered about each college through the Explore phase, including his CDO, CDS review, college visits, college websites and materials, and speaking with his College Support Network and completed his CDO by entering his ratings in 3 of his 6 Keys, Career Match, Personal Match, and Student Support for each college. The ratings are listed on the next page. Sholondo will revisit these ratings as he learns new information.

1 This college has a **little** of what I want and need to be satisfied and successful

2 This college has **some** of what I want and need to be satisfied and successful

3 This college has **much** of what I want and need to be satisfied and successful

4 This college has **most** of what I want and need to be satisfied and successful

5 This college has **everything** I want and need to be satisfied and successful

In Figure 6.5, we provided some of the information in Sholondo's CDO. You can see his fully completed CDO at www.collegeunmazed.com/downloads. Review Sholondo's data in Figure 6.5. Use the information to compare and contrast the colleges on his List.

Figure 6.5

	FGCU	Hodges	Ave Maria	USF	Saint Leo	FAMU	UCF	Keiser	FSW	U of M
Student-to-faculty ratio	22	12	13	22	17	14	31	15	26	12
% admitted	77%		92%	49%	73%	33%	45%	97%		33%
% admit who enroll	22%		21%	30%	18%	33%	37%	51%		18%
ACT Composite 25th Percentile	21		21	25		20	25			28
ACT Composite 75th Percentile	25		28	30		24	30			32
High School GPA	3.2	3.2	3.2	3.6	3.1	3.5	3.4			3.7
# of graduates in field of study	83	2	11	235	106	313	61	23		76
Website review for major(s) you are interested in. Rating of 1 to 5	4	3	3	5	4	5	5	3	3	4
Retention rate	81%	50%	71%	92%	64%	85%	92%	60%		91%
4 year graduation rate	30%	23%	46%	52%	31%	20%	44%	67%	33%	67%
Cohort default rate	4%	6%	4%	3%	8%	8%	4%	9%	9%	2%
Median salary by Field of Study	$47,260	$32,500	$23,000	$38,500	$47,173	$48,883	$43,172	$42,682		$59,124
% of students receiving institutional aid	40%	0%	99%	67%	100%	64%	50%	77%	14%	62%
Avg. amount of institutional aid	$3,087		$15,114	$4,297	$13,321	$4,227	$2,606	$5,453	$3,203	$35,163
Avg. Net Price	$9,053	$20,004	$19,456	$8,756	$19,204	$10,401	$10,754	$32,947	$7,302	$27,874
Career Services Support. Rating of 1 to 5	4	2	3	4	4	5	4	2	3	5
Student Supports available. Rating of 1 to 5	3	1	2	4	3	5	4	1	4	4
Diversity of enrolled students, recreation options, living arrangements, etc. Rating of 1 to 5	4	2	2	4	3	5	5	1	4	4

CHAPTER 6: EXPLORE

Activity 6.7: Eliminating Options

Review Sholondo's College Data Organizer. He identified three colleges that he did not believe matched him well. Based on the information provided, which schools would you remove from his list and why?

1.

2.

3.

Below are the three colleges Sholondo eliminated, and his reasons for doing so.

The first college he crossed off his list was Hodges. He did not feel that Hodges matched the keys important to him. The cost was very high and this private college did not offer any institutional grants to students. Sholondo was also concerned about the very low (14%) 4-year graduation rate. While he would have no trouble getting accepted, he did not feel it was important to him to attend this college.

The second college Sholondo eliminated was Keiser. Cost was a big factor in his decision, as well as the comparatively high loan default rates of students attending this college. Like Hodges, this college was low on 6 Key matching data important to him. While it would be easy to get into, this college held no real personal valuing for being the kind of college he wanted to attend.

The third college Sholondo eliminated was St. Leo. This college moderately matched some of the keys important to him. This is a mission-driven college based on religion and he liked that very much. However, this college is very expensive, has high loan default rates, and low graduation rates. Six to 7 out of every 10 students do not graduate in 4 years. Sholondo felt that he was okay with eliminating this college from his list because he had explored the religious opportunities at the other colleges on his list, including student groups and local churches, that he could take part in if he wanted to.

Sholondo took some time in considering whether or not to include the HBCU on his list. He was concerned about the very low graduation rates, as only about 2 out of every 10 students graduate in 4 years. However, the opportunity to attend such a mission-driven college was very important to him, and when he asked an admission representative about this, he learned that HBCUs serve more low-income students than most other colleges, and this strongly influences their graduation rates. His personal valuing overrode any concerns he had about this college's low graduation rates. He thought to himself that if he were to be accepted and enroll in this college, he would problem solve how he could make himself into the kind of student that graduates from this college in 4 years.

Activity 6.8: Exploring and Reducing Your List

In this activity, you will bring in all the information you have collected in your CDO, along with the personal college values you identified in Activity 6.3, to determine which colleges on your List match you on the 6 Keys most closely. If your List does not contain a good balance of colleges that can provide you what you need and want if you are to be satisfied and successful in college, then this would be a good time for you to go back to the List step (Chapter 5) and develop a set of college choices that does.

Make sure to complete your CDO for Chapter 6, Explore. Please note that in Chapter 7 (Apply) and Chapter 8 (Decide) you will make additional matching ratings of the colleges on your List. You will be able to record these ratings in the CDO. But for now, please don't complete the rating questions in the CDO identified as taking place in the Apply or Decide chapters.

Review each of your college's CDO information. What are some data points you find to be important, either in a positive or negative way? Have you identified any colleges that you do not believe match you well? Based on this information, which colleges would you keep or remove from your list and why? We suggest having 8 to 12 colleges in the Keep section at this point. Write your answers below.

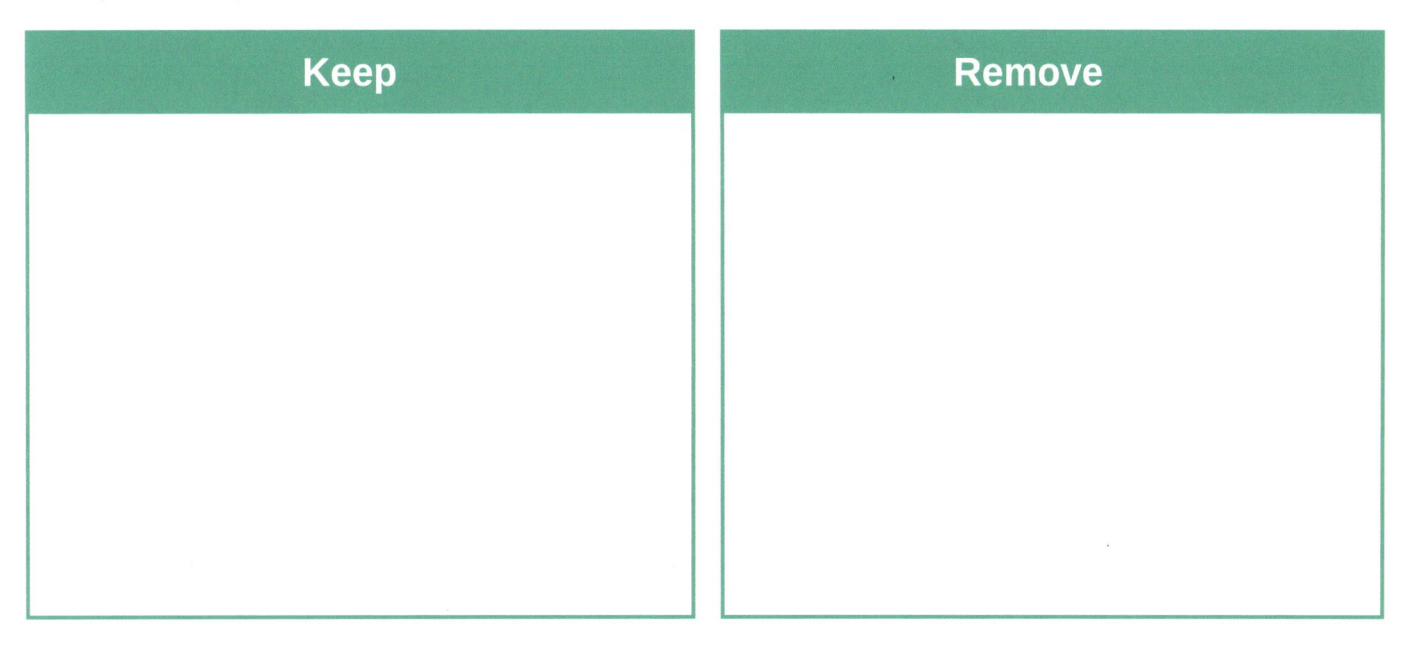

Keep	Remove

Progress Check

You will know if you are ready to move onto the next step of the LEADS process if:
- Colleges on your list match keys important to you.
- Colleges on your list have a reasonable difficulty level of gaining admission. If all the colleges on your List are difficult to get into or too many of your colleges are too easy to get into (meaning you may be undermatching yourself), you may not be ready to move on.
- You personally value the colleges on your list.

Chapter Summary

In the Explore chapter you delved into many things to consider prior to applying to a college. You explored real, useful data, various admissions factors, and how each college fits your You Factor. Developing a thoughtful, comprehensive list takes time and is a very personalized experience. You are now armed with new information that will continue to guide you to making an informed college decision.

At-Home Discussion

If you have not done so, share your College Data Organizer with your family, school counselor, and your College Support Network. Ask them to review the information and discuss the strengths and weaknesses of each college in relation to what they know about you.

Review the High School Planning Checklist in Resources on page 135. What are some next action steps that you need to take in the next month, six months, and year?

CHAPTER 7
Apply
Critiquing and Prioritizing Colleges

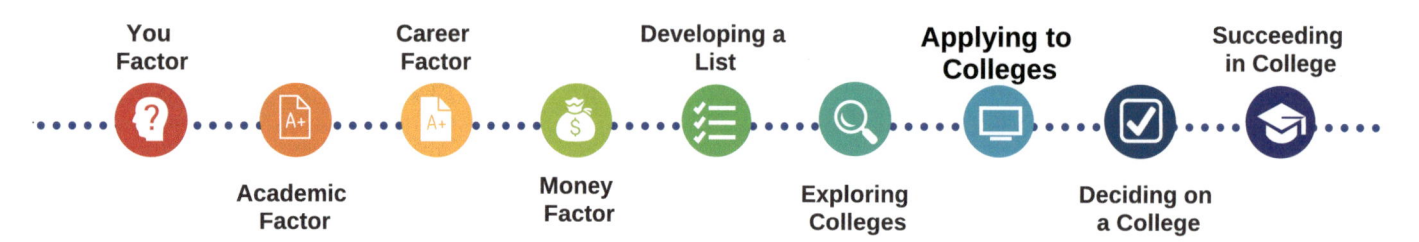

You Factor · Academic Factor · Career Factor · Money Factor · Developing a List · Exploring Colleges · **Applying to Colleges** · Deciding on a College · Succeeding in College

This chapter has two purposes. First, we will help you decide on which colleges to send applications to. Second, we will then show you how to develop and submit strong applications tailored to each of those colleges. In the Explore chapter, you narrowed your List down to approximately 8 to 12 colleges by: eliminating those schools whose characteristics did not fit you, evaluating your options based on the selectivity of each college and understanding what they are looking for when admitting students, conducting in-person and virtual visits, and taking into account what you personally value and want in a college. Now you will select about 5 to 8 colleges from your List that are best for you and where you will Apply. We recommend that you submit applications to at least 5 colleges. Of course, as we have said before, the number of colleges you apply to depends on your personal circumstances and will vary based on you and your family's needs.

To select the best colleges where you will Apply, you will build on the foundation you constructed in List and Explore. You will be shown how to use the 6 Keys of College Fit and your assessment of your chances of being accepted into each college on your list to work together on your behalf. When you evaluate the colleges on your list from these two critical perspectives, you will be able to make a much more informed decision about which colleges you should apply to.

After identifying the specific colleges where you will apply, we will teach you how to craft effective applications for each of them. Our goal here is to enhance your chances of successfully getting into each and every college where you apply by using a targeted application process. This approach will show you how to manage the application process by providing knowledge of the admissions process itself, using organizational tools, understanding what documents are needed, writing a compelling college essay, and learning how to secure the right recommendation letters.

Your Apply Steps

1. Understand Overall Fit and Chance of Admission. Learn how and why it is to your advantage to link how well each college matches you on the 6 Keys of College Fit and what your chances are of being accepted to each college.
2. Review Case Study. Through a case study you will be shown how to use Overall Fit and Chance of Admission to narrow a list to approximately 5 to 8 colleges where this student will apply.
3. Choose the Best Combination of Colleges Where You Will Apply. You will use your Overall Fit and Chance of Admission ratings to make informed decisions about the best combination of colleges to apply to.
4. Develop and Submit Competitive College Applications. After deciding on which colleges to apply to you will learn how to develop and submit applications targeted to what specific colleges are looking for when they admit students.

Step 1: Understand Overall Fit and Chance of Admission

It is in your best interest to learn how to use both the 6 Keys of College Fit and your best estimate of your chances of being accepted into each college to help you determine where you will actually apply. Using one without the other limits your understanding, thus impairing your ability to make informed decisions. For example, when you grasp how you match up with the colleges on your list (in terms of academics, future career possibilities, finances, personal tastes, outcomes for students who go to each college, and support services available) you are in a much better position to determine which colleges are best for you and your own individual circumstances. However, if you stopped here and made up your mind about which colleges to apply to without considering your chances of acceptance, you would not be able to take advantage of considering a college's selectivity, and how selective colleges can provide advantages.

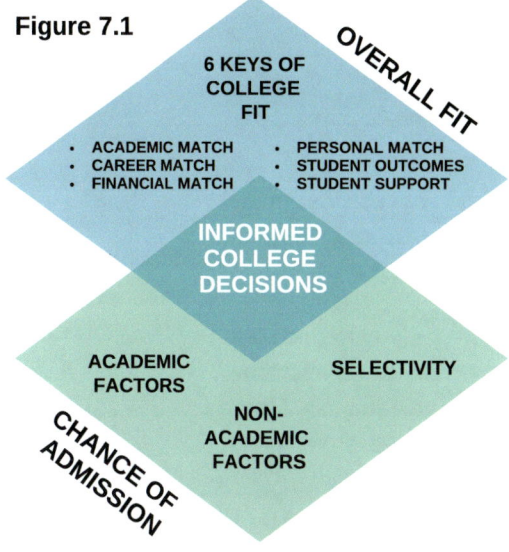

Figure 7.1

OVERALL FIT

6 KEYS OF COLLEGE FIT
- ACADEMIC MATCH
- CAREER MATCH
- FINANCIAL MATCH
- PERSONAL MATCH
- STUDENT OUTCOMES
- STUDENT SUPPORT

INFORMED COLLEGE DECISIONS

ACADEMIC FACTORS — SELECTIVITY

NON-ACADEMIC FACTORS

CHANCE OF ADMISSION

New York Times columnist Frank Bruni wrote a book published in 2016 titled "Where You Go Is Not Who You'll Be." The main premise of the book is that people can find success in college and life at just about any college and that choosing where to attend should be about much more than selectivity. While we agree with his position that colleges don't make students successful (students make themselves successful), and that you have control over your own success, the fact is that students who go to more selective schools, on average, do in fact have better outcomes. This is true for a wide range of reasons; for example, they have more resources and supports available for students, only admit students with a strong record of success in academic settings, give more need-based financial aid, have fewer large lecture hall classes with several hundred students, and have more small, discussion-oriented seminar-type classes that provide valuable writing-intensive training.

The "problem" of choosing which colleges to apply to has traditionally been solved by having students organize their list of colleges in the following categories based on their chance of admission – safety (high chances of admission), match/target (moderate chance of admission) and reach (low chance of admission). Most often, the means used to help students figure out if a college is a safety, a match/target, or a reach is a combination of test scores and GPA. We strongly think that this way of organizing a list of colleges to apply to is very problematic because it overemphasizes selectivity and deemphasizes Overall Fit. Focusing on both Overall Fit and Chance of Admission puts you and your family in the driver's seat.

For example, safety colleges are usually greatly devalued in comparison to match and reach schools. If a student has higher grades and test scores than the typical student attending a safety college and yet they still decide to enroll in that safety school, then they may be "undermatching" themselves and not enroll in a more selective college. Their decision to attend a less selective college is seen as a problem, irrespective of whether or not the safety college matched them the best and provided exactly what they and their family wanted in a college.

To make informed decisions on which colleges to apply to, you must simultaneously investigate and consider how well each college fits you and your chances of being accepted. Doing so allows these two powerful forces – Chance of Admission and Overall Fit – to work together on your behalf. One without the other isn't as good as both together. In Steps 2 and 3 of this chapter, you will be shown how to estimate and merge together Overall Fit and Chance of Admission. By doing this, you will be able to more clearly see the combination of colleges that would be best for you to apply to. Most often, you will find that your optimal combination of colleges to apply to are located at the intersection of Overall Fit and Chance of Admission.

CHAPTER 7: APPLY

Figure 7.2

Assess the Keys

Your 6 Keys
Assess your match to each college on the 6 Keys

- Academic Match
- Career Match
- Financial Match
- Personal Match
- Student Outcomes
- Student Support

Find a Fit

Finding Your Fit
Find your college based on the 6 Keys

- High Fit
- Moderate Fit
- Low Fit

Admission Chances
Estimate your chance of admission

- High Chance
- Moderate Chance
- Low Chance

Get Organized

Getting Organized
- Email Address
- Application Organizer

Understanding Applications
- Common App
- Coalition App
- Institutional Apps

Understanding Deadlines
- Early Decision
- Early Action
- Priority Deadlines
- Regular Decision
- Rolling Admissions

Apply

Building Your Documents
- Résumé
- Essay & Supplementals
- Letters of Recommendation
- Transcript
- ACT/SAT Scores

Scholarships & FAFSA
- FAFSA
- Scholarships

Step 2: Review Case Study – Emily

You were introduced to Emily, then a sophomore, in Chapter 1. Now, Emily is a 12th grader scheduled to graduate at the end of this school year. It is early September, and she wants to move forward on her college applications.

Emily completed the List and Explore steps this past summer and visited several colleges. This helped narrow her list down to 10 colleges. She will complete the FAFSA as soon as it becomes available on October 1st. Also, she is aware of the application options available to her (e.g., Common App, individual college applications) and the different admission deadlines (early action, early decision, and regular). Her goal right now is to decide which colleges she should apply to.

Emily, as you may recall, is a hard-working, first-generation student who took a rigorous course of study in high school, and lives in a suburb outside a large city in the midwestern United States. Her parents own and operate their own small business, earning $90,000 a year. She has 3 younger siblings who are also planning to attend college. Her overall unweighted GPA is a 3.6 and her weighted GPA is a 3.9. Her SAT critical reading score is 620 and math is 650. She also took the ACT and had a composite score of 27. She is worried a little about her GPA and how that might affect her Chance of Admission and getting scholarships. Her school counselor reassured her that anyone reviewing her transcripts would realize that she took additional, and very difficult, science courses. She got mostly Bs in those courses, and mostly As in her other classes. The counselor pointed out that her record also includes impressive achievements outside of coursework – as a peer mediator, president of the Psychology Club, co-captain of the soccer team, great recommendations, and excellent work habits demonstrated in school and in her part-time job, where she has become a shift supervisor.

Emily has decided to be a Psychology major. She is particularly interested in how the brain works and is intrigued with Neuropsychology. While she did not get A's in her science courses, she enjoyed them and more than held her own with difficult academic material. She knows most people who work in Psychology need a graduate degree. She was shocked to find out on College Scorecard that at most of the colleges she is interested in, average starting salaries for General Psychology graduates are less than $30,000 a year. However, when she explored her Career Factor (Chapter 3) using O*Net (www.onetonline.org) she found mental health counselors are in the top 10 for high growth occupations and the median salary is $47,660.

As she approaches her decision on which colleges to apply to, she is mindful of the fact that she has to consider the cost of graduate school in addition to the cost of her undergraduate education. Emily also recognizes that her parents will have other college expenses from her younger siblings. To get a better handle on cost, she used the Net Price Calculator to compare what she and her family would likely pay at each college on her list. After doing this, she is fairly confident that she can afford each college if the financial aid package offered comes close to matching the estimate provided by the Net Price Calculator.

Emily was able to gather all of the information needed about her list of colleges from her College Data Organizer, College Navigator, the College Scorecard, the Net Price Calculator, and the Common Data Set report from each college. While 3 of her choices do not participate in the Common Data Set initiative, she was able to find the information she needed by going to the admissions website for each school and asking questions of admissions.

Following the LEADS process, it is time now to reduce her list of colleges to those colleges where she will apply. She does this by first rating each college on the 6 Keys of College Fit. She has learned much about the colleges on her list and now it is time to make decisions and narrow her options. Then, she estimates her Chance of Admission for each college on her list. Emily is then able to use the graph below to unite Overall Fit and Chance of Admission. This gives her an advantage in identifying the best possible combination of colleges that she will apply to.

Rating Overall Fit

As you can see in the table on the next page (Figure 7.3), Emily wrote the names of each college on her list, then rated how well each college fit her on each of the 6 Keys, using all the information she has gathered on them. She rated each college by first reviewing and reflecting on all the information she has learned about them from her research, college tours, College Data Organizer, websites, and talks with admissions officers. Then, she rated each college on the 6 Keys of College Fit as follows:

1 This college has a **little** of what I want and need to be satisfied and successful

2 This college has **some** of what I want and need to be satisfied and successful

3 This college has **much** of what I want and need to be satisfied and successful

4 This college has **most** of what I want and need to be satisfied and successful

5 This college has **everything** I want and need to be satisfied and successful

She then added the scores for each Key together to determine Overall Fit. She determined the Overall Fit from the total score as follows:

17 or lower = Low Fit   **18–23 = Moderate Fit**   **24–30 = High Fit**

CHAPTER 7: APPLY

A **High Match** college has an average rating of at least 4 points across all 6 Keys.
A **Moderate Match** college has an average rating of at least 3 points but less than 4 points across all 6 Keys.
A **Low Match** college has an average score rating of fewer than 3 points across all 6 Keys.

This rating scale and rationale are used for other 6 Keys of College Fit activities in Chapters 7 & 8.

Figure 7.3

College	Student Outcomes	Academic Match	Personal Match	Career Match	Financial Match	Student Support Services	Total Score	Overall Fit
Lindenwood University	2	3	3	3	2	3	16	Low
Saint Louis University	4	4	3	4	3	4	22	Moderate
Stephens College	3	3	3	3	2	4	18	Moderate
University of Illinois Urbana-Champaign	5	4	3	5	2	5	24	High
University of Missouri-Columbia	4	5	4	4	4	4	25	High
University of Missouri-St Louis	3	3	4	3	5	3	21	Moderate
Missouri State University	3	1	2	3	4	4	17	Low
Truman State University	5	5	3	4	4	4	25	High
Missouri University of Science and Technology	5	5	4	4	4	5	27	High
University of Iowa	4	4	4	4	2	4	22	Moderate

Out of the 10 colleges on her list, Emily has 4 colleges that are a High Fit. These schools have most everything she wants. Four colleges are a Moderate Fit, having much of what she wants. Two colleges are a Low Fit, with only some or a little of what she wants.

Rating Chance of Admission

Now that Emily has decided on what colleges fit her best, she needs to estimate her chances of being accepted into each of the 10 colleges on her list.

The graph on the next page (Figure 7.4) helps Emily better understand her chance of admission to each college. By taking into account her ACT composite score of 27 and SAT composite score of 1270 in relation to the middle 50 percent of students admitted to each college and the average GPA, a clearer picture begins to emerge. Several of the colleges Emily is considering have a test-optional admission policy, which has become increasingly common due, in part, to the COVID-19 pandemic. More than half (55 percent) of all four-year colleges will not require test scores for fall 2022 admissions. Emily decides to submit test scores at each test-optional college as she believes they will strengthen her application because her scores meet or exceed the traditionally accepted student at that college.

COLLEGE UNMAZED

When using her 3.6 unweighted GPA to help her estimate her Chance of Admission, Emily remembers (as discussed in Chapter 2) that many colleges recalculate students' GPA using their own formula. She asked the admissions counselors at the colleges she is considering how they recalculate GPA (e.g., Do they include electives? Do they use a 4.0 or 5.0 scale?) and what the average GPA for admitted students is.

Emily reviews each college's Common Data Set (CDS) as she completed Explore Activity 6.2, focusing on the non-academic factors that the college uses to make an admissions decision. After speaking to her College Support Network, she believes that her character, extracurricular activities, volunteer work, work experience, first-generation status, and ethnicity would help her chances of being admitted.

Based on her academic factors, nonacademic factors, and selectivity of each college, Emily estimates her Chance of Admission as: High (in green) to Lindenwood University, Stephens College, the University of Missouri-St. Louis, and Missouri State University; Moderate (in orange) to Saint Louis University, University of Missouri-Columbia, Truman State University, and the University of Iowa; and Low (in red) to the Missouri University of Science and Technology and the University of Illinois Urbana-Champaign.

Emily's Admissions

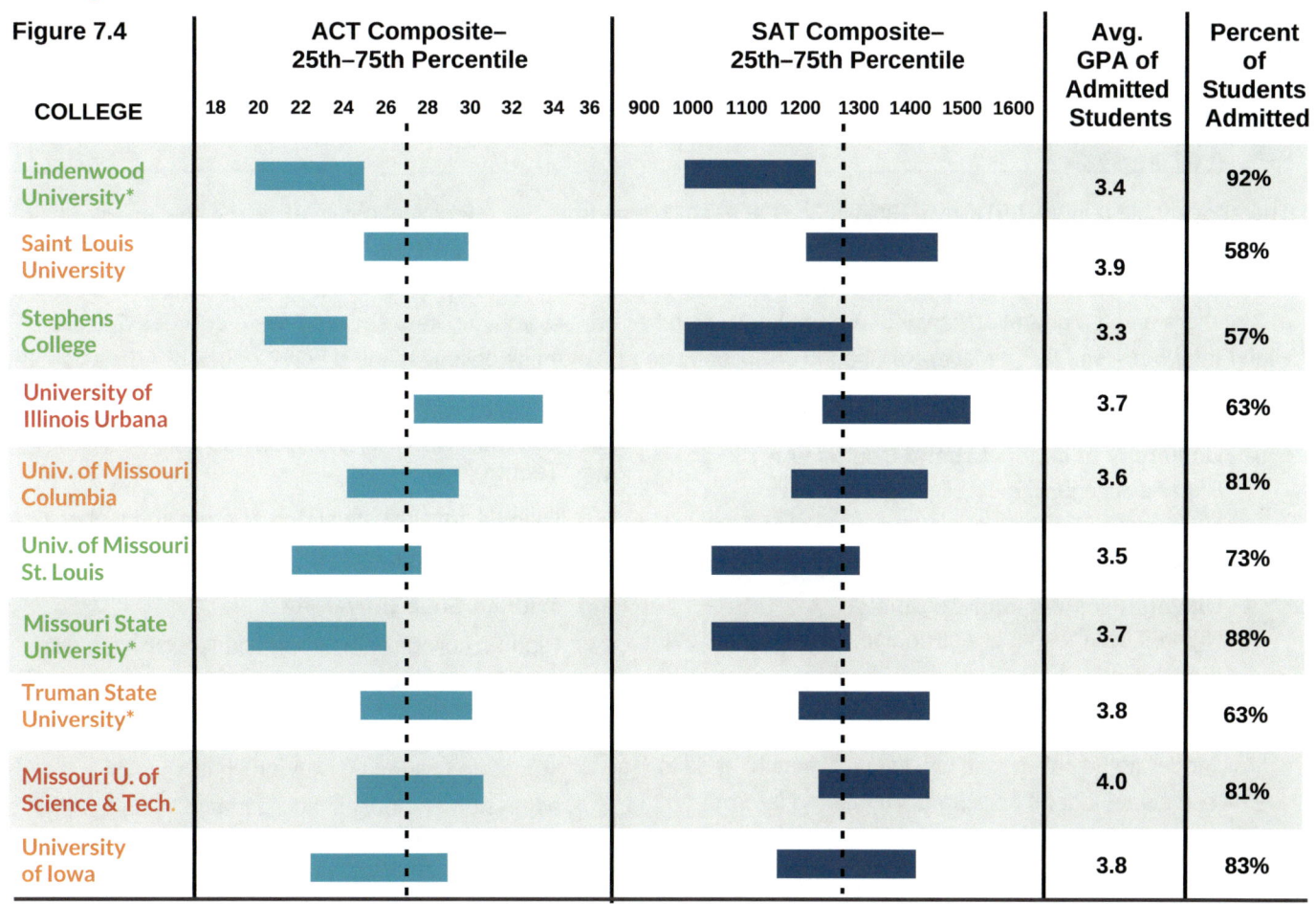

Figure 7.4

COLLEGE	ACT Composite – 25th–75th Percentile	SAT Composite – 25th–75th Percentile	Avg. GPA of Admitted Students	Percent of Students Admitted
Lindenwood University*	20–25	1000–1200	3.4	92%
Saint Louis University	24–29	1200–1400	3.9	58%
Stephens College	20–24	1050–1300	3.3	57%
University of Illinois Urbana	26–32	1250–1500	3.7	63%
Univ. of Missouri Columbia	23–28	1150–1370	3.6	81%
Univ. of Missouri St. Louis	21–27	1070–1280	3.5	73%
Missouri State University*	20–26	1040–1260	3.7	88%
Truman State University*	24–30	1180–1380	3.8	63%
Missouri U. of Science & Tech.	25–31	1210–1410	4.0	81%
University of Iowa	22–28	1140–1340	3.8	83%

- - - - Emily's ACT or SAT score(s)   * Test Optional

● High Chance of Admission   ● Moderate Chance of Admission   ● Low Chance of Admission

Now, Emily is in a position to decide which colleges, out of the 10 on her list, she should apply to. She does this by combining her Overall Fit ratings of each college with her estimates of her Chance of Admission at each college. The table on the next page (Figure 7.5) illustrates her Overall Fit by Chance of Admission for the colleges on her list.

87

CHAPTER 7: APPLY

Figure 7.5

My Overall Fit by Chance of Admission

Overall Fit \ Chance of Admission	High	Moderate	Low
Low	Lindenwood College Missouri State University		
Moderate	Stephens College University of Missouri at St. Louis	Saint Louis University University of Iowa	
High		University of Missouri-Columbia Truman State University	University of Illinois Urbana-Champaign Missouri University of Science & Technology

The above table (Figure 7.5) allows Emily to look at each college from these 2 critical points of view – how good of a fit each college is for her, and her chances of being accepted into that college. Emily has 2 colleges that are a Low Fit for her with a High Chance of Admission. She has 4 colleges that are a Moderate Fit – she has a High Chance of Admission at 2 of them and a Moderate Chance of Admission at the other two. As you can see, she also has 4 colleges that are a High Fit for her – she has a Moderate Chance of Acceptance at 2 of these colleges, and a Low Chance of Admission at 2 of them. Her reasons for eliminating 3 colleges are listed below.

- ✓ **University of Illinois Urbana-Champaign**
  High Fit college with excellent student outcomes, support services, and career match, but low financial match. May be too far away from home and too big.

- ✓ **University of Missouri-Columbia**
  High-Fit college that is a strong academic match, even though big.

- ✓ **University of Iowa**
  Moderate Fit college but low financial match; need to see award letter if accepted. May be too far from home and too big.

- ✓ **Stephens College**
  Moderate Fit college with high chance of admission worth and applying to; award letter will be important. Likes that it is a women's college.

- ⊘ **Lindenwood College**
  There are other colleges with a high chance of admission that are a better overall fit. Also, too close to home.

- ✓ **Missouri University of Science and Technology**
  High Fit college with strong science and technology focus. Preferred distance from home.

- ✓ **Truman State University**
  High Fit college with strong academic match and student outcomes, even though far from home.

- ✓ **University of Missouri-St. Louis**
  Moderate Overall Fit with a high chance of admission and best financial match. Would prefer to be further from home.

- ⊘ **Saint Louis University**
  Other colleges with moderate chance of admission are a better overall fit. Also, very close to home.

- ⊘ **Missouri State University**
  Other colleges with a high chance of admission are a better overall fit, and far from home.

COLLEGE UNMAZED

Step 3: Choose the Best Combination of Colleges Where You Will Apply

It is time now for you to make informed decisions on those colleges where you will apply. We recommend you follow the example of the case of Emily just presented to you. Each college you apply to evaluates you based on the materials you submit. This is the time for you to fully consider how well each college matches the person you are, the person you want to become, and your own individual and family circumstances. You have the power to accept or reject each college as a place worth applying to for you.

Activity 7.1: Your Overall Fit

- Write down the name of each college in the table below and rate how well each college fits you on each of the 6 Keys of College Fit.
- Calculate the total for each college and enter that number in the Total Key Score box.
- Use the scoring rubric presented below and assign each college to a Low, Moderate, or High–Fit group. Put the name of that group in the Overall Fit column provided for each college.
- Enter your scores into your CDO and review the "Chart" tab under Overall Fit (Apply).

1 This college has a **little** of what I want and need to be satisfied and successful

2 This college has **some** of what I want and need to be satisfied and successful

3 This college has **much** of what I want and need to be satisfied and successful

4 This college has **most** of what I want and need to be satisfied and successful

5 This college has **everything** I want and need to be satisfied and successful

17 or lower = Low Fit   **18–23= Moderate Fit**   **24–30 = High Fit**

College	Student Outcomes	Academic Match	Personal Match	Career Match	Financial Match	Student Support Services	Total Key Score	Overall Fit

Please note, sometimes 1 Key is dominant and has veto power over other keys. For example, Financial Match may really override other considerations – however, at this stage without financial aid award letters, you do not have enough information to know exactly what the financial situation will be at each college. Consider for a moment whether or not any of the 6 Keys of College Fit might overrule other Keys. In the Decide chapter, you will be given an opportunity to let more dominant Keys have more influence in your final decision.

CHAPTER 7: APPLY

Activity 7.2: Chance of Admission

Next, determine your Chance of Admission at each college.
Reviewing your College Data Organizer (see Admissions Chart in Chart tab), write down each college name below and rate your Chance of Admission (High = very good Chance of Admission; Moderate = good Chance of Admission; Low = lower Chance of Admission). Record your ratings in your CDO under Academic Match section.

College Name	Chance of Admission	College Name	Chance of Admission

Activity 7.3: Overall Fit by Chance of Admission

Next, find your Overall Fit by Chance of Admission.
- Combine your Overall Fit scores from the table in Activity 7.1 with your estimates of your Chance of Admission at each college into the 3 by 3 table below. Write the name of each college in the box corresponding to its Overall Fit score and your estimated Chance of Admission.
- Make sure each college is included in the box that accurately represents your Overall Fit and Chance of Admission ratings.

My Overall Fit by Chance of Admission

Overall Fit \ Chance of Admission	High	Moderate	Low
Low			
Moderate			
High			

Activity 7.4: Where I Am Applying & Why

Lastly, finalize the list of colleges you wish to apply to using the Overall Fit by Chance of Admission table.

Now, you are in a position to make an informed decision about the colleges on your list you should prepare applications for. In the chart provided below, explain your thinking and justification for why each college is or is not a good place for you to apply. Discuss your list of colleges and the reasons why you should (or should not) apply to each one with your family and others in your College Support Network.

Colleges	Apply? (Yes/No)	Reasoning

Progress Check

You are ready to move on to developing and submitting applications if the final List of colleges you have decided to apply to:

- has a number of colleges that have Moderate and High Overall Fit scores,
- has a reasonable range of difficulty level for gaining admission (some High and Low Admission Chance colleges, with a good number of Moderate admission chance schools),
- has enough colleges with a good intersection of Overall Fit and Chance of Admission.

If the final list of colleges you have decided to apply to doesn't meet these criteria, think about what you need to do to fix the problem. For example, if you do not have enough colleges with Moderate or High Chance of Admission, return to the List and Explore chapters to see if there are any colleges you did not consider that now might work for you. If you do not have enough colleges with a High or Moderate Overall Fit, re-explore your college options based on the 6 Keys of College Fit to see what other possibilities there may be.

CHAPTER 7: APPLY

Step 4: Develop and Submit Competitive College Applications

Now that you know where you will apply and have gathered information about what each college prioritizes when making admission decisions, you are ready to develop and submit applications strategically targeted to each college. To accomplish this, you will integrate the information you have already gathered with the remaining pieces of the college application process. These remaining pieces are: admission documents needed, a college application organizer, understanding college application types, knowing your deadlines, writing your college essay, and obtaining recommendation letters.

Tips to Get Started

1. Create a binder that holds all the information you receive from schools. Organize by college and your Overall Fit according to your List.
2. Create a separate email account that both you and your family have access to. Make the email address professional and easy to identify who you are, such as *firstname.lastname@email.address*. It is recommended that you do not use your high school email account because it may block outside emails due to school policy.
3. Create a spreadsheet with all passwords written down. You will be creating multiple new accounts and with the varying password criteria, it is easy to forget. Emailing college admissions and saying, "I forgot my password" simply looks bad.
4. Know needed documents and deadlines. If you prepare your documents ahead of time, it will truly make the application process easier and more rewarding, in both acceptances and scholarships. Missing deadlines is simply not acceptable.

Admission Documents

Figure 7.6

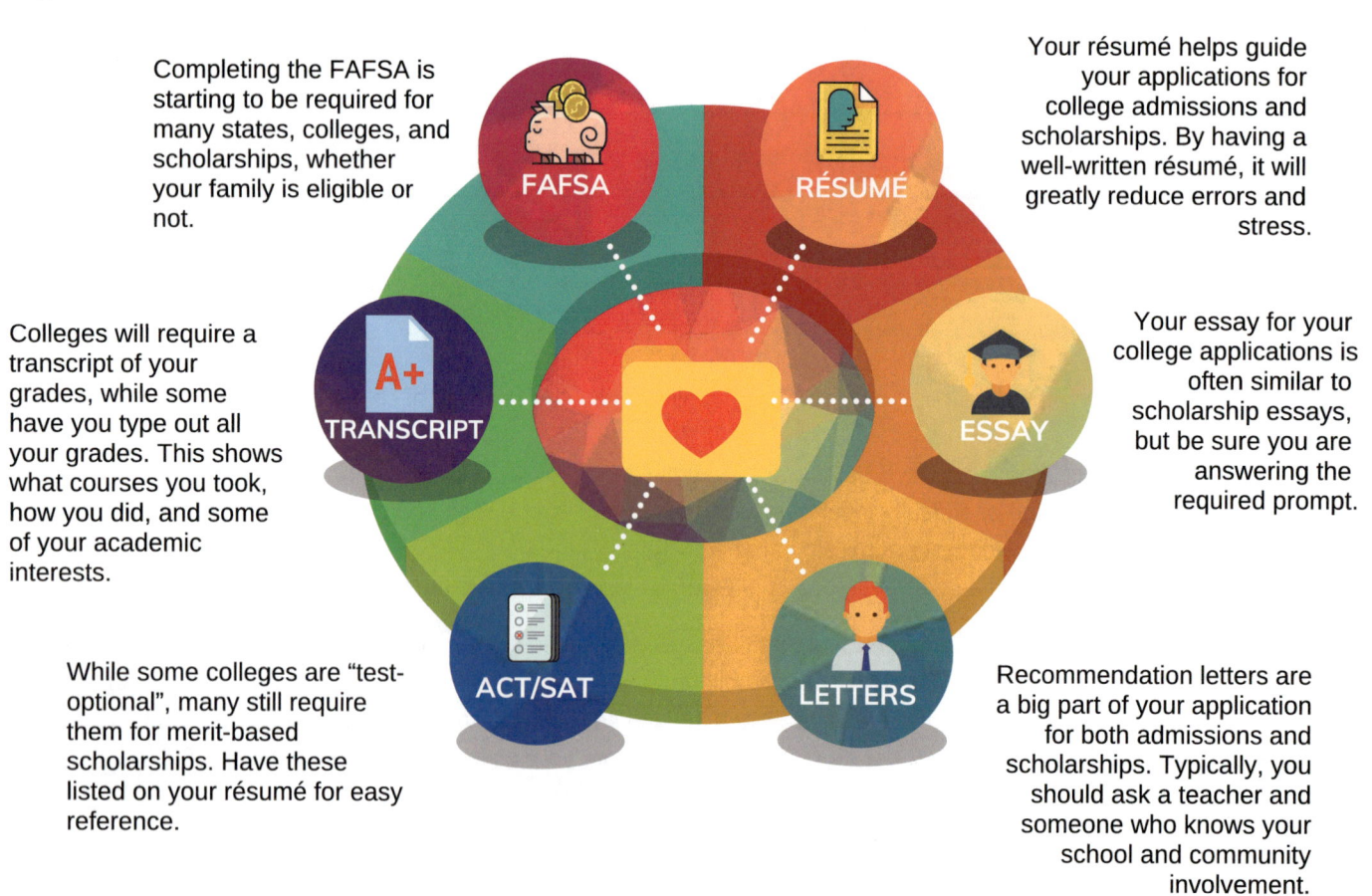

Completing the FAFSA is starting to be required for many states, colleges, and scholarships, whether your family is eligible or not.

Your résumé helps guide your applications for college admissions and scholarships. By having a well-written résumé, it will greatly reduce errors and stress.

Colleges will require a transcript of your grades, while some have you type out all your grades. This shows what courses you took, how you did, and some of your academic interests.

Your essay for your college applications is often similar to scholarship essays, but be sure you are answering the required prompt.

While some colleges are "test-optional", many still require them for merit-based scholarships. Have these listed on your résumé for easy reference.

Recommendation letters are a big part of your application for both admissions and scholarships. Typically, you should ask a teacher and someone who knows your school and community involvement.

College Application Types

There are three major types of applications: the Common App, the Coalition Application, and institutional applications. Many colleges allow you to choose which application to use, while others may give you no choice. Finding which colleges use the same application form can make applying much easier and reduce time spent rewriting or reformatting your documents.

Figure 7.7

1. Common Application

The Common App is used by over 900 colleges and universities around the world. The Common Application also provides students with a variety of resources through a virtual counselor, videos, and advice. Typically, schools using the Common Application take a holistic/selective admissions approach with the requirement of an essay and letters of recommendation.

Transcript
Résumé
Application Fee
Essay*
Recommendations*
(Counselor & 1–2 Teachers)
www.commonapp.org

2. Coalition Application

The Coalition Application is still relatively new, but it is used by over 140 colleges and universities across the United States. The application provides students with a set of free, online college-planning tools, articles, and resources. It also allows students to share their work with others.

Transcript
Résumé
Application Fee
Essay*
Recommendations*
www.coalitionforcollegeaccess.org

3. Institutional Application

Institutional applications are when colleges and universities have their own applications that you can complete. They vary in what is asked and how information is presented. Depending on the school they can either be relatively short or lengthy. Many colleges have a "Free Application Week" or provide waivers when you visit, but this depends on the college.

Transcript
Résumé
Application Fee
Essay*
Recommendations*
Website - see each college's website

*Essay and letters of recommendation requirements are decided by each college.

College application fees can be a considerable cost for many families. On average, a college application fee is $44, with the most common fee being $50 (U.S. News). For example, the Massachusetts Institute of Technology (MIT) application fee is $75. If a student is planning on applying to 8 schools at $44 each, that is $352 just to apply! For students who meet certain financial-need qualifications, such as free and reduced lunch programs, participating in Trio or Upward Bound programs, or meet income eligibility guidelines, there are application fee waivers available to waive these costs. Speak to your school counselor and/or the admission counselors at each college on how to obtain these waivers.

CHAPTER 7: APPLY

College Alternative Admissions

When thinking of college admissions, students generally focus on regular fall admissions. However, over half of all colleges have at least one type of alternative admission program to provide additional enrollment options and/or improve access for students who show academic potential but may need extra support. Each college determines how students can enter these programs and what they offer, but most programs fall into four general categories: support programs, online programs, alternative first-year programs, and alternative-term admission.

As you go through the application process, it is important to know if the colleges you are applying to might have these alternative admission programs. You may want to select an alternative program while applying, or the college may select it for you when they review your application. Your College Support Network may be able to provide some insight and additional support in helping you determine if an alternative admission program is right for you.

Besides alternative admission, you may also be asked to apply to other college-based programs, such as an honor's program, learning communities, direct-entry programs, etc. (see p. 62 for examples). There may be additional application requirements, such as an interview, additional essays, and letters of recommendation.

Figure 7.8

1. Support Programs

Colleges use many names for the programs designed to provide students with additional support during their first year. The college may provide summer programming; limit the number of credits a student can take; provide additional personal, academic, and career counseling; and/or provide financial aid advising. They may also provide additional tutoring, and students may be grouped with similar students for peer support.

2. Online

With online learning becoming more popular, and the lack of dormitory space at some colleges, there may be opportunities to start at a college online then transition to in-person learning. For example, the University of Florida's PaCE program allows students to start online for up to 60 credits and then transition to campus to complete an undergraduate degree.

3. Alternative First-Year Program

The college may partner with other colleges where students can begin their studies. Once students complete this program, they are guaranteed admissions into the primary university's programs. For example, students admitted to Northeastern University's N.U.in Program may be offered the opportunity to study abroad with a partner institution for the fall semester before returning to Northeastern University for the spring semester.

4. Alternative Term

Colleges are increasingly using alternative-term admission options. Because the fall term is highly competitive, they may provide summer or spring admissions to those who do not qualify for fall admission, but are students they would like to admit.

Types of Deadlines

When to submit an application can be confusing, as many colleges offer different deadlines. There are some key differences with each type of deadline that you should pay careful attention to, to increase your chances of being accepted at your preferred colleges. It is extremely important for students to find out what application deadlines each college is using and what is best for their admissions chances. That said, many institutional scholarships, honors programs, and special admission programs require the November 1st deadline.

Figure 7.9

Early Decision

Early decision allows students to apply early, typically in November – and get an admissions decision early (typically in December). However, early decision is a binding agreement, and you can only apply early decision to one college at a time. Using Early Decision means the college is your first choice and if you are accepted, you are committing to attend. Many highly selective colleges offer this option for students to show how committed they are to the college – and doing so can improve your chances of admission. Some colleges also offer early decision II (ED II), which operates very similarly to regular early decision (ED I) except that ED II applications are typically due in January or February, with decisions communicated to applicants 2–4 weeks later. **If you are applying for early decision please read Chapter 8 before doing so!**

Early Action

While similar to early decision, early action is not binding. You can apply early action (typically by November 1st or November 15th) to several colleges and receive their admission decisions earlier as a result. If you are ready to submit your applications and don't think waiting for more grades from your senior year will improve your chances of admission, applying early action might be a good idea for you.

Priority Deadline

Some colleges will have a priority deadline to guarantee your application is reviewed and you are eligible to be considered for things such as scholarships, honors programs, and on-campus housing if accepted. For some colleges, not meeting the priority deadline greatly diminishes your chance of acceptance, even though the regular decision deadline may be several weeks later. We strongly recommend you meet the priority deadline if a college you are applying to uses it.

Regular Decision

The regular decision deadline is the 'normal' deadline for applications to be submitted for consideration, and it is typically in early to mid-January. You may want to apply to a college's regular decision deadline if you would like to submit more grades from your senior year, improve your ACT/SAT scores, or finish more extracurricular activities.

Rolling Admissions

Colleges that use rolling admissions may have deadlines you need to meet to be considered for admission in the next academic term, but they review applications and send decisions on a rolling basis – first come, first served, so to speak. This usually allows you to have more flexibility in deciding when to submit your application materials.

CHAPTER 7: APPLY

Activity 7.5: College Application Organizer

Keeping track of your college applications and their deadlines will help make sure everything is submitted correctly and on time. Use this chart, or create one similar in an Excel or Google sheets file, to help keep track of all your applications. Share with your family, school counselor, and others in your College Support Network so they can help you manage your progress.

- Determine college application type (Common App, Coalition App, institutional).
- Determine what documents are required to complete the application.
- Determine what type of deadline you wish to apply under and what that deadline is.

College Name									
College Application Type									
Documents Required									
• Application									
• Transcript									
• Essay									
• Test Scores									
• Recommendations									
• Résumé									
Types of Deadline									
Deadline Date									

Activity 7.6: Complete Your College Résumé

In Chapter 2: Academic Factor (p.39-42), you started your academic résumé – and for good reason! Now is the time to go back to that document, add any additional activities you have participated in since then, and polish it with any other edits and final touches. You will need to create two different résumés – one for people who will write letters of recommendation for you and scholarship applications, and one for college applications. The main differences between the two résumé types are the word count and number of activities you can include. Your résumé for recommendations and scholarships are not bound by a specific word count or how many activities you can include. While you want to stay succinct in your writing, you can add more personality and explanation. However, for your actual college applications you will need to home in on only 150 characters for each activity description and usually only 8–10 activities can be included.

The College Application Essay

When colleges and universities require essays as part of their application, this tells you that "your story" may be an important piece of information for them. Each college attaches a unique weight to the essay, but your essay can be the thing that makes them say yes to you versus someone else who has similar academic qualifications. For some colleges, the essay is a critical factor in their admission decision.

Unfortunately, too many students either throw their essays together carelessly at the last minute without the benefits of proper editing, reviewing, and feedback. Spelling and grammar errors, in particular, can turn a yes decision into a no.

The essay will be read as part of your application package, as it offers an opportunity to showcase aspects of yourself that would be difficult to convey in other areas of your application. Therefore, it is important that your essay is not repeating material contained elsewhere in the application, but provides a new, unique view into *you*.

Many colleges also ask for supplemental essays, which are smaller in size and are often more specific to the university and why you wish to attend there. Similar to your essay, take your time to put forth a well-written and thoughtful supplemental essay.

Here are some Common Application essay prompts you may be asked to write about (taken from the 2021–2022 Common App, required 250–650 words):

1. Some students have a background, identity, interest, or talent that is so meaningful they believe their application would be incomplete without it. If this sounds like you, then please share your story.

2. The lessons we take from obstacles we encounter can be fundamental to later success. Recount a time when you faced a challenge, setback, or failure. How did it affect you, and what did you learn from the experience? (Third most popular essay at 21.1% chosen)

3. Reflect on a time when you questioned or challenged a belief or idea. What prompted your thinking? What was the outcome?

4. Describe a problem you've solved or a problem you'd like to solve. It can be an intellectual challenge, a research query, an ethical dilemma – anything that is of personal importance, no matter the scale. Explain its significance to you and what steps you took or could be taken to identify a solution.

5. Discuss an accomplishment, event, or realization that sparked a period of personal growth and a new understanding of yourself or others. (Second most popular essay at 23.7% chosen)

6. Describe a topic, idea, or concept you find so engaging that it makes you lose all track of time. Why does it captivate you? What or who do you turn to when you want to learn more?

7. Share an essay on any topic of your choice. It can be one you've already written, one that responds to a different prompt, or one of your own design. (Most popular essay at 24.1% chosen)

Websites
Essays that Worked – Johns Hopkins University
Essays that Worked – Hamilton College
Common Application Personal Statement – Tufts
Babson College Essay Examples

Books
College Essays That Made a Difference
Conquering the College Admissions Essays in 10 Steps
Fiske Real College Essays That Work
100 Successful College Application Essays

CHAPTER 7: APPLY

Figure 7.10

Do's

- Use the essay to reveal something new, a story or idea that showcases your personality and is meaningful to you.
- Show your knowledge of the college, with specific details you have learned through research and visiting.
- Use your voice to tell your story. Don't try to be someone you're not.
- Make sure you answer the prompt.
- Understand all of your deadlines and make a plan to complete a high-quality essay.

Don'ts

- Don't use the essay to repeat what is in your résumé. Use this opportunity to reveal something unique about you.
- Don't copy and paste your essays, even if you are applying to multiple schools. Take the time to write original responses, incorporating the college's values and mission when appropriate.
- Don't write an essay for what you "think" colleges are looking for. This is a time to tell something unique about you.
- Don't rely on spellcheck. Have multiple people read, and check your work before you submit.
- Don't wait until the last minute as it leads to increased stress and poorly written essays.

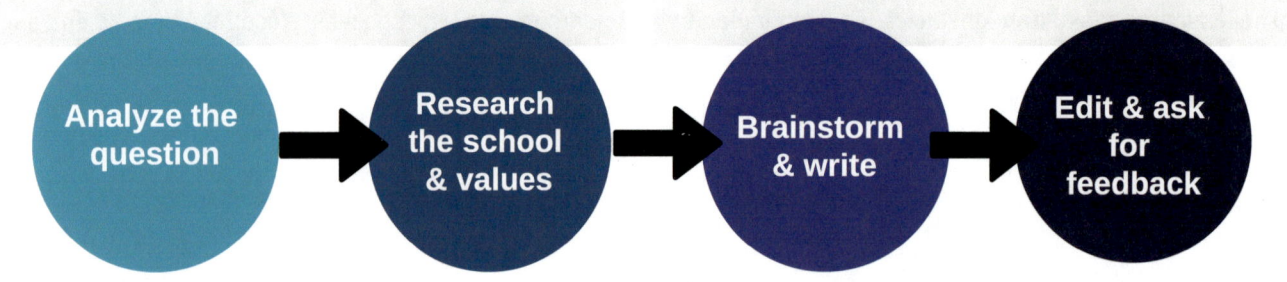

Analyze the question → Research the school & values → Brainstorm & write → Edit & ask for feedback

Emily's Essay Examples

Emily has worked hard in determining the colleges that best fit her on the 6 Key of College Fit, editing and refining her résumé, and making sure she is on track with her college applications. In reviewing her college's CDS information, she found that the colleges she is applying to ranked the college essay as important in deciding to accept a student.

Two of the *College UnMazed* authors independently wrote Emily's college essay and, unsurprisingly, had two very different essays that each thought showcased who Emily was as a person and student. We analyzed her likes and passions in high school, what she finds important in her life, and her academic goals. We reviewed her résumé and considered what else could be expanded upon to provide the college admissions representatives who read her application a deeper dive into what she finds is meaningful.

On the next two pages, you will see the two essays we wrote and what our considerations were in writing each essay. We wanted to demonstrate how two very different essays can be written about the same person. Depending on who the audience is and the intent you want to communicate, your college essay can look quite different. The important point is to be authentic and genuine in what you write. But, please understand, there is no one right way to write a compelling college essay.

Emily's Essay #1

The clanking of the dishes, the sounds of idle chatter, and the yells from the back kitchen all tell me it is another Sunday lunchtime. As the churchgoers funnel into the diner, I see many familiar faces, people I have gotten to know over the years working here. Table 10 is full of the loud choir group that has been known to break out in song. Table 8 is the Marks family. They recently celebrated a birthday for 5-year-old Samantha, who is still proudly wearing her birthday crown. I scan over to Tom sitting at the counter. He ordered his normal biscuits and gravy, and a ham and cheese omelet. After his wife, Marge, died last year, I thought he might order something else as they religiously ordered the same thing and split it. Now, he just takes the other half home, and I always think that he never will eat the other half. However, today he is just staring into his food, looking pensive and slightly agitated.

"Tom, is your food okay today? I don't see you eating much." He slowly looks up at me and says, "It's fine Emily, just not in the mood." If you know Tom, he is always in the mood for Sunday brunch. I look down and expect to see his faithful sidekick, Beau, at his feet, but he's not there. "Tom, where is Beau at today?" I feel a slight hesitation and realize this may be the issue. "He's not well. I took him over to Doc McMiller yesterday, and he needs surgery. But I live on a tight budget and even with the discount Doc would give me, I just don't have the money." I am heartbroken. Tom was our school janitor, and when he retired a few years ago, he would sit with Beau and wave to all the school kids as they walked by his home. That dog is his life.

Having grown up in this community, I feel like I am a part of the life of each person in the restaurant. Especially after working here throughout my high school years so I could help with my family's living expenses, I have a view into people's lives that many are not fortunate enough to have. The small conversations I have throughout my shifts always lead me to ponder people's lives, who they are, what troubles them, and why some are able to overcome obstacles while others simply can't. It's what got me interested in Psychology to begin with, as I wanted to put the pieces together of how the amazing human mind works. I want to be the person that helps others unlock who they are, and are meant to be.

I look around at the busy restaurant and know what I must do. I run to the kitchen and grab a bucket. When I return, I find a chair to stand on and loudly clear my voice. "Excuse me, everyone! Everyone in here knows Tom and what he has done for this community. I don't remember a day not seeing his smiling face as I was growing up. I just heard some sad news that Beau is not well, and unfortunately, the surgery is pretty expensive." I pull a $20 out of my tip bag, "I am going to donate some of my tips today to help Beau and if you would like to as well, I am putting the bucket here. Thank you." Tom looks shocked at first, but as each person from the restaurant comes over and puts money in the bucket, his face lights up.

Seeing Tom and Beau saunter in two weeks later to a round of cheers reinforced to me the importance of noticing the small things, sometimes the things people don't say. It also shows what a community really is, and how supporting one another is what matters.

Author's Thoughts

When we wrote Emily's case in Chapter 2, we tried to describe Emily as a student that was hardworking and cared deeply about her community. Being a first-generation college student and helping her parents in their business, she knew the value of hard work. After she explored her community further through community service, mental health initiatives, and leading her soccer team, we felt that Emily would enjoy a helping career and would be willing to help people when they needed it the most. Her essay, focused on her noticing someone was struggling with a mental health issue and seeking a way to solve it, epitomizes who she is as a person. The personal, story-like feel to this essay is an interesting and engaging way to communicate to an admissions representative what makes her unique.

CHAPTER 7: APPLY

Emily's Essay #2

Our 10th grade Honors Mathematics teacher gave us back our first test. I was nervous. Usually, there was distracting talking going on somewhere in our classroom, but not today. My teacher put the test face down on my desk and said to the whole class, "Okay, now that we have reviewed some basics, we are going to pick up the pace." I turned my test over and saw a B-minus. I had never once received a B in 9th grade. I thought to myself, "I am never going to be able to get a good grade in this course. I need to get into an easier math class."

That night, I spoke to my parents about what I was thinking, and they stated that before I switched math classes I should go and talk to the teacher first. I made the appointment and went in. The teacher listened to my reasons for wanting to switch. Then she said, "So, you're going to give up? You don't give up on the soccer field or in your other classes. I know you are becoming interested in science and the math you will learn in this class will be very useful to you as you take more science classes." I knew she was right about both things. Taking more demanding math courses would help my budding science interests. And I am not a quitter.

We had to conduct a research project on a topic of our own choosing in another class. I did mine on student enrollment in high school mathematics courses. I was surprised to learn that, on average, grades in mathematics courses go down across the high school years. Research published in the *Journal for Research in Mathematics Education* suggested that this was an important reason why so many students stopped taking advanced math courses in high school. I decided not to be a statistic.

I took charge of the situation like I do when playing defense on the soccer team and working at my part-time job. I started attending extra-help sessions the math teacher offered after school. I quickly discovered that I wasn't alone. There were many classmates, girls and boys, who felt the same. I started a study group for mutual help and support and kept it going until the end of the year. Even though I decided to stay in the class and worked hard to study and get extra help, I still found it difficult to get the grades I was accustomed to getting as a high school freshman. I made an appointment with my school counselor to discuss this. He reassured me that taking on more rigorous courses and pushing myself would help me be more successful in the future, both in college and in my career.

Now, I am a 12th grader pushing myself in courses that I may or may not pursue in college. I focus not on the grade earned, but on the knowledge that I can take away from the course. I also continue to pursue my passions in the field of Psychology that links the brain and the body. Synapses and neurons and how they affect our mood and behavior is something I find weirdly riveting.

I have turned a weakness into a strength. I am getting better at both math and science as I move along. I have worked very hard to build an academic foundation that will help me to excel in college. Last week, I was listening to the woman who won last year's Nobel Peace Prize for her and her colleague's work. The human genome is fascinating. I want to learn more about how things like this work and can help us make a better world. I am ready, able, and willing to take on this next challenge.

Author's Thoughts

In this example, we tried to highlight Emily's demonstrated perseverance and initiative in the face of adversity. Mathematics and science are gateway courses where college majors and careers, ones you might greatly enjoy, are prematurely ruled out. This is not the case for Emily. She is becoming intrigued with Biology and how it connects to Psychology. Her fascination with how the human nervous system and the brain work might lead her to study Neuropsychology in graduate school.

Activity 7.7: Essay Brainstorm

Look at the Common App prompts and brainstorm ideas that can help you convey aspects of your You Factor that may not be evident to the people reviewing your applications.

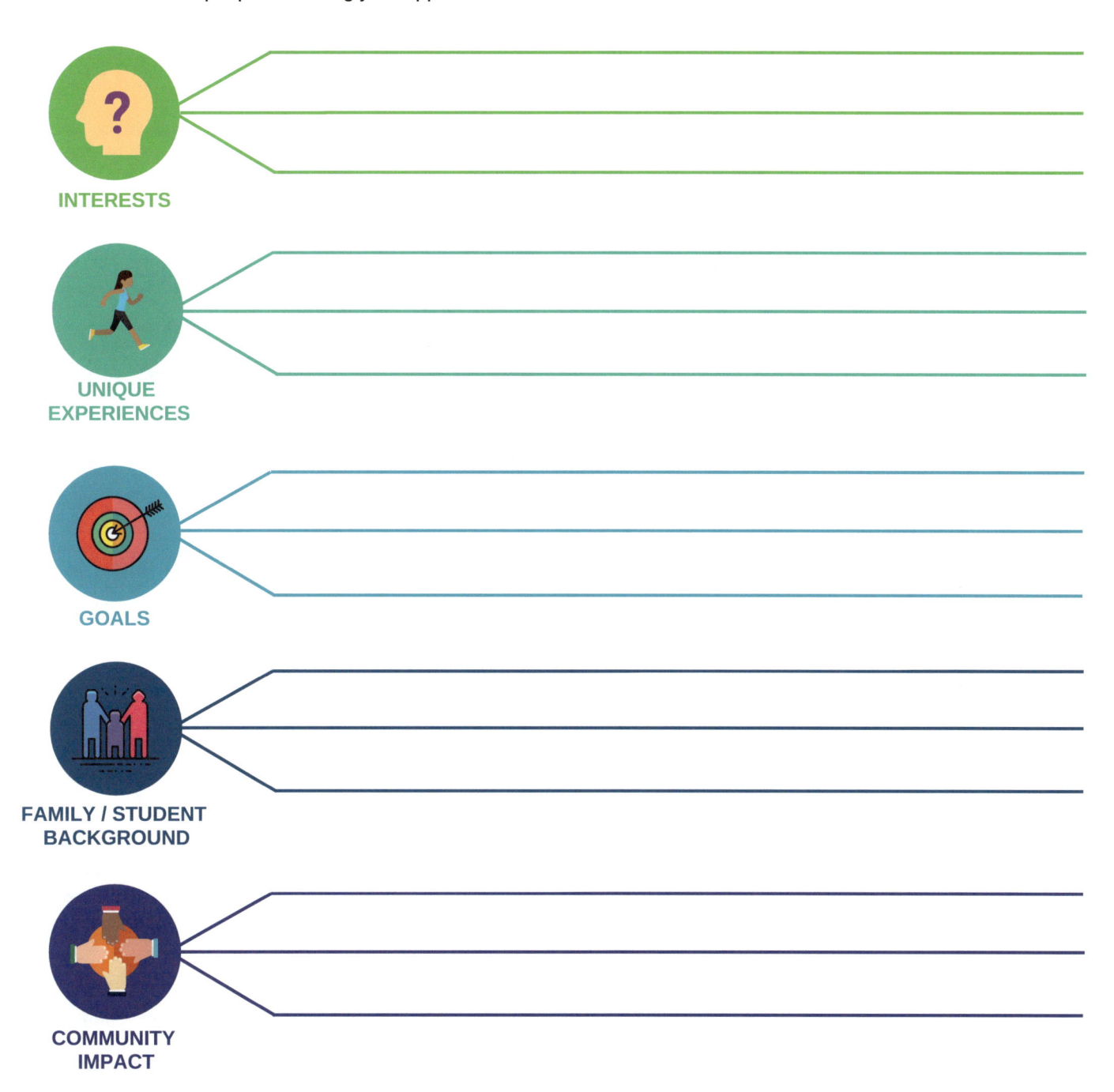

INTERESTS

UNIQUE EXPERIENCES

GOALS

FAMILY / STUDENT BACKGROUND

COMMUNITY IMPACT

Activity 7.8: Writing the Essay

Writing your essay is a process, and you will likely want to revise your essay several times after reading it for yourself and getting feedback from your teachers, counselor, and others in your college support network. Using word processing software such as Microsoft Word or Google Docs, write an outline of your essay using ideas from your brainstorming (Activity 7.7) to get started, then write the essay itself.

CHAPTER 7: APPLY

Letters of Recommendation

Letters of recommendation are an important part of the application review. If a college you are considering participates in the CDS initiative, you can get a sense of how important recommendation letters are in relation to other parts of your application. Using the steps below and the Teacher and Counselor Recommendation forms (Activity 7.9 & 7.10) will help you obtain letters that reflect who you are as a student.

Figure 7.11

1 Identify counselors, teachers, and other professionals that can attest to your academic and personal character. Follow guidelines on which recommendations to submit.

2 Create a well-written résumé that details your high school career, including academic achievements, extracurriculars, and other important factors that may be useful when talking about you.

3 Allow your recommenders plenty of time to write the recommendation. Provide a copy of your résumé, the schools you are applying to, your recommendation form, and all documents needed.

4 These letters take considerable time. Follow up before the deadline with your sincere appreciation, like a nice thank you card, to show your gratitude for their extra effort.

Why Non-Required Recommendations Are Important

Not every college requires recommendations, but here are five reasons why you should have them.

1. Poor grades in high school. Even if you did not amass the strongest academic record in high school, there is hope. Well-written recommendations can instruct the college admissions team to look beyond the numbers on your transcript. This is an opportunity for an outside individual to describe your character, personal journey through high school, and other attributes that would make you a strong addition to a college – and perhaps provide some reasons why the grades on your transcript do not reflect your potential to succeed in college.

2. Explain a special circumstance. There may be reasons you chose a particular academic program, had a bad semester, or do not have a lot on your résumé. Using recommendations to answer some of these key questions will help admissions reviewers understand more about your context and situation.

3. Supports an application or unique trait. Letters of recommendation allow a professional that knows the student well to describe the student and something that is unique about them. This could include their personality, involvement in a particular activity or club, or something that sets them apart from other students that is often hard to communicate on an application.

4. Use it as a piece of the application. When developing your application, review your résumé, transcript, essay, and other documents and ask, What is missing? Guiding recommenders to help round out your story will provide admissions officers a more comprehensive understanding of who you are and what you are capable of.

5. Additional scholarship opportunities. While many colleges do not require recommendations, many programs and scholarships do. Unfortunately, if you don't have your documents ready, you will be at a disadvantage for applying to these opportunities.

Activity 7.9: Teacher Recommendation

Teacher's Name: _____

Student Name: _____

Course(s) with this Teacher (i.e., English 2): _____

Date of Request: _____ Date Needed: _____

Thank you so much for agreeing to write this letter of recommendation for me. I asked you because I think you are a teacher who knows me well and can accurately evaluate my potential for success in college. The information below may be helpful to you as you write my recommendation.

1. I think my academic strengths are …

2. I think my personal strengths are …

3. I am considering the following college majors because …

4. Some of the things I want the college admission and/or scholarship committee to know about me are …

5. The specific things I hope you discuss in this letter are …

6. What I remember most about your class is …

7. Additional information that might be helpful includes …

Colleges I am applying to:

Again, thank you. I know writing a strong letter of recommendation is a big time commitment, and I greatly appreciate your help.

CHAPTER 7: APPLY

Activity 7.10: Counselor Recommendation

Counselor's Name: _____

Student Name: _____

Date of Request: _____ Date Needed: _____

Thank you so much for agreeing to write this letter of recommendation for me. I understand your letter is important because it helps describe me personally and academically. The information below are factors that you may not have known about me and may be helpful to you as you write the recommendation. I would be happy to plan a meeting with you to discuss further.

1. My academic interests are ...

2. I am considering the following college majors because ...

3. I have had some situations that have affected my academic performance, and they are (such as family issues, illnesses, moving, etc.) ...

4. Some significant extracurricular activities (could include summer experiences, major study programs, work, volunteer, etc.) that have been of significant importance to me are ... because ...

5. I consider my greatest strength or talent to be ...

6. I believe I am unique because (suggest adding three to four adjectives that best describe you and why) ...

7. I feel very passionate about (could be school, community, or society related) ...

8. I believe my family background is important to me because (suggest including information that the counselor might not know) ...

FAFSA & CSS Profile

As we discussed in Chapter 4: Money Factor, completing your Free Application for Federal Student Aid (FAFSA) is a critical part of the application process. Universities and colleges use this vital document to provide additional grant and loan money to families to reduce the cost of higher education. While some families may think they do not qualify, they could be missing out on additional scholarships and aid money they did not know existed. We recommend *all* families complete the FAFSA whether they think they qualify or not.

Some colleges require an additional form called the College Scholarship Service (CSS) Profile (CSS Profile) that allows colleges to have a more comprehensive look at the financial and family situation as they determine eligibility for institutional financial aid.

Figure 7.12

1. **PRIOR-PRIOR YEAR:** The income reported on the FAFSA is from taxes filed two years before you start college. Example – Start date of fall 2022, would be your 2020 tax return.

2. **OCTOBER 1:** FAFSA opens to be submitted for the next school year. To receive the highest amount of aid, you should submit as close to October 1 as possible.

3. **COMPLETE THE FAFSA ONLINE:** Complete the FAFSA online at https://studentaid.gov/. Check your school/community for free support workshops to aid in the process.

4. **COLLEGES:** The colleges you put into your FAFSA application will receive your financial aid materials and determine what financial aid you can receive in the form of grants, work-study, or loans. The FAFSA review is done after the college has accepted you.

5. **AWARD LETTER:** Each institution you are accepted to will provide you an award letter that breaks down your FAFSA award (further discussion of award letters in Chapter 8: Decide).

Chapter Summary

In this chapter, you learned how to determine which colleges to apply to by connecting the 6 Keys of College Fit to your Chance of Admission. You also learned what documents and information you need to assemble and gather to submit high-quality applications to those colleges. Since you can only choose to attend a college you have been accepted to, the decisions you make about where to apply are among the most important ones you will make in your college-going journey.

At-Home Discussion

Unless you have applied early decision to a college, you will have a lot of time between when you finish submitting applications and May 1st (the date you need to make your final decision). Discuss with your family what other information you may need to be ready to make an informed decision about which college you should attend. For example, you may want to visit a college you applied to but did not have time to visit or you may want to plan to revisit a college you were accepted to.

Review the High School Planning Checklist in Resources on page 135. What are some next action steps that you need to take in the next month, six months, and year?

CHAPTER 8
Decide

Comparing Offers and Making a Commitment

You Factor • Academic Factor • Career Factor • Money Factor • Developing a List • Exploring Colleges • Applying to Colleges • **Deciding on a College** • Succeeding in College

This chapter has three purposes. First, we will help you better understand and compare college acceptance offers you have now received. Congratulations! Second, we will show you how to rank order those colleges where you have earned admission to more accurately compare and evaluate how each college can help you meet your educational and career goals. Based on new information you have received (e.g. acceptance and award letters), you will revisit your ratings of the 6 Keys of College Fit and judge the Desirability of each college. And third, you will learn how to effectively get and use feedback from your family and College Support Network, and then make an informed final decision on which college you will attend.

Making an informed choice as to which college to attend requires higher-order thinking. You need to reflect on and think through how both your factual knowledge and your emotional, personal reaction to each college – i.e., how desirable each college is to you – work together to help you make a good decision. The figure on the next page (Figure 8.1) uses Bloom's Taxonomy to describe how you will employ higher-order thinking in this chapter to make an informed college decision.

The 6 steps of higher-order thinking described on the next page (Figure 8.1) connect to specific activities you will complete in this chapter and the next chapter. First, it is important that you *Remember* all you have learned about the colleges you have been accepted into (e.g., information you learned while assessing the 6 Keys of College Fit or visiting the college) and fully *Understand* the financial offers they have made to you. Next, you will compare financial aid award letters from the colleges you were accepted into, revise your ratings of the 6 Keys of College Fit based on this new information, and make judgments about how acceptable and desirable each college is to you. You will then *Apply* this knowledge to interpret how your Overall Fit and Desirability ratings work together to help you see which colleges are stronger options for you. Next, you will *Analyze* each option by explaining your reasons why each college does or does not fit you and arrange colleges into a decision tree that helps you identify your top choice. Finally, you will get feedback from your College Support Network about your choices and reasoning and *Evaluate* this information in order to make your final decision. In the next chapter (Chapter 9: Succeed), you will *Create* a plan to help you succeed in college financially, academically, and socially.

We will show you how to use an informed decision-making sequence to choose a specific college through the case of Emily. The decisions about where Emily applied were presented to you in the last chapter. Now, you will learn which colleges she has been accepted into and work through her final decision-making steps with her.

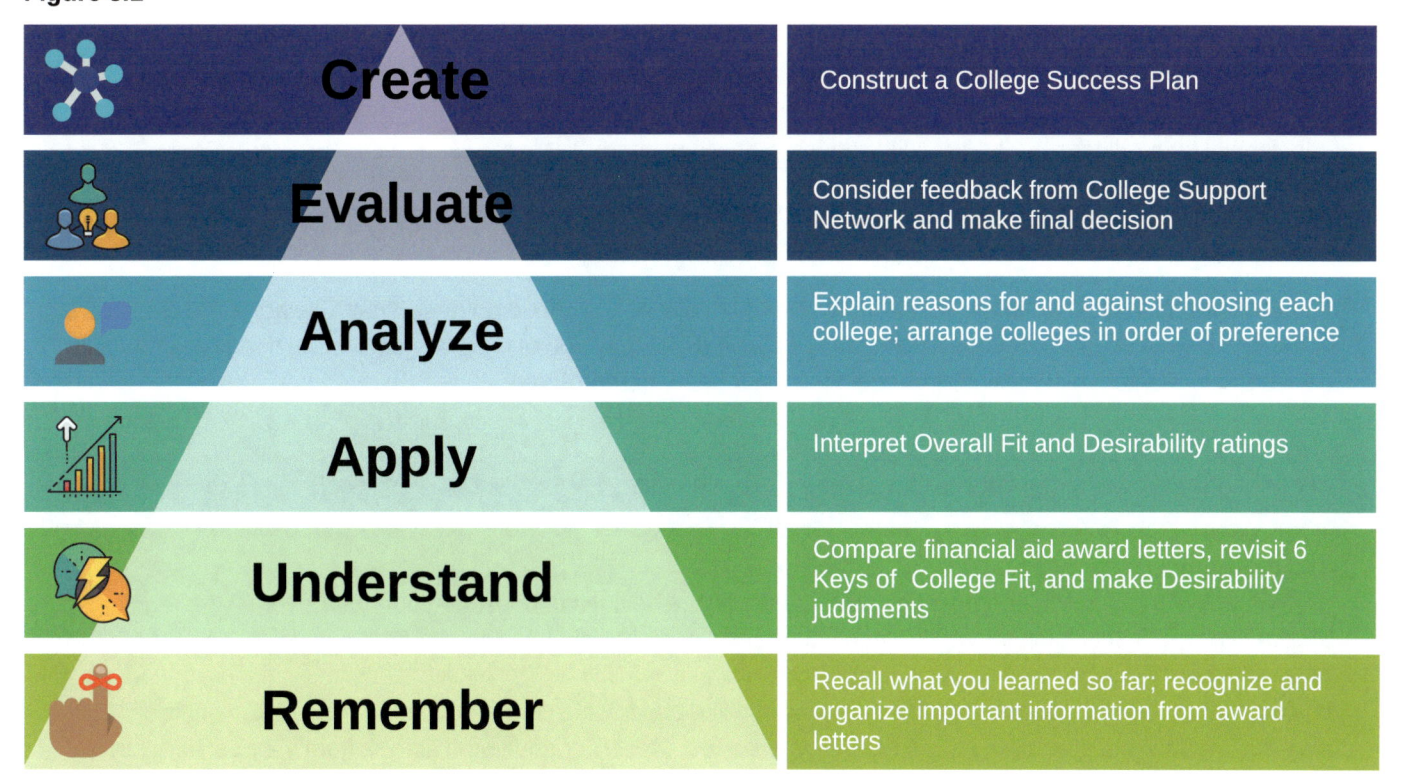

Figure 8.1

	Create	Construct a College Success Plan
	Evaluate	Consider feedback from College Support Network and make final decision
	Analyze	Explain reasons for and against choosing each college; arrange colleges in order of preference
	Apply	Interpret Overall Fit and Desirability ratings
	Understand	Compare financial aid award letters, revisit 6 Keys of College Fit, and make Desirability judgments
	Remember	Recall what you learned so far; recognize and organize important information from award letters

Your Decide Steps

1. Learn about Types of College Admission Decisions. You will understand the various decision options a college might make and what your next steps may be for each type of decision.

2. Review Case Study – Emily. Through a case study you will be shown how to work your way through a higher-order thinking process to make an informed decision about which college this student should attend.

3. Make Your Final Decision. You will now use this higher-order thinking process to make an informed decision about which college you will attend.

Step 1: Learn about Types of College Admission Decisions

Colleges receive applications from many qualified applicants every year. Each college has its own way of reviewing applications, especially when they receive so many. For example, the University of California – Los Angeles received over 203,700 (up from 97,112 in 2016!) applications, New York University received 75,037, and the University of Michigan – Ann Arbor received 65,021. Traditionally, your application review starts with your area's representative, as they know your school and academic choices. There is a rubric or criteria that each college sets each year that guides the review of applicants. The college will review all of your materials and decide to either accept, accept with conditions, defer/waitlist, or deny you as a student.

While we hope that through your List building you chose to submit applications to colleges that fit you well, there is always a chance that you will not be admitted. Often it is not because you were not a great student, but that the college can only accept a limited number of students. The sheer number of applicants at some colleges can make it difficult for anyone to get in. You will be notified of each college's decision on your application by mail, email, or through their application portal. It is important to check these often, so nothing is missed. There are several decision options colleges might make with your application, such as:

CHAPTER 8: DECIDE

Figure 8.2

Admit

The college has determined you are qualified for admissions. They provide you with an offer of admission, traditionally for a fall term seat. They will start the process of sending you required documents (see Figure 8.3).

Alternative Admissions

The college has decided to admit you with one of the conditions described on page 94. While not a "regular" admit to the college, you can still choose to attend the college as long as you also agree to the condition specified, such as starting in the spring semester or attending a summer support program.

Defer

The college may defer deciding on your application when:
a. You applied early action or early decision and the college decides to consider your application in the regular application pool. If this happens at a college you applied early decision to, you are free to consider offers from other schools.
b. You applied regular decision and the college would like additional information before rendering a decision. They may ask for additional letters of recommendation, new test scores, or additional grades from your senior year.

Waitlist

The college has finished reviewing your application and has decided to put you on a waitlist. In this situation, new information is not needed, and the college is waiting as other students who were fully admitted decide if they will be attending or not. Once seats open, the college may then offer you admission. At some colleges, students rarely get off the waitlist, and at some, most do. You can see how many students have been accepted from the waitlist at colleges that participate in the Common Data Set initiative in section C2.

Deny

The college has decided not to accept you. While you can appeal this decision, unless there was something that significantly alters your application in your favor, succeeding in the appeal process is unlikely. If this was your dream college, continue to do your research as you may be able to attend a different college and transfer in later.

If you are admitted, the college may review your application to check your eligibility for other programs, such as honors programs and specialized learning communities. The college will also review your FAFSA and application to see if you qualify for scholarships, grants, loans and work-study. Some scholarships and grants are automatically added to your award letter and some you may have to apply for separately. It is important to review the college's application portal and check your email frequently so you do not miss any opportunities. From here, the college will send you your award letter, discussed later in the chapter. The next page provides an overview of the process each college will take when reviewing your application and next steps if admitted.

Application Review Process

Figure 8.3

Application Review
The college's admission team reviews all necessary documents and discusses the student based on their admission criteria.

Scholarship & Program Review
If admitted, a student's application is reviewed for scholarships and additional programs (honors, direct-entry, etc.). There may be an essay or interview process.

Housing & Orientation
Once the spot is accepted, additional documents will need to be provided to the college, such as official transcripts, and residency verification. Students will need to select housing (if applicable) and an orientation time.

Application Decision
Admissions determines if the student is accepted, accepted with conditions, deferred, waitlisted or denied. The college sends the student notification of the decision either by mail or through their college application portal.

Award Letter
Admitted students are sent an estimated award letter, including cost of attendance, scholarships and grant aid, and loans. Includes an expected net price. Students will need to accept or decline their award letter and confirm attendance.

Step 2: Review Case Study – Emily

You will now work your way through the higher-order thinking process described in the beginning of this chapter to help Emily make a more informed decision about which college she should choose to attend. After that, you will do the same thing for yourself.

> Emily was accepted into 5 of the 7 colleges where she applied, with 1 being a special summer term program. She was accepted into 2 colleges where she accurately estimated her chances were High for being accepted, with both schools also being Moderate in Fit – Stephens College and the University of Missouri – St. Louis. She was accepted into another 2 colleges that she estimated her chances for acceptance as being Moderate, with both schools rated as being High in Overall Fit – the University of Missouri-Columbia and Truman State University. And finally, Emily was accepted into 1 college that she believed she had a Low chance of being accepted into but she felt that this college was a High Fit for her – Missouri University of Science and Technology.
>
> The all-important question now is which of these 5 colleges should Emily choose to attend? To answer this question, follow the higher-order thinking strategy outlined throughout Emily's case study.
>
> **Remember:** Recall what you have learned so far (You, Academic, Career, and Money Factors; 8 Strengths; LEADS), and recognize and organize important information from admission and award letters
>
> Before receiving her acceptance and award letters, Emily reviews not only the financial aid information in Chapter 4 but all of what she has learned in Section 1 and Section 2 of this book. When her letters do arrive, the first thing Emily does is read them carefully and thoroughly. She needs to make sure that she understands any acceptances, including alternative admissions, that she knows deadlines each college goes by, and any other important information she may need to know. Letters vary between colleges, so it is incumbent on Emily to fully understand what is in each of them and to ask questions if she doesn't. Emily carefully reviews each letter. After doing this, she is quite sure that she understands what is required of her and what type of admissions she was given. She takes notes and organizes that information to help her recall important information when she needs it to complete the informed decision-making work to come.

CHAPTER 8: DECIDE

Understand: Compare financial aid award letters, revisit the 6 Keys of College Fit, make Desirability judgments

Once Emily received all her award letters (example from Truman below, Figure 8.4), she created the comparison table on the next page (Figure 8.5) to more easily evaluate the financial information colleges were providing. While not all the terminology was exactly the same, she made sure she was clear on what all the costs were minus grant and scholarship money. She paid particular attention to loans she would have to pay back, something she is strongly trying to avoid. If you were going to interpret the financial numbers in this table, what would you say to Emily?

Figure 8.4

Dear Emily,
The Financial Aid Office at Truman State University is pleased to offer you this financial aid package for the above academic year in response to your FAFSA results. Need-based offers are calculated using your Expected Family Contribution (EFC) from your FAFSA. Initial offers are based on an expected enrollment status of full-time and are contingent upon continued funding from federal, state, and institutional sources. Your actual costs will be calculated when you receive your first bill in August.

Direct Costs
Represents costs that are directly associated with enrollment. Tuition, fees, and room and board (if you live on campus) are directly charged to your Truman account.

Indirect Costs
These costs vary by student and are provided by the college as an estimate to help you budget additional expenditures. Represents items such as transportation, books, supplies, and other personal expenses which are calculated using an average amount per academic year. You are in control of how much you spend on these items. Indirect costs are NOT charged to your Truman account.

Scholarships & Grants
Grants and scholarships are considered gift aid that does not require repayment. Gift aid for which you are eligible may include awards from federal and state programs, as well as institutional grants and scholarships. You must reapply through the FAFSA each year to be considered for federal, state, and institutional grants. If you receive additional scholarships and / or grants that are not listed on this notification, your student loans and/or Work-Study funds may need to be reduced or cancelled. If private scholarships are listed, you may log into TruView for individual award amounts.

Options to Pay Remaining Costs
A portion of your cost can be funded through self-help aid like federal student loans, federal parent PLUS loans, or private loan programs. Loans are optional and must be repaid. It is best to only borrow what you need to cover your educational expenses. In addition, Federal Work-Study provides part time jobs for students with financial need, allowing them to earn money to pay educational expenses. Many students are also employed on and off campus in non Work-Study positions.

Average Annual (Fall and Spring Estimated Costs)	Total
Direct Costs	
Annual Tuition (12–17 credits per semester)	$8,365
Required and Academic Fees	$804
Housing & Meals	$9,417
Average Total Direct Costs	**$18,586**
Indirect Costs	
Books & Supplies	$1,000
Personal Expenses	$2,500
Transportation Expenses	$1,300
Average Total Indirect Costs	**$4,800**
Scholarships & Grants	
Pell Grant	$2,045
Access Missouri Grant	$2,450
TruMerit Scholarship	$4,000
TruOpportunity Scholarship	$2,000
Total Scholarships & Grants	**$10,585**
Options to Pay Remaining Costs	
Federal College Work-Study	$2,800
Federal Subsidized Direct Loan	$3,500
Federal Unsub. Direct Loan	$2,000
Total Self Help Aid	**$8,300**

*We reached out to each of Emily's potential colleges to see if they were willing to provide an example award letter. This financial aid award letter was an example provided by Truman State University. Some information was removed due to space limitations.

Figure 8.5

	Stephens College	University of Missouri-Columbia	University of Missouri-St. Louis	Truman State University	Missouri University of Science and Technology
Cost of Attendance					
• Tuition & Fees	$24,570	$13,128	$13,114	$9,169	$10,934
• Room & Board	$9,324	$10,964	$10,796	$9,417	$11,028
• Books & Supplies	$2,000	$1,032	$1,032	$1,000	$782
• Travel & Other Expenses	$4,020	$5,350	$4,580	$4,840	$4,140
TOTAL COST OF ATTENDANCE	**$39,914**	**$30,474**	**$29,522**	**$24,426**	**$26,884**
Gift Aid					
• Institution Grants & Scholarships	$16,545	$11,369	$9,280	$8,540	$10,899
• Federal Grants	$2,045	$2,045	$2,045	$2,045	$2,045
• State Grants	$0	$0	$0	$0	$0
• Other Grants & Scholarships	$0	$0	$0	$0	40
Total Gift Aid	**$18,590**	**$13,414**	**$11,325**	**$10,585**	**$12,944**
NET COST	**$21,324**	**$17,060**	**$18,197**	**$13,841**	**$13,940**
Loans & Work-Study					
• Loan: Subsidized	$3,500	$3,500	$3,500	$3,500	$3,500
• Loan: Unsubsidized	$2,000	$2,000	$2,000	$2,000	$2,000
• Federal Work-Study	$3,000	$3,000	$3,000	$2,800	$3,000
• Other Loans	$0	$0	$0	$0	$0
Total Loans & Work-Study	**$8,500**	**$8,500**	**$8,500**	**$8,300**	**$8,500**
REMAINING BALANCE AFTER LOANS	**$12,824**	**$8,560**	**$9,697**	**$5,541**	**$5,440**

Information for Emily's award letters included in the table above (Figure 8.5) were estimated from the Net Price Calculator for each college and/or College Navigator, and are not based on award letters from each college – except for the one we received from Truman (Figure 8.4). The actual cost and financial aid amounts presented in the table will vary based on each college's own review process. The information above is for illustrative purposes only.

There may be a substantial gap of time between being admitted and receiving your award letter. While many students are excited to make their admission decisions as soon as they get an acceptance letter, we recommend waiting until all information is in and you can compare the financial aspects of each college and what they are offering. You have until May 1st, which is known as National College Decision Day, to decide which college to attend. Do your best not to let your excitement, or requests from colleges to place a deposit, rush you into deciding before you are ready.

CHAPTER 8: DECIDE

It will now be helpful for you to go back and review Chapter 4 before reviewing the case study, paying particular attention to the sections on institutional scholarships and financial aid. This will greatly help you understand financial information contained in your award letters.

Overall Fit

Since applying, Emily has put effort into learning as much as she can about each college. In addition to the new information about Financial Match detailed in the award letters, she has talked to admission officers, went on additional college visits – both in-person and virtual – spoken to academic counselors and tutors at the resource centers at each college – (e.g., writing centers and academic support services), explored career services and spoken to alumni who have gone on to graduate school in Psychology, and discussed what she was learning about each college she applied to with her family and college support network. She has been intentional about learning all she can and has organized the new information and reassessed each college on the 6 Keys of College Fit, as shown below.

1 This college has a **little** of what I want and need to be satisfied and successful

2 This college has **some** of what I want and need to be satisfied and successful

3 This college has **much** of what I want and need to be satisfied and successful

4 This college has **most** of what I want and need to be satisfied and successful

5 This college has **everything** I want and need to be satisfied and successful

17 or lower = Low Fit   **18–23= Moderate Fit**   **24–30 = High Fit**

Figure 8.6

Colleges	Student Outcomes	Academic Match	Personal Match	Career Match	Financial Match	Student Support Services	Total Score	Overall Fit
Stephens College	3	2	3	3	3	4	18	Moderate
University of Missouri-Columbia	4	4	3	4	5	4	24	High
University of Missouri-St Louis	2	1	2	3	5	3	16	Low
Truman State University	5	4	4	5	4	4	26	High
Missouri University of Science and Technology	5	5	4	4	5	4	27	High

As you can see by comparing Emily's rating table in this chapter against her rating table in the Apply chapter, some of her ratings have remained the same while others have markedly changed. The 3 High Fit colleges (University of Missouri-Columbia, Truman State University, Missouri University of Science and Technology) still remain very strong matches for Emily. Also, the Moderate Fit private college (Stephens College) is still ranked by Emily at that level. But, the remaining in-state public university (University of Missouri-St. Louis) has fallen from a Moderate Fit to a Low Fit. In doing additional exploration, Emily believed that other colleges she applied to could help her better achieve her academic and career goals.

Desirability

While Emily has worked hard at understanding how each college fits her needs on the 6 Keys of College Fit, which provides strong objective data, she needed to also consider for her own feelings, including her values (Activity 6.3) and her likes and dislikes on a wide range of areas, including, but not limited to, proximity to home, the overall feel of the campus, extracurricular activities, etc. According to a recent study (Higher Education Research Institute at UCLA), 71% of first-year college students report feeling homesick and 57% stated they felt isolated from campus life. Knowing this, Emily realizes the importance of using her own subjective thoughts as she understands this is the place she is wanting to learn and grow at for the next four years.

After reviewing her Overall Fit, she had to ask herself, "How desirable is it that I attend this college?"

To include the Desirability perspective, Emily rates each college using one of the following three Desirability categories:

Low Desirability: It is not really desirable to me to attend this college.
Moderate Desirability: It is desirable to me to attend this college.
High Desirability: It is very desirable to me to attend this college.

Figure 8.7

Colleges	Desirability Rating
Stephens College	High
University of Missouri-Columbia	Moderate
University of Missouri-St Louis	Low
Truman State University	High
Missouri University of Science and Technology	High

As you can see above (Figure 8.7), Emily rated the University of Missouri-St. Louis as Low Desirability because when she visited campus, it felt too close to home and the urban campus wasn't as appealing to her. She rated the University of Missouri-Columbia as Moderate Desirability because it felt too large both in terms of the number of students and physical size of the campus. Emily rated the remaining three colleges as High Desirability. At Stephens College, she really liked the mission-driven, all-women focus and small campus feel. At Truman State University, she liked the small liberal arts feel and more rural setting. At the Missouri University of Science and Technology, Emily felt good about the science and technology focus, the more rural campus setting, and the smaller Psychology program.

Connecting Fit and Desirability

An informed decision about which college to attend needs both the evidence-supported Overall Fit side and the emotion-based Desirability side to work together. To include these two critical perspectives, Emily assigns each college to the box in the table on the next page (Figure 8.8) that matches her Overall Fit rating from Figure 8.6 and Desirability rating from Figure 8.7.

Apply: Interpret Overall Fit and Desirability Ratings

By bringing her Overall Fit ratings together with her Desirability ratings, a hierarchy of choices becomes clearer for Emily. She has two colleges (Missouri University of Science and Technology and Truman State University) that are highly rated on both Overall Fit and Desirability. She also has 1 college (University of Missouri-Columbia) that is a High Fit on the 6 Keys and rated as Moderate on Desirability. Interestingly, Emily has one college (Stephens College) that is a Moderate Fit on the 6 Keys but is of High Desirability to her. As her college explorations continued, Emily found that the appeal of this mission-driven, private women's college grew stronger and stronger. But, she came to more clearly see that she has 3 colleges that are a much stronger Overall Fit for her. And lastly, the University of Missouri-St. Louis, which fell in her estimations of Overall Fit, and was rated as Low in Desirability.

CHAPTER 8: DECIDE

Figure 8.8

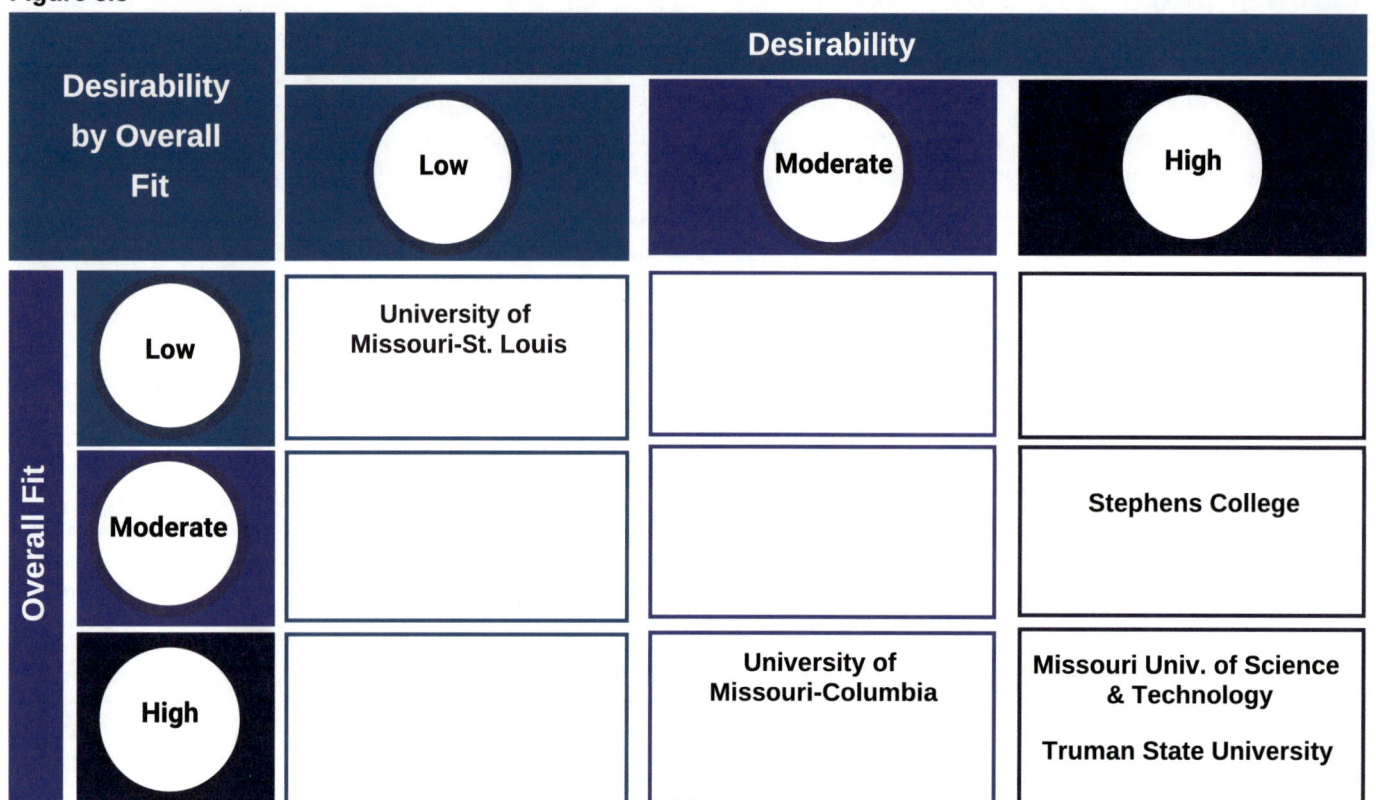

	Desirability		
Desirability by Overall Fit	Low	Moderate	High
Overall Fit — Low	University of Missouri-St. Louis		
Overall Fit — Moderate			Stephens College
Overall Fit — High		University of Missouri-Columbia	Missouri Univ. of Science & Technology Truman State University

Analyze: Explain reasons for and against choosing each college, and arrange colleges in order of preference

With the Overall Fit by Desirability table completed, Emily selects her top choices. She feels that she has four good choices – University of Missouri-Columbia, Truman State University, Stephens College, and Missouri University of Science and Technology. She then writes out the most important pros and cons related to her decision about whether or not to attend each college. Writing out these reasons will help Emily accomplish two things: analyze her best options, and prepare her to discuss her reasoning with her family and college support network.

Figure 8.9

Stephens College	This mission-driven, all-women college is very appealing, and grew in desirability the more I learned about it. However, there are other colleges that fit me better in terms of Student Outcomes, Academic Match, what I want to do for a career, and how much it costs. I found myself liking the larger universities more, where they had better student outcomes, appealing academic programs, and pathways to what I want to do after graduating from college.
University of Missouri-Columbia	I could see myself being successful and satisfied at this college as it does fit me to some extent. However, this may be too big of a college for me, and I feel that I may be in a better position to link my interests in science and technology to possible careers in psychology by attending one of the other colleges. I don't think I would be able to play varsity-level soccer here.

Truman State University	I liked how Truman felt very comfortable the minute I walked on campus. It is known as a good liberal arts college, and has good student outcomes. There is a large Research and Experimental Psychology major, which if combined with the Cognitive Science minor would fulfill what I am looking for. After talking with the soccer coach, I feel I would have a reasonably good chance of earning a spot on the women's soccer team.
Missouri University of Science and Technology	I liked how this campus felt, as well as the dorm options available. It has a good reputation for science and technology education. While the Psychology program is relatively small, the combined minor in Computer Science, Mathematics and Biology is very intriguing to me. I feel the summer term admissions with the additional advisors could really benefit me, and I have a good chance at playing on the women's soccer team.

Emily's Decision Tree

After writing out and analyzing her reasons, Emily then uses the decision tree below to prioritize and organize her preferences.

Figure 8.10

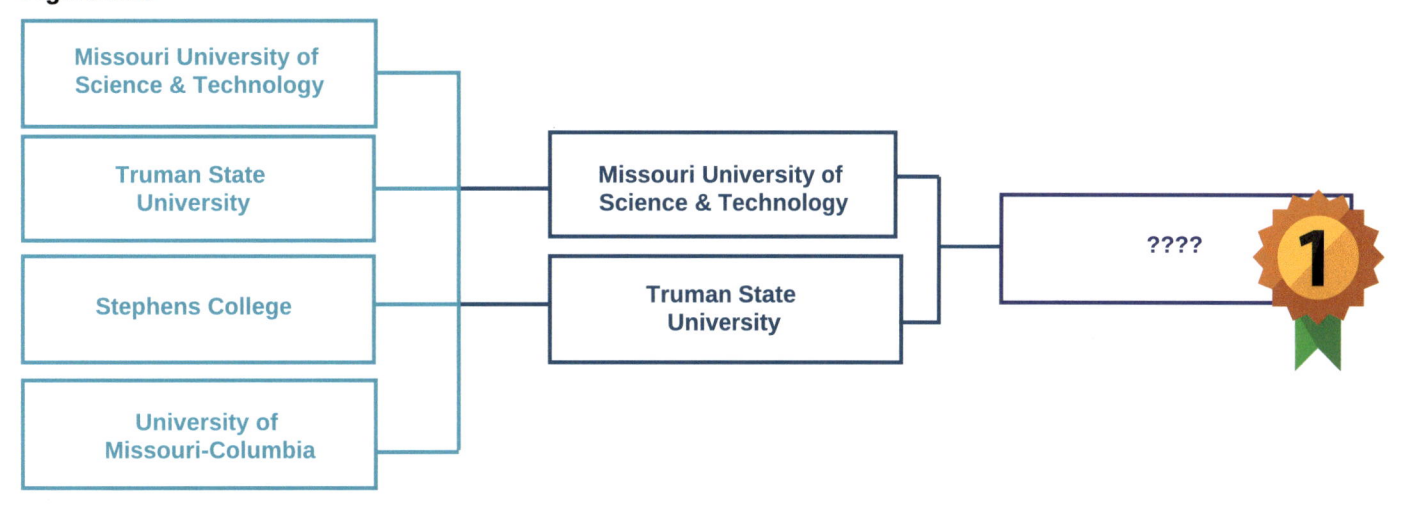

On the left of the decision tree above are the four colleges Emily considers to be her best options. By bringing her Overall Fit ratings together with her Desirability ratings and analyzing her reasons, a hierarchy of choices becomes clear for Emily and she is able to narrow those four choices down to two – Missouri University of Science and Technology and Truman State University. She feels that these two colleges have the best combination of Fit, Desirability, and reasons to attend. Both are colleges she would be happy to attend, but she is unsure at this point about which one of her top 2 colleges she should choose.

Evaluate: Consider feedback from family and your College Support Network, and then make your final decision

It is important now for Emily to get feedback from her family and College Support Network. She shares with them her reasoning and the decision tree, listening carefully to their reactions and feedback. She asks them clarifying questions to better understand their points of view.

Emily's College Support Network compliments her for her diligent work, as it shows she has become very informed about each college. Because she has developed a strong College Support Network, she is eager to hear their thoughts on each college. Emily writes down their thoughts (Figure 8.11) so she will remember them when making her final decision.

CHAPTER 8: DECIDE

Figure 8.11

College Support Network Thoughts

- Her coach was excited about her possibly staying in soccer at both Truman and the Missouri University of Science and Technology, as she has excelled as a player and leader on her high school team.
- Her parents are a little concerned about the distance to Truman and how that could impact their attending parent events, visiting, and providing transportation.
- Her family thought the costs of her top choices were reasonable for her family to manage without using substantial loans.
- Her school counselor and the director of the National Association of Mental Illness, where she volunteers, thought the liberal arts nature of Truman, good graduate school placement, and the Cognitive Science minor would nicely fit her career goals.

Emily's Final Decision

It is now time for Emily to decide. We place that decision in your capable hands. Which of her two top choices do you think she should choose and why? Write your answer and reasoning in the space provided below.

Step 3: Make Your Final Decision

Now is your turn to make an informed college decision.

Remember: Recall what you have learned so far (You, Academic, Career, and Money Factors; 8 Strengths; LEADS) and recognize and organize important information from admission and award letters

Before receiving your acceptance and award letters, you should review not only the financial aid information in Chapter 4, but also remember all of what you have learned in Section 1 and Section 2 of this book. When your letters do arrive, the first thing you should do is read them carefully and thoroughly. Make sure you know deadlines for each college and any other important information you may need to know. Award letters vary between colleges, so it is incumbent on you to fully understand what is in each of them and to ask questions if you don't. Carefully review each letter. After doing this, be quite sure that you understand what is required of you.

Understand: Compare financial aid award letters, revisit 6 Keys of College Fit, and make Desirability judgments

Once you have received your award letters, you can create the comparison table below to more easily evaluate the financial information colleges have provided to you. While not all the terminology will be exactly the same, make sure you are clear on what all the costs are and any grant and scholarship money they may be offering. Pay particular attention to loans you will have to pay back.

It can sometimes be difficult to understand exactly how much attending a college will cost you from the information provided to you on an award letter. For example, loans and work-study are often reported under the heading of "Self-Help Aid" and it is not always clear that the loans need to be repaid, or that work-study aid offered will be paid directly to you and not deducted from your bill. This is why we have organized the table below in the manner we have, to help you focus on the net cost – the actual amount of money it will cost you to attend that year.

Your financial aid award letter is based on your family's finances as reported for the prior tax year. Between the time that information was submitted and when you attend college, your financial status could change drastically by, for example, the death of parent/guardian, layoffs, divorce, illness, or deportation. If your family's financial status has changed in a way that makes paying for college more difficult, you can appeal your financial aid award at the college you will attend. Typically, there is a form you complete to request a review, and you are asked to send supporting documentation. Visit the college's financial aid website for more information.

Activity 8.1: Award Letter Comparison

Once you have received your financial aid award letters from your accepted colleges, use the chart below to compare their aid offers. Visit www.collegeunmazed.com/downloads for an Excel sheet you can complete for more colleges.

COLLEGE NAME						
Cost of Attendance						
• Tuition & Fees						
• Room & Board						
• Books & Supplies						
• Travel & Other Expenses						
TOTAL COST OF ATTENDANCE						
Gift Aid						
• Institution Grants & Scholarships						
• Federal Grants						
• State Grants						
• Other Grants & Scholarships						
Total Gift Aid						
NET COST						
Loans & Work Study						
• Loan: Subsidized						
• Loan: Unsubsidized						
• Federal Work-Study						
• Other Loans						
Total Loans & Work-Study						
REMAINING BALANCE AFTER LOANS						

CHAPTER 8: DECIDE

Overall Fit

After applying, you should put effort into learning as much as you possibly can about each of your colleges. In addition to the new information about Financial Match detailed in your award letters, you can talk to admission officers, go on additional in-person and virtual college visits, speak to academic counselors and tutors at the resource centers at these colleges (e.g., writing centers and academic support services, career services, counseling center), speak to alumni, and discuss what you have learned about each college you applied to with your family and College Support Network.

Activity 8.2: Reassessing the 6 Keys of College Fit

Now it is time to reassess the 6 Keys of College Fit for each of the colleges where you have been accepted. With the additional information you now have about each college from your hard work in researching, visiting, and engaging with the college, complete the chart below to see if your Overall Fit rating has changed from the Explore chapter. For example, your Financial Match ratings may change now that you have specific information from award letters, or you were admitted through an alternative program. As Emily did, list each college you have applied to in the table below. Rate each college for how well they match you on the 6 Keys, and then recalculate each college's Total Score and determine Overall Fit. If you do this in the CDO, the calculations are done for you.

1 This college has a **little** of what I want and need to be satisfied and successful

2 This college has **some** of what I want and need to be satisfied and successful

3 This college has **much** of what I want and need to be satisfied and successful

4 This college has **most** of what I want and need to be satisfied and successful

5 This college has **everything** I want and need to be satisfied and successful

17 or lower = Low Fit   **18–23 = Moderate Fit**   **24–30 = High Fit**

Colleges	Student Outcomes	Academic Match	Personal Match	Career Match	Financial Match	Student Support Services	Total Score	Overall Fit

As we mentioned in the Explore chapter, some Keys may have become much more important to you than others. For example, after receiving your award letters and more fully understanding the actual cost to attend each college, you realize that some colleges that fit you well in other areas are not a good Financial Match. Financial Match may now be an overriding priority for you and your family. If one of the 6 Keys has become a dominating priority, you can change the Overall Fit rating to reflect your situation. For example, if your total score for a college is in the High Fit range, you can lower the Overall Fit rating to Moderate or Low based on your compelling priorities. Likewise, a Low Fit college might change to a Moderate or High Fit college if your priorities warrant such an improvement.

COLLEGE UNMAZED

Desirability

Up to this point, you have worked your way through a decision-making process that is heavily fact and evidence-based. Now is the time for you to listen to your feelings about which colleges are most desirable to you. Which of the colleges that you have been accepted into do you feel really good about attending? For example, upon visiting a college many people report having a feeling they describe as just knowing that "This is the right college for me!" There are many different reasons people may experience that feeling – the campus setting, students and faculty, diversity of students, campus activities, and living arrangements just to name a few. Now that you have rated the objective, factual fit between yourself and each college that has accepted you, it is time for you to rate how desirable and acceptable each college is to you.

Activity 8.3: Rate Desirability

Rate the Desirability of each college to you as Low, Moderate, or High.

Low Desirability: It is not really desirable to me to attend this college.

Moderate Desirability: It is desirable to me to attend this college.

High Desirability: It is very desirable to me to attend this college.

Colleges	Desirability Rating

Apply: Interpret Overall Fit and Desirability ratings

Activity 8.4: Combine Overall Fit and Desirability for Best Options

An informed decision about which college to attend needs both the evidence-supported Overall Fit side and the emotion-based Desirability side to work together. To merge these two critical perspectives, assign each college to the box in the table below that matches your Overall Fit rating from Activity 8.2 and Desirability rating from Activity 8.3. By bringing your Overall Fit ratings together with your Desirability ratings, a hierarchy of choices will become clearer for you.

Overall Fit by Desirability	Desirability: Low	Desirability: Moderate	Desirability: High
Overall Fit: Low			
Overall Fit: Moderate			
Overall Fit: High			

CHAPTER 8: DECIDE

Bringing your Overall Fit and Desirability ratings together, as you did in the table above, will help you identify your top choices. We recommend you select your top four choices based on Overall Fit and Desirability. While we recommend you narrow your options to no more than four at this point, you may have more or less than four given your individual circumstances – and that is OK! For example, if you were accepted into your dream college, you may wonder why you need to consider other colleges at all. The reason you should consider at least one other college in addition to your dream college is to ensure you fully understand how your preferred college compares to other choices you have. As well, if you get to this point and have more than 4 top choices, that is OK – you do not need to rule them out at this point. However, the tasks that follow will be easier for you if you can prioritize and narrow your options now. If you only have 1 viable option at this point, it is still important that you complete the remaining activities to make your choice to attend that college an informed decision.

Analyze: Explain reasons for and against choosing each college, and arrange colleges in order of preference

Activity 8.5: Rank Colleges in Order of Preference and Explain Reasons

With the Overall Fit by Desirability table completed, it is now time for you to explain your reasons and prioritize your college options. First, write out the most important pros and cons related to your decision about whether or not to attend each college. Writing out these reasons in the boxes below will help you accomplish two things: analyze your best options and prepare you to discuss your reasoning with your family and college support network. We have provided space below for you to do this for 5 colleges; you may need more or less space depending on your personal situation.

College	Pros	Cons

Activity 8.6: Your Decision Tree

After writing out and analyzing your reasons, use the decision tree below to prioritize and organize your preferences, and make your initial decision. Start with your top 4 colleges and write their names in the boxes on the far left of the decision tree. Then, pick your top 2 choices. And, then if you can, make a tentative selection of your top choice. You will be able to confirm or change your decision in the next section after getting feedback from your family and College Support Network.

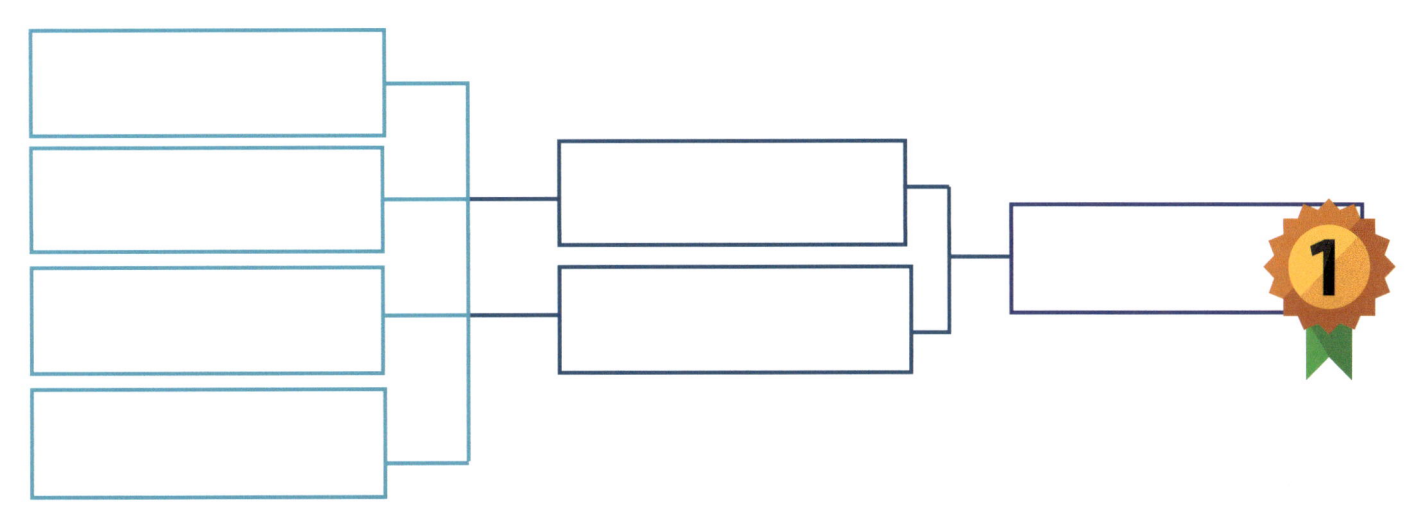

Evaluate: Consider feedback from family and your College Support Network and then make Final Decision

Activity 8.7: Discuss Reasoning and Decision Tree with Your College Support Network

It is important now for you to get feedback from your family and college support network. Share with them your reasoning and decision tree, listen carefully to their reactions and feedback. Ask them clarifying questions to better understand their points of view. Share with your College Support Network your reasons and decision tree for your top choices. Use the space below to write down their thoughts and reactions.

College Support Network

In general, you are ready to make a final decision if you have at least one college choice that is a reasonable Overall Fit and holds at least some Desirability for you. Similar to Emily, you may have two or more colleges that are all good fits where you could be academically successful. While it may feel stressful to not have a clear choice, it shows your hard work and perseverance in choosing great colleges that you would be successful at. The fact is that you can be successful and satisfied at many different colleges.

CHAPTER 8: DECIDE

If you have gotten to this point and, unfortunately, do not have such a choice, you should 100 percent not give up. You have options. Everyone does not have to go to college right after high school. Low college graduation rates are due to many factors, one of which is that many young people are not ready to commit themselves right out of high school to do what it will take to graduate from college. Deciding to not attend college at this particular moment isn't a bad thing, even though you may be hearing a different message. You may take a "Gap Year" where you can wait a year and re-apply, making sure you reflect on what you have learned to better position yourself for next year's admissions process. You can get a job and save money. You can enroll in classes as a non-matriculated student, and demonstrate your ability and develop your skills, talents, and interests. You can serve in the military and earn substantial money for college. It is better for you to go to college when you are academically and personally ready to succeed.

Make Your Final Decision

Congratulations! You have used the LEADS college decision-making strategy to determine what college you will attend! Please write it down here:

Chapter Summary

Again, congratulations! You have completed the LEADS process and made an informed decision. We would like to compliment you on the hard work you and your family have put into this process. In this chapter, you have followed steps that allowed you to use higher order thinking skills to make this decision. You *Remembered* what you learned throughout this book and recognized important information from your award Letters. You *Understood* the financial offers made to you, and rated the Fit and Desirability of each college. You *Applied* the Overall Fit and Desirability ratings by creating a 3 x3 table to help you interpret these ratings. You *Analyzed* reasons for and against attending each college, organized colleges in order of preference, and explained your reasoning to your family and College Support Network. You *Evaluated* the feedback you received from your family and College Support Network, and then made your final decision. This was an intentional, deliberate, self-directed journey that you should feel very proud of. This is the kind of determined effort, engagement, and responsibility taking that will greatly help you to be successful in college and your future career. In the next chapter, Succeed, you will *Create* a College Success Plan to help you make a successful transition into college.

At-Home Discussion

Now is the time for you and your family to prepare for what needs to happen next. You should speak to your family and College Support Network, including your school counselor, about your final decision and what steps to take next – e.g., submitting a final high school transcript, paying the housing deposit, and providing residency documents. You will also want to talk with your family and determine a more detailed budget – also discussed in the next chapter. Finally, enjoy the moment and thank the people who have helped you through the maze that is the college-choice process!

Review the High School Planning Checklist in Resources on page 136. What are some next action steps that you need to take in the next month, six months, and year?

CHAPTER 9
Succeed

Creating Financial, Academic & Social Plans

You Factor • **Academic Factor** • **Career Factor** • **Money Factor** • **Developing a List** • **Exploring Colleges** • **Applying to Colleges** • **Deciding on a College** • **Succeeding in College**

You have now made an informed decision about which college to attend, great work! By putting in the effort and self-direction needed to go through this book you have put a lot of yourself into making a good decision. Make sure you and your family take some time to celebrate this genuine accomplishment. But not too much time, because the final step in the LEADS process begins right now - to Succeed at the college you have chosen! You have been intentional and deliberate in following a higher-order thinking sequence. You have *Remembered*, *Understood*, *Applied*, *Analyzed*, and then *Evaluated* information critical to the heart of the decision you have just made about which college to attend.

It is now time to take everything you have learned and accomplished and climb up to the top level of higher-order thinking – *Create*. Many scholars believe that the apex of high-order thinking is when a learner is able to use everything they have been working on to create something new. They compose, construct, and invent new ways of expressing themselves and solving difficult problems. In this chapter, you will organize and creatively craft all you have worked through to make your informed decision into a College Success Plan. This multilayered approach will include specific strategies for dealing with the financial, academic, and social challenges you will need to navigate to be satisfied and successful in college.

College debt without a degree is a very bad deal. As we have pointed out earlier in this book, almost 6 out of every 10 students who enroll in a 4-year college in the United States do not graduate in 4 years. Six-year graduation rates aren't much better – only 6 out of every 10 students who enroll in a 4-year college graduate in 6 years. We want you to be one of the 4 out of every 10 students who graduate in 4 years. The financial savings alone of graduating in 4 years are substantial – the cost of extra tuition plus lost wages is estimated to be at least $50,000 a year! Further, far too many high school seniors who get accepted into a college for the upcoming fall semester don't follow through and enroll, a phenomenon known as "summer melt". Summer melt affects every high school, and estimates suggest that anywhere from 10–40 percent of graduating seniors who are accepted to college don't show up on a college campus that fall.

Three major challenges need to be addressed to make it more likely that you will be successful and satisfied in college. You have to deal effectively with money issues, negotiate the academic demands of doing college-level work, and, figure out how you will manage the social environment and opportunities available to you at college. Successfully handling your finances, and building strong academic and social connections between yourself and your college will increase your feelings of comfort and belonging to your college. When you feel at home, that you belong, that things are working out for you, then you will be less anxious and much more confident about your chances of success in college. This positive mindset puts you in a position where you can do your best academic work and be your best person. This chapter will help you develop a plan for college success to help you effectively handle these financial, academic, and social challenges.

CHAPTER 9: SUCCEED

Colleges have recognized the importance of helping their students build strong networks of academic and social integration to increase student success and satisfaction. It is truly impressive how colleges have evolved over time to offer an abundance of well-designed resources, support programs, and intentionally constructed recreational and social activities. College administrators know the value of these assets in promoting the success of their students. It is your job to take charge of these opportunities and thoughtfully select those programs, services, and activities that will be of most benefit to you. For example, summer support and enrichment programs (often called bridge programs) lead to better outcomes, such as making it more likely freshmen will return as sophomores. This increases the college's retention rates, something that is in everyone's best interest. This is a tremendous opportunity being made available to you. All that your college has to offer you is being laid out in front of you. Now, is the time to pick and choose which opportunities are in your best interest to take advantage of.

You have now made a good college decision that fits you and your family. To realize your goals to attend and graduate from this college, you should be just as planful and intentional with your approach to starting college as you have been with applying to and choosing a college to attend. This chapter will show you how to do just that. First, we will discuss financial integration, academic integration, and social integration, and then get you started building strong connections with your college. We will show you how to build a College Success Plan through a case study. Then, you will create your own. And lastly, we will briefly summarize for you the skills you have developed by completing the tasks in this book, and how these skills are transferable to your educational and career future.

Your Succeed Steps

1. Establish Financial, Academic, and Social Strategies to Succeed in College. You will learn about financial, academic, and social integration in college and how to begin building strong connections in each of these three areas with your college.

2. Learn about College Success Plans. Learn how to construct an effective plan through the aid of a case study.

3. Develop Your Own College Success Plan. Design a College Success Plan fit and tailored to the college you will attend that includes financial, academic, and social strategies.

4. Reflect on What You Have Accomplished. Reflect on all you have achieved by completing the LEADS process and working through this book.

Step 1: Establish Financial, Academic, and Social Strategies to Succeed in College

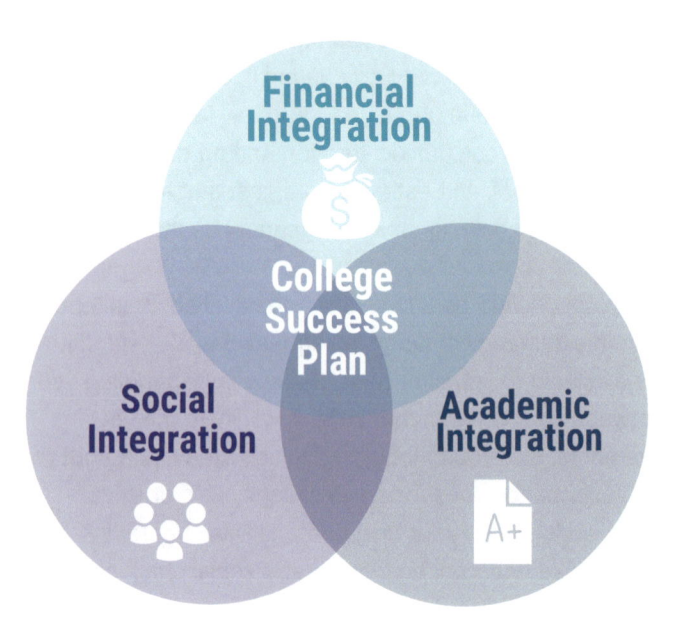

There are three critical components to an effective College Success Plan – Financial, Academic, and Social Integration.

Financial, academic, and social integration overlap and interact to influence critical college outcomes. These three challenges work together to determine, to a great extent, whether or not you will be successful and satisfied with the college you will be attending. For example, they influence whether or not you will return as a sophomore to the college, and whether or not you will persist to graduation and earn your degree. These are very influential sources of support that promote and enhance student well-being and achievement. It is to your advantage to make allies out of these three factors, to get them working for you to promote your success and satisfaction in college.

Financial Integration

One of the biggest challenges to students and families is managing their finances to deal with debt as it accumulates from one year to the next. Students who are the first in their families to attend college and students from lower-income backgrounds are less likely to graduate from college. One of the reasons for not persisting to graduation is that the cost of college becomes unmanageable – for example, a parent loses their job, the cost of attending the college increases, or the cost of each additional year depletes family resources. Having a plan for managing your finances for the first year through graduation will help you be resilient to financial challenges as they arise.

Students and their families should ask and answer questions such as:

- How and when to appeal a financial aid award?
- What will my total loan debt be, and what would my monthly payments be? (See https://studentaid.gov/loan-simulator/)
- For private loans, what is the interest rate, does it vary, and when does repayment start?
- How do I maintain eligibility for my grants and scholarships for four years?
- What will I use my work-study money for?
- What financial aid forms need to be completed each year aside from the FAFSA (e.g., CSS profile)?
- What additional funding opportunities are available at my college (e.g., paid internships, research assistantships)?
- Who should I connect with at the financial aid office each year, and how do I contact them?
- Does the state I live in have a non-profit higher education finance organization, and if so, how might that help me? (See https://www.efc.org/page/efc_member_map to check)

Academic Integration

Researchers have clearly established the importance of academic and social integration to student success and satisfaction in college. Academic integration focuses on whether or not you are meaningfully connected to the intellectual life of the college you are attending.

- Are you doing well in your classes?
- Do you feel connected to faculty and staff?
- Do you find your studies engaging, relevant, and of practical value to your present life and future career possibilities?
- Is your major working out for you?

Social Integration

Social integration focuses on whether or not you feel a sense of belonging and comfort with your campus culture, climate, environment, and relationships outside of the classroom.

- Do you feel a sense of psychological comfort with the culture, climate, and relationships available at your college?
- Do you feel some sense of common cause with other students?
- Have you developed meaningful friendships and relationships important to you?
- Do you feel secure and safe?
- Do you feel accepted into groups of other students with shared affinity in values and interests?

Step 2: Learn about College Success Plans (Case Study)

Let's use the case study of Emily to show how you can get started making financial, academic, and social Integration work on your behalf. In our view, Emily has three very good choices (Truman State University, Missouri University of Science and Technology, and the University of Missouri-Columbia). Each of these colleges can be the means by which she gets what she wants from college. Her personal desires elevated two of these colleges (Truman and Missouri University of Science and Technology), but all three colleges are a good fit for her.

Let's assume Emily chose to attend Truman State University. What would she do next? How would she begin to build financial, academic, and social integration into an advantage for her at this specific college? First off, in addition to the materials she has likely received from Truman, Emily should go directly to her college's website and learn all she can about what admitted students need to do before their classes start in the fall (e.g., https://www.truman.edu/admitted-students). Most colleges will have the information you and your family need organized and available to you on a website very similar to this. Critical information, like when deposits and payments are due, and the next steps to take are laid out for you. Take the time to explore and learn all you can about your college. Topics covered on this page of Truman's website include: visiting campus, housing, FAFSA, attending a summer orientation, returning medical forms, sending in your final transcripts, preparing for move-in day, and Truman Week, which helps all new students make a smooth transition from high school to college.

Emily should pay particular attention to summer orientation, Truman Week, and move-in day. There are 9 orientations offered in the summer and Emily must attend one. In-person and virtual options are both offered. At the orientation, she will choose her classes for the fall semester with the help of advisors and faculty in her intended major, meet other students, and collect additional information both she and her parents need. There are options she can select to personalize her schedule and tailor Truman Week to better meet her needs and interests. And, move-in day lays out all the detailed information Emily and her family should know as she moves into her room on campus – e.g., COVID vaccination rules and dates and times for arrival.

Emily's College Success Plan is summarized in the tables below and on the next page.

FINANCIAL PLAN

Summer	School Year
Part-time job: Increase hours to build up savings	Part-time job: Pick up shifts, if possible, when on break from college
Loans: Determine amounts to accept from award letter	Loans: Research private loans in case they are needed for year 2
Work-Study: Apply for work-study	Work-Study: Build work-study hours into a weekly schedule, save half for year 2, apply for year 2
Scholarships: Complete requirements to ensure you meet and maintain eligibility	Scholarships: Maintain eligibility for full scholarships (e.g., GPA above 3.25)
FAFSA: Be prepared to respond if selected for verification of FAFSA information	FAFSA: Reapply for financial aid for year 2 by completing the FAFSA
Budget: Emily and her family create a budget that includes personal expenses	Budget: Follows budget, and modifies as needed

There are two main issues Emily needs to attend to related to finances – maintaining eligibility for her awarded financial aid package, and how she will use her work-study money. She was awarded financial aid from the federal government (Pell Grant, subsidized and unsubsidized loans), the state of Missouri (Access Missouri grant), and Truman (TruMerit and TruOpportunity scholarships). Each of these aid sources has different requirements to maintain eligibility.

- **Federal Loans & Pell Grants:** To keep her federal loans and the Pell Grant, Emily needs to submit a FAFSA each year and maintain what is called *satisfactory academic progress*, which can vary from college to college. At Truman, *satisfactory academic progress* requires Emily to maintain full-time student status and earn above a 1.7 GPA the first 4 semesters (2.0 thereafter).
- **Access Missouri Grant:** The Access Missouri grant requires Emily to earn at least a 2.5 GPA, and is available for up to 10 semesters.
- **Institutional Scholarships:** The institutional scholarships (TruMerit and TruOpportunity) have more stringent requirements. Emily needs to earn at least a 3.25 GPA to maintain 100% of her funding from these two scholarships. If she gets between a 3.0 to 3.24 GPA, her funding will be reduced to 70% to 90% of the original scholarship amount – and she will lose these scholarships entirely if her GPA falls below 3.0. Beginning in her third semester, she will need to complete 55 hours of "scholarship renewal service" each semester – she is hoping to do research with a faculty member in her major to complete her hours. Emily can decide to not do the service requirement, but her scholarships will be cut in half.

Emily and her parents both realized they needed to discuss how work-study money would be used. At first, Emily was planning on using her work-study funding for personal expenses such as recreational and social activities. Her parents, on the other hand, saw the work-study money going towards college expenses (room and board, and tuition) as it was specified in the financial aid award letter. They realize that if the work-study money is not used in this way, then the family will need to find additional funds to cover their expenses. Also, they learn that work-study money is subject to state and federal taxes. Emily and her parents discussed this and compromised. Emily will put half of the money she earns from work-study into a savings account and keep the remaining half for her own personal expenses. Her parents agree to cover the additional $1,400 needed to attend Truman in the first year. The family anticipates needing to take out private loans for year 2. Emily's savings and additional income she earns from part-time work over semester breaks and the summer will be used to keep these additional loan amounts as low as possible.

Emily and her family should also understand that the financial aid award letter provided estimates only. Oftentimes costs for personal and textbook expenses can vary greatly. Emily can explore other ways to reduce these costs such as purchasing used or digital copies of textbooks, limiting eating off-campus, or using public transportation. Choices like these can make a significant impact on a college student's and family's budget.

ACADEMIC PLAN

Summer	School Year
Advisor: Major in Psychology and Minor in Cognitive Science; develop a 4-year plan of study	Advisor: Meet with an academic advisor to continue the discussion of major and minor; review and revise 4-year plan of study
Courses: Enroll in fall semester classes	Courses: Enroll in spring semester classes
Learning Resources: Learn about all support services and resources available	Learning Resources: Take advantage of: academic advising, career center, Mathematics support, Office of Student Research and the Student Research Conference, and the writing center.
Psychology Club: Contact student representative and faculty advisor; join	Psychology Club: Attend meetings and participate in club activities

CHAPTER 9: SUCCEED

The summer is a critical time for newly admitted students. Emily is planning to begin talking to her advisor and Psychology faculty during summer orientation to learn all she can about this major and gather information on a possible minor in Cognitive Science. This will help her to continue nurturing her developing interests in science. She will then be more informed about which classes to enroll in. She knows it is to her advantage to learn all she can about the academic resource programs available to her (like most good colleges, Truman has many from diversity, to the career center, to disability services). She will need to get in touch with the student and faculty advisors of the Psychology Club to join.

As the academic year begins, Emily will meet with her academic advisor to continue the discussion about her major and possible minor. She will continue to develop and revise her 4-year plan of study and enroll in classes for spring semester. There are five learning resource programs and support services that she has decided to take advantage of. In particular, she is intrigued with the opportunities for students to get involved in research and present at the Student Research Conference. Given her interest in pursuing graduate study in Psychology, she is aware of how helpful this opportunity would be to her growth and development. Also, the writing center offers a wide range of support services that will help her become the best writer she can be. Writing is a skill she knows will be of great value to her, regardless of what she decides to do with her Psychology major after graduating. And, there is a special service to assist students with Mathematics. She knows her interests in science can only be enhanced if she establishes a strong foundation for herself in Mathematics. She will become an active member of the Psychology Club and fit her work-study hours into her weekly schedule.

SOCIAL PLAN

Summer	School Year
Truman Week Social Activities: Meet and make friends	Calendar Year Social Events: Participate and deepen relationships with peers and friends
Athletics: Contact soccer coach and fill out online questionnaire to be considered for the women's team; try out for the team	Athletics/Intramurals: Become a member of the women's soccer team; if this doesn't work out select Intramurals (individual and team sports) to stay physically fit and active across the academic year; take advantage of wellness programs and exercise classes; meet students with like interests
Residence Hall: Explore on-campus options and become an active participant in choosing college roommate	Residence Hall: Become an active member in residence hall governance and social activities; effectively manage relationship with college roommate
Family: Engage family in information gathering and discussions; get their feedback and insights	Family/Parent Day: Invite family to Family Day scheduled in early October of each school year at Truman, plan for regular contact with family and extended support network across the academic year

Emily will lean in this summer and be open to meeting new people and establishing new friendships. Truman Week will be a great place to begin building a network of peer friendships. She will complete and submit the required online questionnaire for joining the women's soccer team and try out, if invited. Emily will research her living options on campus and be an active participant in roommate selection. And finally, during the summer, Emily will make sure her family is engaged in discussions, gather the information they need, and be open to feedback from her College Support Network.

During the academic year, Emily will be intentional about participating in organized social events that are scheduled on her college's academic year calendar. She will be mindful of strengthening her relationships with peers and deepening friendship bonds important to her. If she is not successful in joining the women's soccer team, Emily will stay active and keep fit through intramural sports, recreational activities, and the health and wellness programs offered on campus. She knows that physical exercise will support her overall emotional balance and help her to do better in her classes. Time taken for physical activity is a good investment in aiding her academic and social development in college. Emily will become an active member of her residence hall community. And finally, Emily will not isolate herself from her family and support networks. Parent Day is called Family Day at Truman, and Emily intends to surround herself with the people that love and support her.

Step 3: Develop Your Own College Success Plan

Write out your financial, academic, and social plans using the space provided below, and discuss with your family and College Support Network to see if anything needs to be added or modified. Space is provided below each table for you to note whatever you find important in carrying out your College Success Plan.

As you do so, be sure to do a final review of the High School Planning Checklist in Resources on page 137. What are some next action steps that you need to take in the next month, six months, and year?

Activity 9.1: Your College Success Plan

FINANCIAL PLAN	
Summer	**School Year**

Notes:

CHAPTER 9: SUCCEED

ACADEMIC PLAN

Summer	School Year

Notes:

SOCIAL PLAN

Summer	School Year

Notes:

Step 4: Reflect on Accomplishments and Next Steps

In Section 1 of this book, you learned about factors that, when fully developed, prepare you for future educational and career success. You increased your chances for success and satisfaction in whatever educational and career pathways you choose to pursue by utilizing the 8 Strengths of College and Career Readiness (your You Factor), paying attention to the growth of your Academic Factor, getting direction from your Career Factor, and learning how to negotiate the Money Factor. These are lifelong skills. They will pay dividends to you as you persist to graduate from college and then pursue a career in a pathway that adds meaning and fulfillment to your life.

In Section 2 of this book, you learned how to make an informed decision about which college to attend. The LEADS process helped you to List possible options, Explore colleges in ways that let you narrow your choices, figure out which colleges you actually wanted to Apply to, and then Decide on the one college best for you. In this last chapter of the book, you have started to make the transition from a successful high school student to Succeed as a college student. If you have faithfully worked through this book, you have acquired tools to help you be successful as you move your life forward after high school.

The attitudes, knowledge, and skills you can learn from this book are really lifelong skills. By age 30, you are likely to have had between 8 to 10 different jobs. Across your working lifetime, you are also likely to change your occupation several times (e.g., change from being a teacher to a website developer). This means that you will likely need further education and training after you graduate from college. One of the things industrialized countries agree on is that they want their citizens to be lifelong learners. You can transfer what you have learned in this book to successfully deal with the major educational and career transitions and challenges you will face in college and in your working adult life. You will be called on to make many difficult decisions related to education and work throughout your life. The strategies you have learned in this book can be applied to these future transitions to help you make truly informed decisions.

In the world we are living in, chance events will present you with challenges and opportunities. The attitudes, knowledge, and skills you have learned in this book will help you embrace these as problems to be solved that can lead you to a better future. As the famous French chemist and microbiologist, Louis Pasteur said, "Chance favors only the prepared mind." You are now prepared and ready to take the next steps. Enjoy your successes!

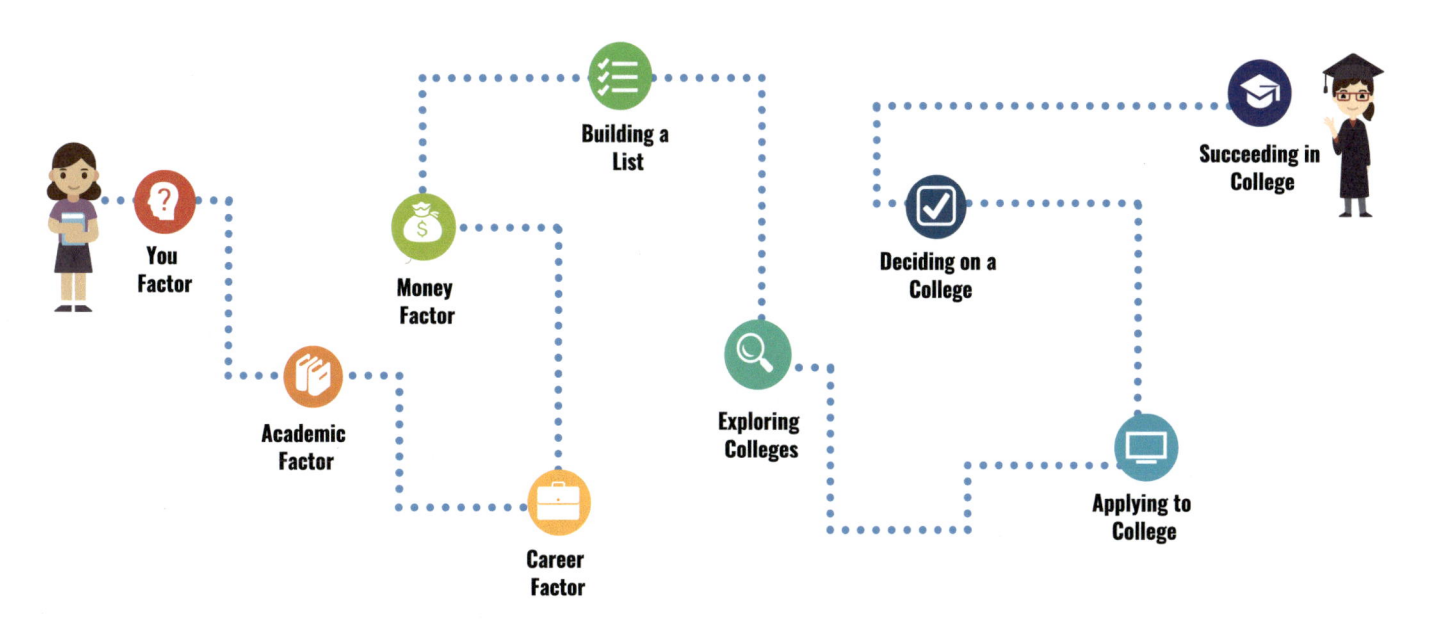

RESOURCES

College UnMazed High School Planning Checklist & Links

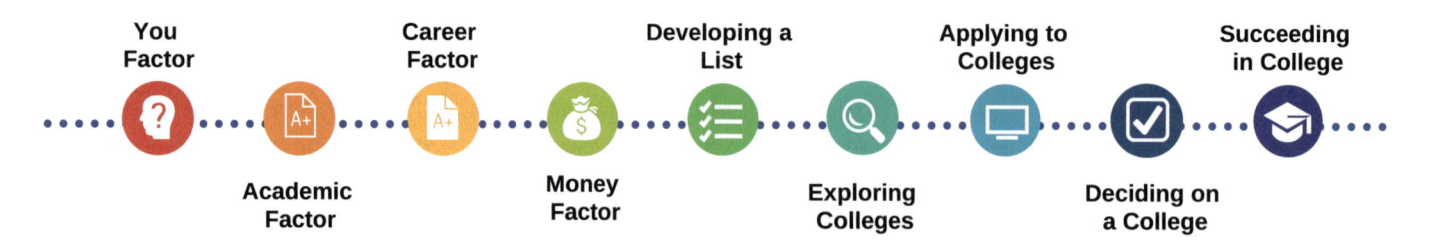

You Factor • Academic Factor • Career Factor • Money Factor • Developing a List • Exploring Colleges • Applying to Colleges • Deciding on a College • Succeeding in College

High School Planning Checklist for Success

The checklist that follows provides ideal times to work through the activities contained in this book so that you are college and career ready when it is your time to make an informed college decision. However, if you don't pick up this book until fall of your senior year, please do not think you are so far behind that you cannot catch up! You can work through this book at your own pace, at whatever point in the college-going process you happen to be at. Cross off each number as you progress through the High School Planning Checklist for Success.

9th–10th Grade

	Introduction: Section 1
1.	Talk to your family about how you want to work together with them across your high school years so you are ready for postsecondary education
2.	Discuss with your school counselor why it is in your best interest to further your education after high school
3.	Know the financial benefits of postsecondary education
4.	Understand that knowing who you are as a person, when combined with academic, career, and financial aid knowledge (Section 1 of this book) lays the foundation you need to make an informed college decision (Section 2 of this book)
	Chapter 1: You Factor
1.	Discuss with your school counselor the 4 Factors that help prepare you for college – the You Factor, Academic Factor, Career Factor, and Money Factor
2.	Understand and make a commitment to develop each of the 8 Strengths of College and Career Readiness – Agency, Positive Beliefs, Effective Goals, Knowing Yourself, Becoming a Successful Student, Character for Workplace Success, College Knowledge, and College Support Network
3.	Participate in activities that develop each of the 8 College and Career Readiness Strengths, give examples of at least 2 ways you have strengthened them through work experiences, community involvement, creative pursuits, major-specific activities, school clubs and activities, or leadership
4.	Describe how you are becoming a well-rounded and strength-focused "T"-shaped student
5.	Discuss with your family and College Support Network the ways you are developing your You Factor – your strengths and areas for improvement

9th–10th Grade

	Chapter 2: Academic Factor
1.	Discuss with at least one member of your College Support Network what the Academic Factor is and why it is so important for college and career readiness
2.	Understand the importance of academic coursework, grades, and standardized test scores in the college admissions process
3.	Know the importance of rigorous academic coursework for college admission
4.	Identify the different academic courses and programs available to you in high school, such as credit by-examination, dual enrollment, MOOCs, and industry certification
5.	Know what your grade point average is, how it is calculated in your school, and how some colleges recalculate and weight GPAs differently when deciding on which students to admit
6.	Identify the similarities and differences between the SAT and the ACT
7.	Plan out what standardized tests you will take across your high school years, as well as when you should register and take them
8.	Construct an Individualized Academic Plan (IAP) for your 4-years in high school
9.	Understand what role the 8 Strengths of the You Factor play in helping you develop your Academic Factor
10.	Discuss with family and your College Support Network the ways you are developing your Academic Factor – your strengths and areas for improvement
	Chapter 3: Career Factor
1.	Discuss with your school counselor what the Career Factor is and why it is important
2.	Understand what Career Pathways are
3.	Assess which Career Pathways, right now, best match your interests, abilities, and career values
4.	Critique how informed career decision-making focuses on those Career Pathways found at the intersection between self-knowledge and occupational knowledge
5.	Understand the role that educational attainment plays in Career Pathways and salaries
6.	Know the hierarchy of college degrees – from an Associate to a Doctoral Degree
	Chapter 4: Money Factor
1.	Discuss what the Money Factor is with your school counselor and why it is important
2.	Know what the FAFSA is, why it is important, and when and how to apply for it
3.	Understand what financial need is in relation to going to college
4.	Calculate the net price for 3 colleges you may be interested in, and compare to their listed cost of attendance
5.	Realize why it is that sometimes private colleges may actually be cheaper for you to attend than public colleges
6.	Understand what a 4-year plan to pay for college is and what you and your family will need to do to develop one
7.	Distinguish between federal, state, and local aid

RESOURCES

9th–10th Grade

	Chapter 4: Money Factor (Continued)
8.	Understand what subsidized, unsubsidized, and Direct PLUS federal student loans are
9.	Understand what Expected Family Contribution is
10.	Explain how you and your family will manage the costs of you going to college
11.	Use a Net Price Calculator to estimate the likely cost of attending a college you might be interested in
12.	Understand the different sources of gift aid
13.	Identify the different kinds and sources of scholarships you could apply for
14.	Explore how you can earn micro-scholarships for college while still in high school by participating in programs like Raise.Me
15.	Understand what work-study is
16.	Understand what role the 8 College and Career Readiness Strengths play in helping you develop your Money Factor
17.	Discuss with your family and College Support Network the ways in which you and your family are developing your Money Factor – your strengths and areas for improvement

11th Grade

	Introduction: Section 2, LEADS
1.	Describe to someone in your College Support Network what each step of the LEADS informed college decision making strategy is
2.	Understand what the 6 Keys of College Fit are and why each of the 6 Keys is important
3.	Know why it is important to evaluate each college you are interested in using each of the 6 Keys of College Fit
4.	Consider how the LEADS process and the 6 Keys of College Fit work together to help you make an informed college decision
5.	Discuss with family and your College Support Network what the LEADS process means for you and your family
	Chapter 5: List
1.	Use College Navigator to identify colleges (approximately 10 to 15) you may be interested in exploring in more depth
2.	Identify at least one other college exploration tool you can use in addition to the College Navigator
3.	Summarize those college attributes from the Academic Match, Career Match, and Personal Match Keys that you learned are important to you in developing your list of colleges
4.	Name the top 3 college attributes (e.g., distance from home, available majors) that you found to be the most important matches for you when including colleges on your List
5.	Talk to your school counselor about at least 3 of the 9 different college programs you might consider (e.g., honors, HBCU, 2+2 programs)
6.	Discuss with family and your College Support Network your list of colleges; highlight the pros and cons of each

11th Grade

	Chapter 6: Explore
1.	Complete and use the College Data Organizer (CDO) from www.collegeunmazed.com/downloads to more thoroughly explore each college on your list across all 6 Keys of College Fit
2.	Review websites of colleges you are interested in to learn about their support programs (e.g., tutoring, career services, counseling)
3.	Use the Common Data Set to better understand what college admission officers at the colleges on your list are looking for when they admit new students
4.	Understand what academic and nonacademic factors are in college admissions
5.	Make in-person and virtual college visits to explore colleges
6.	Speak to college admissions personnel at colleges you are interested in
7.	Reflect on your personal values for what you want in a college
8.	Identify approximately 8 to 12 colleges you value (the exact number varies depending on what your needs and personal circumstances are) and that match you on Keys important to you; make sure your List contains a mix of colleges in terms of your Chance of Admission

12th Grade (Summer and Fall)

	Chapter 7: Apply
1.	Explain how each college you are considering applying to can be more completely understood by seeing it from two different perspectives – Fit and Chance of Admission
2.	Explain what undermatching is to someone in your College Support Network and explore what that means for you
3.	Calculate Overall College Fit scores for each college you are considering and then assign each college to 1 of 3 categories – Low Fit, Moderate Fit, or High Fit
4.	Rank each college into 1 of 3 categories based on your estimated Chance of Admission into each college – High, Moderate, and Low chance of admission
5.	Complete the My Overall Fit by Chance of Admission table
6.	Use the My Overall Fit by Chance of Admission table to select the best combination of 5 to 8 colleges where you will apply
7.	Write out your reasons for why you will apply to each of the 5 to 8 colleges that remain on your List
8.	Discuss with family and your College Support Network each of the 5 to 8 colleges you are considering applying to; if after talking to them, you don't feel there are enough colleges that have Moderate or High Fit, a reasonable range of admission chances, or are lacking in colleges you personally value, then revisit prior chapters and identify additional colleges that do
9.	However, if your combination of 5 to 8 colleges meets these criteria then you are ready to develop and submit competitive and effective applications to each college on your final list
10.	Gather admission documents you need for your applications

RESOURCES

12th Grade (Summer and Fall)

	Chapter 7: Apply (Continued)
11.	Know the different application types – Common App, Coalition App, and institutional applications
12.	Know the different types of college admissions and their deadlines – early decision, early action, priority deadlines, regular decision, and rolling admissions
13.	Complete your College Application Organizer
14.	Complete your college résumé
15.	Write an effective college essay
16.	Obtain positive and influential letters of recommendations from key allies – e.g., teachers, school counselor, mentors
17.	Submit competitive and effective college applications
18.	Know what applications for financial aid need to be submitted every year – e.g., FAFSA for every college and the College Scholarship Service (CSS) for those colleges that require the CSS
19.	Discuss with your family and your College Support Network how your applications are progressing and ask for their help as you need it

12th Grade (Fall and Spring)

	Chapter 8: Decide
1.	Know different types of decisions colleges make when admitting students - admit, deny, waitlist, defer, and alternate admissions
2.	Explain acceptance and financial aid award letters to your family and at least 1 person in your College Support Network
3.	Compare financial aid award letters and interpret what the cost of attendance, net cost, and remaining balance owed after loans are for each college
4.	Revisit Overall College Fit ratings for each college you have been accepted into by considering new information you have learned from acceptance and award letters, as well as your continued exploration of colleges you have applied
5.	Rate the Desirability of each college you have been accepted into
6.	Complete the Overall Fit by Desirability table
7.	Using the Desirability by Overall Fit table, analyze and explain reasons for and against choosing each college as the college you will attend – arrange colleges in order of preference
8.	Complete the decision tree to identify your tentative top pick
9.	Share reasons for top choices and your decision tree with your family and College Support Network
10.	Evaluate your top choices by gathering and considering feedback from your family and College Support Network.
11.	Make your final decision on which college you will attend only after completing the first 5 steps of the higher-order thinking strategy outlined in Chapter 8 – Remember, Understand, Apply, Analyze, and Evaluate
12.	Discuss with your family and College Support Network next steps that need to be taken after you have committed to attend 1 specific college – e.g., submitting transcripts and signing and returning documents

12th Grade– Freshman Year of College (Summer and Fall)

	Chapter 9: Succeed
1.	Develop and begin implementing a College Success Plan that includes financial, academic and social integration
2.	Understand the costs of accumulating college debt
3.	Identify what summer melt is and how you will not succumb to it
4.	Learn everything you can about the college you are going to attend on their website – e.g., admissions information, deadlines, payment dates, choosing classes, student orientations, and unique learning opportunities
5.	Explain to family and your College Support Network what financial, academic, and social integration are and why they are important to your success and satisfaction in college
6.	Develop a set of questions that you and your family should be able to answer about financial, academic, and social Integration at the college you will attend. Ask these questions to your college's advisors and representatives.
7.	As part of your College Success Plan, list specific things you will do the summer before you enroll and during your freshman year at your college to successfully integrate financially into your college – e.g., apply for work-study and re-apply for FAFSA to get funding for your sophomore year in college, as soon as you can during your first semester in college
8.	As part of your College Success Plan, list specific things you will do the summer before you enroll and during your freshman year at your college to successfully integrate academically into your college – e.g., complete student orientation and take advantage of learning resources available to you, such as the writing center and the career center
9.	As part of your College Success Plan, list specific things you will do the summer before you enroll and during your freshman year at your college to successfully integrate socially into your college – e.g., make new friends by participating in social activities organized by your college and choosing recreational and athletic activities you will do to keep physically fit, such as intramural sports and clubs that interest you
10.	Reflect on all you have learned and accomplished by making an informed decision about which college to attend, and now starting to use a College Success Plan to improve your chances of being satisfied and successful in college
11.	Explain to your school counselor how the knowledge, skills, and attitudes you focused on in Section 1 of this book, e.g., the 8 Strengths of College and Career Readiness, have moved you forward to now become college and career ready
12.	Discuss with your family and your College Support Network how the higher-order thinking strategy embedded in the LEADS informed decision-making process can be used again and again when you are faced with making important educational and career decisions over the course of your lifetime
13.	Recognize how the LEADS process can help you take advantage of chance opportunities to promote your educational and career success

RESOURCES

Referenced Links and Resources

The referenced website links listed were active as of February 2022. Note that websites and links may change.

Page	Website Link
p. 4	www.collegeunmazed.com
p. 5	https://www.luminafoundation.org/stronger-nation/report/#/progress
p. 6	https://www.bls.gov/careeroutlook/2020/data-on-display/education-pays.htm
p. 13	www.collegeunmazed.com/downloads
p. 18	https://www.nacacnet.org/news--publications/publications/state-of-college-admission/
p. 20	https://ap.collegeboard.org/
p. 20	https://www.ibo.org/
p. 20	https://www.cambridgeinternational.org/
p. 20	https://clep.collegeboard.org/
p. 20	https://www.coursera.org/
p. 20	https://www.edx.org/
p. 20	https://www.khanacademy.org/
p. 20	https://www.futurelearn.com/
p. 20	https://www.kadenze.com/
p. 20	https://www.udacity.com/
p. 20	https://www.udemy.com/
p. 21	https://journals.sagepub.com/doi/full/10.3102/0013189X20902110
p. 22	https://www.act.org/content/act/en/products-and-services/the-act.html
p. 22	https://www.collegeboard.org/
p. 23	https://www.khanacademy.org/
p. 29	https://nces.ed.gov/programs/digest/d20/tables/dt20_326.10.asp
p. 30	https://completecollege.org/article/data-snapshot-on-time-graduation-and-the-credits-needed-to-get-there/
p. 30	https://careertech.org/career-clusters
p. 32	https://www.onetonline.org/find/descriptor/browse/Interests/
p. 37	https://www.onetonline.org/find/career
p. 43	https://www.salliemae.com/about/leading-research/how-america-pays-for-college/
p. 45	https://educationdata.org/average-cost-of-college
p. 45	https://collegecost.ed.gov/net-price
p. 48	https://studentaid.gov/help/fafsa-worksheet
p. 48	https://bigfuture.collegeboard.org/pay-for-college/calculate-your-cost/expected-family-contribution
p. 48	https://www.fastweb.com/
p. 48	https://www.scholarships.com/
p. 48	https://www.cappex.com/
p. 49	https://www.raise.me/home
p. 52	https://nces.ed.gov/collegenavigator/
p. 53	https://bigfuture.collegeboard.org/pay-for-college/paying-your-share/expected-family-contribution-calculator
p. 53	https://smartasset.com/student-loans/student-loan-calculator
p. 59	https://collegenavigator.gov/
p. 60	https://bigfuture.collegeboard.org/
p. 60	https://www.cappex.com

Resource Links

Page	Website Link
p. 60	https://www.cappex.com/greenlight/landing
p. 60	https://www.niche.com/
p. 60	https://www.princetonreview.com/college-search
p. 64	https://nces.ed.gov/collegenavigator/
p. 67	https://collegescorecard.ed.gov/
p. 67	https://nces.ed.gov/collegenavigator/
p. 67	https://www.collegeunmazed.com/downloads
p. 73	https://www.kaptest.com/blog/press/2021/01/28/kaplan-survey-college-admissions-officers-increasingly-say-applicants-social-media-content-is-fair-game/
p. 79	https://www.collegeunmazed.com/downloads
p. 93	https://www.commonapp.org/
p. 93	https://www.coalitionforcollegeaccess.org/
p. 93	https://www.usnews.com/education/best-colleges/the-short-list-college/articles/colleges-with-the-highest-application-fees
p. 97	https://www.commonapp.org/blog/2021-2022-common-app-essay-prompts
p. 97	https://apply.jhu.edu/application-process/essays-that-worked/
p. 97	https://www.hamilton.edu/admission/apply/college-essays-that-worked
p. 97	https://admissions.tufts.edu/apply/advice/past-essays/common-application-essays/
p. 97	https://www.babson.edu/admission/undergraduate-school/college-career-advice-for-high-school-students/how-to-write-a-college-essay/
p. 105	https://cssprofile.collegeboard.org/
p. 105	https://studentaid.gov/
p. 113	https://www.heri.ucla.edu/briefs/YFCY/YFCY-2016-Brief.pdf
p. 117	https://www.collegeunmazed.com/downloads
p. 125	https://studentaid.gov/loan-simulator/
p. 125	https://www.efc.org/page/efc_member_map
p. 126	https://www.truman.edu/admitted-students/